A HISTORY

OF

THE PHILIPPINES

BY

DAVID P. BARROWS, Ph.D.

General Superintendent of Public Instruction for the Philippine Islands

NEW YORK ·· CINCINNATI ·· CHICAGO

AMERICAN BOOK COMPANY

COPYRIGHT, 1905, BY
DAVID P. BARROWS

———

Entered at Stationers' Hall, London

———

Barrows, Philippines

W. P. I

PREFACE

THIS book has been prepared at the suggestion of the educational authorities for pupils in the public high schools of the Philippines, as an introduction to the history of their country. Its preparation occupied about two years, while the author was busily engaged in other duties, — much of it being written while he was traveling or exploring in different parts of the Archipelago. No pretensions are made to an exhaustive character for the book. For the writer, as well as for the pupil for whom it is intended, it is an introduction into the study of the history of Malaysia.

Considerable difficulty has been experienced in securing the necessary historical sources, but it is believed that the principal ones have been read. The author is greatly indebted to the Honorable Dr. Pardo de Tavera for the use of rare volumes from his library, and he wishes to acknowledge also the kindness of Mr. Manuel Yriarte, Chief of the Bureau of Archives, for permission to examine public documents. The occasional reprints of the old Philippine histories have, however, been used more frequently than the original editions. The splendid series of reprinted works on the Philippines, promised by Miss Blair and Mr. Robertson, was not begun in time to be used in the preparation of this book. The appearance of this series will make easy a path which the present writer

(3)

has found comparatively difficult, and will open the way for an incomparably better History of the Philippines than has ever yet been made.

The drawings of ethnographic subjects, which partly illustrate this book, were made from objects in the Philippine Museum by Mr. Anselmo Espiritu, a teacher in the public schools of Manila. They are very accurate.

Above every one else, in writing this book, the author is under obligations to his wife, without whose constant help and encouragement it could not have been written.

DAVID P. BARROWS.

MANILA, PHILIPPINE ISLANDS,
MARCH 1ST, 1903.

CONTENTS.

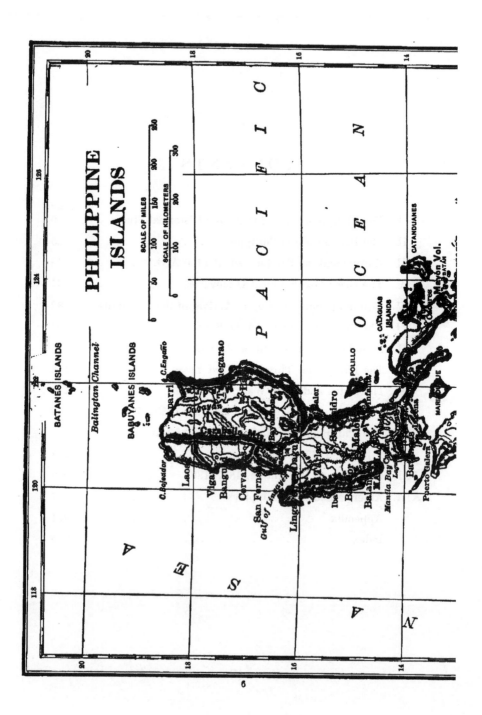

PHILIPPINE
ISLANDS

SCALE OF MILES
0   50   100   150   200   250

SCALE OF KILOMETERS
0   100   200   300

LIST OF MAPS.

HISTORY OF THE PHILIPPINES.

CHAPTER I.

THE PHILIPPINES AS A SUBJECT FOR HISTORICAL STUDY.

Purpose of this Book. — This book has been written for the young men and young women of the Philippines. It is intended to introduce them into the history of their own island country. The subject of Philippine history is much broader and more splendid than the size and character of this little book reveal. Many subjects have only been briefly touched upon, and there are many sources of information, old histories, letters and official documents, which the writer had not time and opportunity to study in the preparation of this work. It is not too soon, however, to present a history of the Philippines, even though imperfectly written, to the Philippine people themselves; and if this book serves to direct young men and young women to a study of the history of their own island country, it will have fulfilled its purpose.

The Development of the Philippines and of Japan. — In many ways the next decade of the history of the Philippine Islands may resemble the splendid development of the neighboring country of Japan. Both countries have in past times been isolated more or less from the life and thought of the modern world. Both are now open to the full current of human affairs. Both countries promise to play an important part in the politics and commerce of

9

the Far East. Geographically, the Philippines occupy the
more central and influential position, and the success of
the institutions of the Philippines may react upon the
countries of southeastern Asia and Malaysia to an extent
that we cannot appreciate or foresee. Japan, by reason
of her larger population, the greater industry of her people,
a more orderly social life, and devoted public spirit, is at
the present time far in the lead.

The Philippines. — But the Philippines possess certain .
advantages which, in the course of some years, may tell
strongly in her favor. There are greater natural resources,
a richer soil, and more tillable ground. The population,
while not large, is increasing rapidly, more rapidly, in fact,
than the population of Japan or of Java. And in the
character of her institutions the Philippines have certain
advantages. The position of woman, while so unfortunate
in Japan, as in China and nearly all eastern countries, in
the Philippines is most fortunate, and is certain to tell
effectually upon the advancement of the race in competition with other eastern civilizations. The fact that Christianity is the established religion of the people makes
possible a sympathy and understanding between the Philippines and western countries.

Japan. — Yet there are many lessons which Japan can
teach the Philippines, and one of these is of the advantages
and rewards of fearless and thorough study. Fifty years
ago, Japan, which had rigorously excluded all intercourse
with foreign nations, was forced to open its doors by an
American fleet under Commodore Perry. At that time
the Japanese knew nothing of western history, and had no
knowledge of modern science. Their contact with the
Americans and other foreigners revealed to them the in-
feriority of their knowledge. The leaders of the country

awoke to the necessity of a study of western countries and their great progress, especially in government and in the sciences.

Japan had at her service a special class of people known as the *samurai*, who, in the life of Old Japan, were the free soldiers of the feudal nobility, and who were not only the fighters of Japan, but the students and scholars as well. The young men of this *samurai* class threw themselves earnestly and devotedly into the study of the great fields of knowledge, which had previously been unknown to the Japanese. At great sacrifice many of them went abroad to other lands, in order to study in foreign universities. Numbers of them went to the United States, frequently working as servants in college towns in order to procure the means for the pursuit of their education.

The Japanese Government in every way began to adopt measures for the transformation of the knowledge of the people. Schools were opened, laboratories established, and great numbers of scientific and historical books were translated into Japanese. A public school system was organized, and finally a university was established. The Government sent abroad many young men to study in almost every branch of knowledge and to return to the service of the people. The manufacturers of Japan studied and adopted western machinery and modern methods of production. The government itself underwent revolution and reorganization upon lines more liberal to the people and more favorable to the national spirit of the country. The result has been the transformation, in less than fifty years, of what was formerly an isolated and ignorant country.

The Lesson for the Filipinos. — This is the great lesson which Japan teaches the Philippines. If there is to be transformation here, with a constant growth of knowledge and advancement, and an elevation of the character of the people as a whole, there must be a courageous and unfaltering search for the truth: and the young men and young women of the Philippines must seek the advantages of education, not for themselves, but for the benefit of their people and their land; not to gain for themselves a selfish position of social and economic advantage over the poor and less educated Filipinos, but in order that, having gained these advantages for themselves, they may in turn give them to their less fortunate countrymen. The young Filipino, man or woman, must learn the lessons of truthfulness, courage, and unselfishness, and in all of his gaining of knowledge, and in his use of it as well, he must practice these virtues, or his learning will be an evil to his land and not a blessing.

The aim of this book is to help him to understand, first of all, the place that the Philippines occupy in the modern history of nations, so that he may understand how far and from what beginnings the Filipino people have progressed, toward what things the world outside has itself moved during this time, and what place and opportunities the Filipinos, as a people, may seek for in the future.

The Meaning of History. — History, as it is written and understood, comprises many centuries of human life and achievement, and we must begin our study by discussing a little what history means. Men may live for thousands of years without having a life that may be called historical; for history is formed only where there are credible written records of events. Until we have these records, we have no ground for historical study, but leave the field to another study, which we call Archeology, or Prehistoric Culture.

Historical Races. — Thus there are great races which

have no history, for they have left no records. Either the people could not write, or their writings have been destroyed, or they told nothing about the life of the people.. The history of these races began only with the coming of a historical, or more advanced race among them.

Thus, the history of the black, or negro, race begins only with the exploration of Africa by the white race, and the history of the American Indians, except perhaps of those of Peru and Mexico, begins only with the white man's conquest of America. The white, or European, race is, above all others, the great historical race; but the yellow race, represented by the Chinese, has also a historical life and development, beginning many centuries before the birth of Christ.

The European Race. — For thousands of years the white race was confined to the countries bordering the Mediterranean Sea. It had but little contact with other races of men and almost no knowledge of countries beyond the Mediterranean shores. The great continents of America and Australia and the beautiful island-world of the Pacific and Indian oceans were scarcely dreamed of. This was the status of the white race in Europe a little more than five hundred years ago. How different is the position of this race to-day! It has now explored nearly the entire globe. The white people have crossed every continent and every sea. On every continent they have established colonies and over many countries their power.

During these last five centuries, besides this spread of geographical discoveries, the mingling of all the races, and the founding of great colonies, has come also the development of scientific knowledge — great discoveries and inventions, such as the utilization of steam and electricity, which give to man such tremendous power over the

material world.   Very important changes have also marked
the religious and political life of the race.   Within these
years came the Protestant revolt from the Roman Catholic Church, destroying in some degree the unity of Christendom; and the great revolutions of Europe and America,
establishing democratic and representative governments.

The European Race and the Filipino People. —
This expansion and progress of the European race early
brought it into contact with the Filipino people, and the
historical life of the Philippines dates from this meeting
of the two races.   Thus the history of the Philippines has
become a part of the history of nations.   During these
centuries the people of these islands, subjects of a European nation, have progressed in social life and government, in education and industries, in numbers, and in
wealth.   They have often been stirred by wars and revolutions, by centuries of piratical invasion, and fear of conquest by foreign nations.   But these dangers have now
passed away.

There is no longer fear of piratical ravage nor of foreign
invasion, nor is there longer great danger of internal revolt; for the Philippines are at the present time under a
government strong enough to defend them against other
powers, to put down plunder and ravage, and one anxious
and disposed to afford to the people such freedom of opportunity, such advantages of government and life, that
the incentive to internal revolution will no longer exist.
Secure from external attack and rapidly progressing toward
internal peace, the Philippines occupy a position most fortunate among the peoples of the Far East.   They have
representative government, freedom of religion, and public education, and, what is more than all else to the aspir-
ing or ambitious race or individual, freedom of opportunity.

How History is Written. — One other thing should be explained here. Every child who reads this book should understand a little how history is written. A most natural inquiry to be made regarding any historical statement is, "How is this known?" And this is as proper a question for the school boy as for the statesman. The answer is, that history rests for its facts largely upon the written records made by people who either lived at the time these things took place, or so near to them that, by careful inquiry, they could learn accurately of these matters and write them down in some form, so that we to-day can read their accounts, and at least know how these events appeared to men of the time.

But not all that a man writes, or even puts in a book, of things he has seen and known, is infallibly accurate and free from error, partiality, and untruthfulness. So the task of the historian is not merely to read and accept all the contemporary records, but he must also compare one account with another, weighing all that he can find, making due allowance for prejudice, and on his own part trying to reach a conclusion that shall be true. Of course, where records are few the task is difficult indeed, and, on the other hand, material may be so voluminous as to occupy a writer a lifetime, and make it impossible for any one man completely to exhaust a subject.

Historical Accounts of the Philippines. — For the Philippines we are so fortunate as to have many adequate sources of a reliable and attractive kind. In a few words some of these will be described. Nearly all exist in at least a few libraries in the Philippines, where they may sometime be consulted by the Filipino student, and many of them, at least in later editions, may be purchased by the student for his own possession and study.

The Voyages of Discovery. — European discovery of the Philippines began with the great voyage of Magellan; and recounting this discovery of the islands, there is the priceless narrative of one of Magellan's company, Antonio Pigafetta. His book was written in Italian, but was first published in a French translation. The original copies made by Pigafetta have disappeared, but in 1800 a copy was discovered in the Ambrosian Library of Milan, Italy, and published. Translations into English and other languages exist. It may be found in several collections of Voyages, and there is a good Spanish translation and edition of recent date. (*El Primer Viaje alrededor del Mundo*, por Antonio Pigafetta, traducido por Dr. Carlos Amoretti y anotado por Manuel Walls y Merino, Madrid, 1899.) There are several other accounts of Magellan's voyage; but Pigafetta's was the only one written by an eye-witness, and his descriptions of the Bisaya Islands, Cebu, Borneo, and the Moluccas are wonderfully interesting and accurate.

There were several voyages of discovery between Magellan's time (1521) and Legaspi's time (1565). These include the expeditions of Loaisa, Saavedra, and Villalobos, and accounts of them are to be found in the great series of publications made by the Spanish Government and called *Coleccion de documentos ineditos*, and, in another series, Navarrete's *Coleccion de los viajes y descubrimientos*.

Spanish Occupation and Conquest. — As we come to the history of Spanish occupation and conquest of the Philippines, we find many interesting letters and reports sent by both soldiers and priests to the king, or to persons in Spain. The first complete book on the Philippines was written by a missionary about 1602, Father Predo Chirino's *Relacion de las Islas Filipinas*, printed in Rome in 1604. This important and curious narrative is exceedingly rare, but a reprint, although rude and poor, was made in Manila in 1890, which is readily obtainable. The *Relacion de las Islas Filipinas* was followed in 1609 by the work of Judge Antonio de Morga, *Sucesos de las Islas Filipinas*. This very rare work was printed in Mexico. In 1890 a new edition was brought out by Dr. José Rizal, from the copy in the British Museum. There is also an English translation.

These two works abound in curious and valuable information upon the Filipino people as they were at the time of the arrival of the Spaniards, as does also a later work, the *Conquista de las Islas Filipinas*, by Friar Gaspar de San Augustin, printed in Madrid in 1698. This latter is perhaps the most interesting and most important early work on the Philippine Islands.

As we shall see, the history of the Philippines is closely connected with that of the East Indian Spice Islands. When the Spanish forces took the rich island of Ternate in 1606, the triumph was commemorated by a volume, finely written, though not free from mistakes, the *Conquista de las Islas Moluccas*, by Leonardo de Argensola, Madrid, 1609. There is an old English translation, and also French and Dutch translations.

To no other religious order do we owe so much historical information as to the Jesuits. The scholarship and literary ability of the Company have always been high. Chirino was a Jesuit, as was also Father Francisco Colin, who wrote the *Labor Evangelica*, a narrative of the Jesuit missions in the Philippines, China, and Japan, which was printed in Madrid in 1663. This history was continued years later by Father Murillo Velarde, who wrote what he called the *Segunda Parte*, the *Historia de la Provincia de Filipinas de la Compania de Jesus*, Manila, 1749.

There is another notable Jesuit work to which we owe much of the early history of the great island of Mindanao: this is the *Historia de Mindanao y Jolo*, by Father Francisco Combes. The year 1663 marked, as we shall see, an epoch in the relations between the Spaniards and the Mohammedan Malays. In that year the Spaniards abandoned the fortress of Zamboanga, and retired from southern Mindanao. The Jesuits had been the missionaries in those parts of the southern archipelago, and they made vigorous protests against the abandonment of Moro territory. One result of their efforts to secure the reoccupancy of these fortresses was the notable work mentioned above. It is the oldest and most important writing about the island and the inhabitants of Mindanao. It was printed in Madrid in 1667. A beautiful and exact edition was brought out a few years ago, by Retana.

A Dominican missionary, Father Diego Aduarte, wrote a very important work, the *Historia de la Provincia del Sancto Rosario de la Orden de Predicadores en Filipinas, Japon y China*, which was printed in Manila at the College of Santo Tomas in 1640.

We may also mention as containing a most interesting account of the Philippines about the middle of the seventeenth century, the famous work on China, by the Dominican, Father Fernandez Navarrete, *Tratados históricos, politicos, ethnicos, y religiosos de la Monarchia de China*, Madrid, 1767. Navarrete arrived in these islands in 1648, and was for a time a cura on the island of Mindoro. Later he was a missionary in China, and then Professor of Divinity in the University of Santo Tomas. His work is translated into English in Churchill's *Collection of Voyages and Travels*, London, 1744, second volume.

The eighteenth century is rather barren of interesting

historical matter. There was considerable activity in the production of grammars and dictionaries of the native languages, and more histories of the religious orders were also produced. These latter, while frequently filled with sectarian matter, should not be overlooked.

Between the years 1788 and 1792 was published the voluminous *Historia General de Filipinas*, in fourteen volumes, by the Recollect friar, Father Juan de la Concepcion. The work abounds in superfluous matter and trivial details, yet it is a copious source of information, a veritable mine of historical data, and is perhaps the best known and most frequently used work upon the Philippine Islands. There are a number of sets in the Philippines which can be consulted by the student.

Some years after, and as a sort of protest against so extensive a treatment of history, the sane and admirable Augustinian, Father Joaquin Martinez de Zuniga, wrote his *Historia de las Islas Filipinas*, a volume of about seven hundred pages. It was printed in Sampaloc, Manila, in 1803. This writer is exceptional for his fairmindedness, his freedom from the narrow prejudices which have characterized most of the writers on the Philippines. His language is terse and spirited, and his volume is the most readable and, in many ways, the most valuable attempt at a history of the Philippines. His narrative closes with the English occupation of Manila in 1763.

Recent Histories and Other Historical Materials. — The sources for the conditions and history of the islands during the last century differ somewhat from the preceding. The documentary sources in the form of public papers and reports are available, and there is a considerable mass of pamphlets dealing with special questions in the Philippines. The publication of the official journal of

the Government, the *Gazeta de Manila,* commenced in
1861. It contains all acts of legislation, orders of the
Governors, pastoral letters, and other official matters,
down to the end of Spanish rule.

A vast amount of material for the recent civil history
of the islands exists in the Archives of the Philippines, at
Manila, but these documents have been very little ex-
amined. Notable among these original documents is the
series of Royal Cedulas, each bearing the signature of the
King of Spain, " Yo, el Rey." They run back from the last
years of sovereignty to the commencement of the seventeenth century. The early cedulas, on the establishment
of Spanish rule, are said to have been carried away by the
British army in 1763, and to be now in the British Museum.

Of the archives of the Royal Audiencia at Manila, the
series of judgments begins with one of 1603, which is
signed by Antonia de Morga. From this date they appear to be complete. The earliest records of the cases
which came before this court that can be found, date
from the beginning of the eighteenth century.

Of modern historical writings mention must be made of
the *Historia de Filipinas,* three volumes, 1887, by Montero
y Vidal, and the publications of W. E. Retana. To the
scholarship and enthusiasm of this last author much is
owed. His work has been the republication of rare and
important sources. His edition of Combes has already
been mentioned, and there should also be mentioned, and
if possible procured, his *Archivo del Bibliofilo,* four volumes, a collection of rare papers on the islands, of different dates; and his edition, the first ever published, of
Zuniga's Estadismo de las Islas Filipinas, an incomparable
survey of the islands made about 1800, by the priest and
historian whose history was mentioned above.

Accounts of Voyagers Who Visited the Philippines. — These references give some idea of the historical literature of the Philippines. They comprise those works which should be chiefly consulted: There should not be omitted the numerous accounts of voyagers who have visited these islands from time to time, and who frequently give us very valuable information. The first of these are perhaps the English and Dutch freebooters, who prowled about these waters to waylay the richly laden galleons. One of these was Dampier, who, about 1690, visited the Ladrones and the Philippines. His *New Voyage Around the World* was published in 1697. There was also Anson, who in 1743 took the Spanish galleon off the coast of Samar, and whose voyage is described in a volume published in 1745. There was an Italian physician, Carreri, who visited the islands in 1697, in the course of a voyage around the world, and who wrote an excellent description of the Philippines, which is printed in English translation in Churchill's *Collection of Voyages.*

A French expedition visited the East between 1774 and 1781, and the Commissioner, M. Sonnerat, has left a brief account of the Spanish settlements in the islands as they then appeared. (*Voyage aux Indes Orientales et à la Chine*, Paris, 1782, Vol. 3.)

There are a number of travellers' accounts written in the last century, of which may be mentioned Sir John Bowring's *Visit to the Philippine Islands*, 1859, and Jagor's *Reisen in der Philippinen*, travels in the year 1859 and 1860, which has received translation into both English and Spanish.

Bibliographies. — For the historical student a bibliographical guide is necessary. Such a volume was brought out in 1898, by Retana, *Catalogo abreviado de la Biblioteca*

Filipina. It contains a catalogue of five thousand seven hundred and eighty works, published in or upon the Philippines. A still more exact and useful bibliography has been prepared by the Honorable T. H. Pardo de Tavera, *Biblioteca Filipina,* and is published by the United States Government.

It is lamentable that the Philippines Government possesses no library of works on the Archipelago. The foundation of such an institution seems to have been quite neglected by the Spanish Government, and works on the Philippines are scarcely to be found, except as they exist in private collections. The largest of these is said to be that of the Compañia General de Tabacos, at Barcelona, which has also recently possessed itself of the splendid library of Retana. In Manila the Honorable Dr. Pardo de Tavera possesses the only notable library in the islands.

Since the above was written the Philippines Government has commenced the collection of historic works in the Philippines, and a talented young Filipino scholar, Mr. Zulueta, has gone to Spain for extensive search, both of archives and libraries, in order to enrich the public collection in the Philippines.

The publication of a very extensive series of sources of Philippine history has also been begun by the Arthur H. Clark Company in the United States, under the editorship of Miss E. H. Blair and Mr. J. A. Robertson. The series will embrace fifty-five volumes, and will contain in English translations all available historical material on the Philippines, from the age of discovery to the nineteenth century. This notable collection will place within the reach of the student all the important sources of his country's history, and will make possible a more extensive and accurate writing of the history of the islands than has ever before been possible.

In addition to the published works, there repose numerous unstudied documents of Philippine history in the the Archives of the Indies at Seville.

Historical Work for the Filipino Student. — After reading this book, or a similar introductory history, the student should procure, one by one, as many as he can of the volumes which have been briefly described above, and, by careful reading and patient thought, try to round out the story of his country and learn the lessons of the history of his people. He will find it a study that will stimulate his thought and strengthen his judgment; but always he must search for the truth, even though the truth is sometimes humiliating and sad. If there are re-regrettable passages in our own lives, we cannot find either happiness or improvement in trying to deny to ourselves that we have done wrong, and so conceal and minimize our error. So if there are dark places in the history of our land and people, we must not obscure the truth in the mistaken belief that we are defending our people's honor, for, by trying to conceal the fact and excuse the fault, we only add to the shame. It is by frank acknowledgment and clear depiction of previous errors that the country's honor will be protected now and in the future.

Very interesting and important historical work can be done by the Filipino student in his own town or province. The public and parish records have in many towns suffered neglect or destruction. In all possible cases these documents should be gathered up and cared for. For many things, they are worthy of study. They can show the growth of population, the dates of erection of the public buildings, the former system of government, and social conditions.

This is a work in which the patriotism of every young

man and woman can find an expression. Many sites throughout the islands are notable for the historic occurrences which they witnessed. These should be suitably marked with tablets or monuments, and the exact facts of the events that took place should be carefully collected, and put in writing. Towns and provinces should form public libraries containing, among other works, books on the Philippines; and it should be a matter of pride to the young Filipino scholar to build up such local institutions, and to educate his townsmen in their use and appreciation.

But throughout such studies the student should remember that his town or locality is of less importance, from a patriotic standpoint, than his country as a whole; that the interests of one section should never be placed above those of the Archipelago; and that, while his first and foremost duty is to his town and to his people, among whom he was born and nurtured, he owes a greater obligation to his whole country and people, embracing many different islands and different tongues, and to the great Government which holds and protects the Philippine Islands, and which is making possible the free development of its inhabitants.

CHAPTER II.

THE PEOPLES OF THE PHILIPPINES.

The Study of Ethnology. — The study of races and peoples forms a separate science from history, and is known as *ethnology*, or the science of races. Ethnology informs us how and where the different races of mankind originated. It explains the relationships between the races as well as the differences of mind, of body, and of mode of living which different people exhibit.

All such knowledge is of great assistance to the statesman as he deals with the affairs of his own people and of other peoples, and it helps private individuals of different races to understand one another and to treat each other with due respect, kindness, and sympathy. Inasmuch, too, as the modern history which we are studying deals with many different peoples of different origin and race, and as much of our history turns upon these differences, we must look for a little at the ethnology of the Philippines.

The Negritos. — *Physical Characteristics.* — The great majority of the natives of our islands belong to what is usually called the Malayan race, or the Oceanic Mongols. There is, however, one interesting little race scattered over the Philippines, which certainly has no relationship at all with Malayans. These little people are called by the Tagálog, "Aeta" or "Ita." The Spaniards, when they arrived, called them "Negritos," or "little negroes," the name by which they are best known. Since they

25

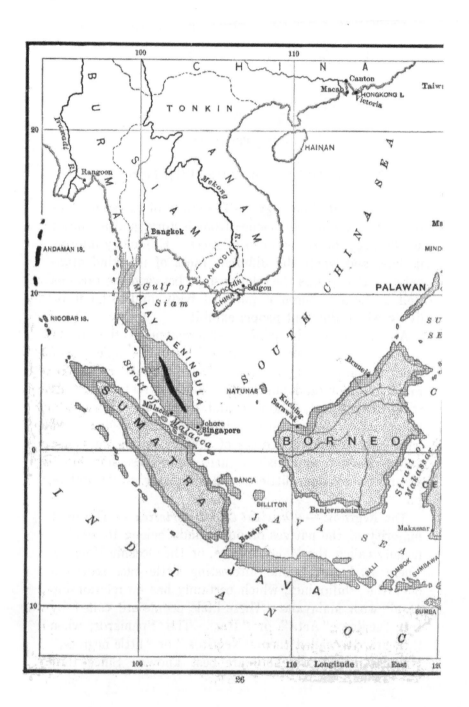

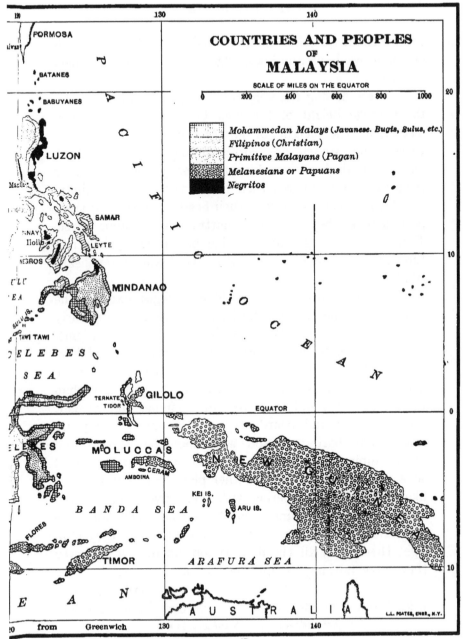

COUNTRIES AND PEOPLES
OF
MALAYSIA

SCALE OF MILES ON THE EQUATOR

0   200   400   600   800   1000

Mohammedan Malays (*Javanese, Bugis, Sulus, etc.*)
Filipinos (*Christian*)
Primitive Malayans (*Pagan*)
Melanesians or Papuans
Negritos

were without question the first inhabitants of these islands
of whom we have any knowledge, we shall speak of them
at once.

They are among the very smallest peoples in the world,
the average height of the men being about 145 centi-
meters, or the height of an American boy of twelve
years ; the women are correspondingly smaller. They
have such dark-brown skins that many people suppose
them to be quite black ; their hair is very wooly or kinky,
and forms thick mats upon their heads. In spite of these
peculiarities, they are not unattractive in appearance.
Their eyes are large and of a fine brown color, their features are quite regular, and their little bodies often beau-
tifully shaped.

The appearance of these little savages excited the
attention of the first Spaniards, and there are many early
accounts of them. Padre Chirino, who went as a missionary in 1592 to Panay, begins the narrative of his labors
in that island as follows: "Among the Bisayas, there are
also some Negroes. They are less black and ugly than
those of Guinea, and they are much smaller and weaker,
but their hair and beard are just the same. They are
much more barbarous and wild than the Bisayas and
other Filipinos, for they have neither houses nor any fixed
sites for dwelling. They neither plant nor reap, but live
like wild beasts, wandering with their wives and children
through the mountains, almost naked. They hunt the
deer and wild boar, and when they kill one they stop
right there until all the flesh is consumed. Of property
they have nothing except the bow and arrow." [1]

Manners and Customs. — The Negritos still have this
wild, timid character, and few have ever been truly civ-

[1] *Relacion de las Islas Filipinas*, 2d ed., p. 38.

ilized in spite of the efforts of some of the Spanish missionaries. They still roam through the mountains, seldom building houses, but making simply a little wall and roof of brush to keep off the wind and rain. They kill deer, wild pigs, monkeys, and birds, and in hunting they are very expert; but their principal food is wild roots and tubers, which they roast in ashes. Frequently in traveling through the mountains, although one may see nothing of these timid little folk, he will see many large, freshly dug holes from each of which they have taken out a root.

The Negritos ornament their bodies by making little rows of cuts on the breast, back, and arms, and leaving the scars in ornamental patterns; and some of them also file their front teeth to points. In their hair they wear bamboo combs with long plumes of hair or of the feathers of the mountain cock. They have curious dances, and ceremonies for marriage and for death.

Distribution. — The Negritos have retired from many places where they lived when the Spaniards first arrived, but there are still several thousand in Luzon, especially in the Cordillera Zambales, on the Pacific coast, and in the Sierra Madre range; and in the interior of Panay, Negros, Tablas, and in Surigao of Mindanao.

Relation of the Negritos to Other Dwarfs of the World. — Although the Negritos have had very little effect on the history of the Philippines, they are of much interest as a race to scientists, and we can not help asking, Whence came these curious little people, and what does their presence here signify? While science can not at present fully answer these questions, what we do actually know about these pygmies is full of interest.

The Aetas of the Philippines are not the only black dwarfs in the world. A similar little people, who must

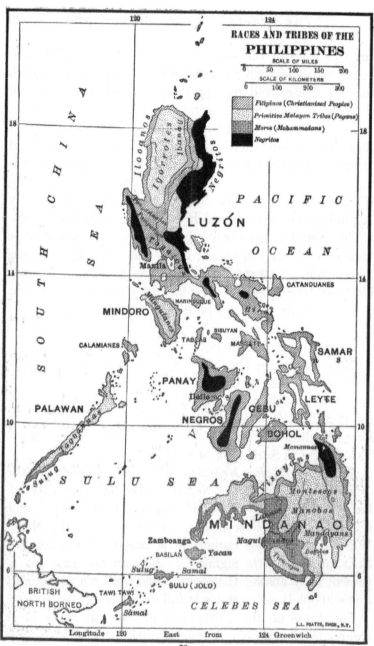

RACES AND TRIBES OF THE
PHILIPPINES

SCALE OF MILES
0   50   100   150   200

SCALE OF KILOMETERS
0   100   200   300

Filipinos (Christianized Peoples)
Primitive Malayan Tribes (Pagans)
Moros (Mohammedans)
Negritos

120   124

18   18

S
O
U
T
H   C
H
I
N
A

Iloquans
Igorrotes
Ibanag
Negritos

P   A   C   I   F   I   C

LUZÓN

O   C   E   A   N

14   14

Manila

CATANDUANES

MINDORO   MARINDUQUE
SIBUYAN
TABLAS   MASBATE

CALAMIANES   SAMAR
s

PANAY
Iloilo   LEYTE

PALAWAN   NEGROS   CEBU

10   10
BOHOL
Mamanuas
Sulug Caganes
Montesos
S   U   L   U   S   E   A   Visayans   Manobos

MINDANAO   Mandayans
Zamboanga   Maguindanaos   Bilanes
BASILAN   Yacan
Sulug   Samal

BRITISH
NORTH BORNEO   TAWI TAWI   SULU (JOLO)   C   E   L   E   B   E   S   S   E   A
Sámal

L.L. POATES, ENGR., N.Y.

Longitude   120   East   from   124 Greenwich

30

belong to the same race, live in the mountains and jungles of the Malay peninsula. On the Andaman Islands in the Indian Ocean, all the aboriginal inhabitants are similar pygmies, called "Mincopies." Some traces of their former existence are reported from many other places in the East Indies.

Thus it may be that there was a time when these little men and women had much of this island-world quite to themselves, and their race stretched unbrokenly from the Philippines across Malacca to the Indian Ocean. As it would have been impossible for so feeble a people to force their way from one island to another after the arrival of the stronger races, who have now confined them to the mountainous interiors, we are obliged to believe that the Negritos were on the ground first, and that at one time they were more numerous. The Indian archipelago was then a world of black pygmies. It may be that they were even more extensive than this, for one of the most curious discoveries of modern times has been the finding of similar little blacks in the equatorial forests of Africa.

The Negritos must not be confused with the black or negro race of New Guinea or Melanesia, who are commonly called Papuans; for those Negroes are of tall stature and belong with the true Negroes of Africa, though how the Negro race thus came to be formed of two so widely separated branches we do not know.

The Malayan Race. — *Origin of the Race.* — It is thought that the Malayan race originated in southeastern Asia. From the mainland it spread down into the peninsula and so scattered southward and eastward over the rich neighboring islands. Probably these early Malayans found the little Negritos in possession and slowly drove them backward, destroying them from many islands until they no longer exist except in the places we have already named.

With the beginning of this migratory movement which carried them from one island to another of the great East Indian Archipelago, these early Malayans must have invented the boats and praos for which they are famed, and have become skillful sailors living much upon the sea.

Effect of the Migration. — Life for many generations, upon these islands, so warm, tropical, and fruitful, gradually modified these emigrants from Asia, until they became in mind and body quite a different race from the Mongol inhabitants of the mainland.

Characteristics. — The Malayan peoples are of a light-brown color, with a light yellowish undertone on some parts of the skin, with straight black hair, dark-brown eyes, and, though they are a small race in stature, they are finely formed, muscular, and active. The physical type is nearly the same throughout all Malaysia, but the different peoples making up the race differ markedly from one another in culture. They are divided also by differences in religion. There are many tribes which are pagan. On Bali and Lombok, little islands south of Java, the people are still Brahmin, like most inhabitants of India. In other parts of Malaysia they are Mohammedans, while in the Philippines alone they are mostly Christians.

The Wild Malayan Tribes. — Considering first the pagan or the wild Malayan peoples, we find that in the interior of the Malay Peninsula and of many of the islands, such as Sumatra, Borneo and the Celebes, there are wild Malayan tribes, who have come very little in contact with the successive civilizing changes that have passed over this archipelago. The true Malays call these folk "Orang

benua," or "men of the country." Many are almost
savages, some are cannibals, and others are headhunters
like some of the Dyaks of Borneo.

In the Philippines, too, we find what is probably this
same class of wild people living in the mountains. They are
warlike, savage, and resist approach. Sometimes they eat
human flesh as a ceremonial act, and some prize above all
other trophies the heads of their enemies, which they cut
from the body and preserve in their homes. It is probable
that these tribes represent the earliest and rudest epoch
of Malayan culture, and that these were the first of this
race to arrive in the Philippines and dispute with the Negritos for the mastery of the soil. In such wild state of
life, some of them, like the Manguianes of Mindoro, have
continued to the present day.

The Tribes in Northern Luzon. — In northern Luzon,
in the great Cordillera Central, there are many of these primitive tribes. These people are preëminently mountaineers.
They prefer the high, cold, and semi-arid crests and valleys of the loftiest ranges. Here, with great industry, they
have made gardens by the building of stone-walled terraces on the slopes of the hills. Sometimes hundreds of
these terraces can be counted in one valley, and they rise one
above the other from the bottom of a cañon for several
miles almost to the summit of a ridge. These terraced
gardens are all under most careful irrigation. Water is
carried for many miles by log flumes and ditches, to be distributed over these little fields. The soil is carefully fer-
tilized with the refuse of the villages. Two and frequently
three crops are produced each year. Here we find undoubtedly the most developed and most nearly scientific
agriculture in the Philippines. They raise rice, cotton,
tobacco, the taro, maize, and especially the camote, or

sweet potato, which is their principal food. These people
live in compact, well-built villages, frequently of several
hundred houses. Some of these tribes, like the Igorrotes
of Benguet and the Tinguianes of Abra, are peaceable as
well as industrious. In Benguet there are fine herds of
cattle, much excellent coffee, and from time immemorial
the Igorrotes here have mined gold.

Besides these peaceful tribes there are in Bontoc, and
in the northern parts of the Cordillera, many large tribes,
with splendid mountain villages, who are nevertheless in a
constant and dreadful state of war. Nearly every town
is in feud with its neighbors, and the practice of taking
heads leads to frequent murder and combat. A most
curious tribe of persistent headhunters are the Ibilao, or
Ilongotes, who live in the Caraballo Sur Mountains between
Nueva Ecija and Nueva Vizcaya.

On other islands of the Philippines there are similar
wild tribes. On the island of Paragua there are the Tag-
banúa and other savage folk.

Characteristics of the Tribes of Mindanao. — In
Mindanao, there are many more tribes. Three of these
tribes, the Aetas, Mandaya, and Manobo, are on the eastern
coast and around Mount Apo. In Western Mindanao,
there is quite a large but scattered tribe called the Sub-
anon. These people make clearings on the hillsides and
support themselves by raising maize and mountain rice.
They also raise hemp, and from the fiber they weave truly
beautiful blankets and garments, artistically dyed in very
curious patterns. These peoples are nearly all pagans,
though a few are being gradually converted to Mohammedanism, and some to Christianity. The pagans occasionally practice the revolting rites of human sacrifice and
ceremonial cannibalism.

The Civilized Malayan Peoples. — *Their Later Arrival.*
— At a later date than the arrival of these primitive
Malayan tribes, there came to the Philippines others
of a more developed culture and a higher order of intelligence. These peoples rapidly mastered the low country
and the coasts of all the islands, driving into the interior
the earlier comers and the aboriginal Negritos. These later
arrivals, though all of one stock, differed considerably,
and spoke different dialects belonging to one language
family. They were the ancestors of the present civilized
Filipino people.

Distribution of These Peoples. — All through the central islands, Panay, Negros, Leyte, Samar, Marinduque,
and northern Min-
danao, are the Bi-
saya, the largest of
these peoples. At the
southern extremity
of Luzon, in the
provinces of Sorso-
gon and the Cama-
rines, are the Bicol.

Mindanao Belt of Bamboo Fiber.

North of these, holding central Luzon, Batangas, Cavite,
Manila, Laguna, Bataan, Bulacan, and Nueva Ecija, are
the Tagálog, while the great plain of northern Luzon is
occupied by the Pampango and Pangasinan. All the
northwest coast is inhabited by the Ilocano, and the
valley of the Cagayan by a people commonly called Caga-
yanes, but whose dialect is Ibanag. In Nueva Vizcaya
province, on the Batanes Islands and the Calamianes,
there are other distinct branches of the Filipino people,
but they are much smaller in numbers and less important
than the tribes marked above.

Importance of These Peoples. — They form politically and historically the Filipino people. They are the Filipinos whom the Spaniards ruled for more than three hundred years. All are converts to Christianity, and all have attained a somewhat similar stage of civilization.

Early Contact of the Malays and Hindus. — These people at the time of their arrival in the Philippines were probably not only of a higher plane of intelligence than any

Mindanao Brass Vessels.

who had preceded them in the occupation of the islands, but they appear to have had the advantages of contact with a highly developed culture that had appeared in the eastern archipelago some centuries earlier.

Early Civilization in India. — More than two thousand years ago, India produced a remarkable civilization. There were great cities of stone, magnificent palaces, a life of splendid luxury, and a highly organized social and political system. Writing, known as the Sanskrit, had been developed, and a great literature of poetry and philosophy produced. Two great religions, Brahminism and Buddhism, arose, the latter still the dominant religion of Tibet, China, and Japan. The people who produced this civilization are known as the Hindus. Fourteen or fifteen hundred years ago Hinduism spread over Burma, Siam, and Java. Great cities were erected with splendid temples and huge idols, the ruins of which still remain, though their magnificence has gone and they are covered to-day with the growth of the jungle.

Influence of Hindu Culture on the Malayan Peoples. — This powerful civilization of the Hindus, established thus in Malaysia, greatly affected the Malayan people on these islands, as well as those who came to the Philippines. Many words in the Tagálog have been shown to have a Sanskrit origin, and the systems of writing which the Spaniards found in use among several of the Filipino peoples had certainly been developed from the alphabet then in use among these Hindu peoples of Java.

The Rise of Mohammedanism. — *Mohammed.* — A few hundred years later another great change, due to religious faith, came over the Malayan race, — a change which has had a great effect upon the history of the Philippines, and is still destined to modify events far into the future. This was the conversion to Mohammedanism. Of all the great religions of the world, Mohammedanism was the last to arise, and its career has in some ways been the most remarkable. Mohammed, its founder, was an Arab, born about 572 A.D. At that time Christianity was established entirely around the Mediterranean and throughout most of Europe, but Arabia was idolatrous. Mohammed was one of those great, prophetic souls which arise from time to time in the world's history. All he could learn from

Hebrewism and Christianity, together with the result of his own thought and prayers, led him to the belief in one God, the Almighty, the Compassionate, the Merciful, who as he believed would win all men to His knowledge through the teachings of Mohammed himself. Thus inspired, Mohammed became a teacher or prophet, and by the end of his life he had won his people to his faith and inaugurated one of the greatest eras of conquest the world has seen.

Spread of Mohammedanism to Africa and Europe. — The armies of Arabian horsemen, full of fanatical enthusiasm to convert the world to their faith, in a century's time wrested from Christendom all Judea, Syria, and Asia Minor, the sacred land where Jesus lived and taught, and the countries where Paul and the other apostles had first established Christianity. Thence they swept along the north coast of Africa, bringing to an end all that survived of Roman power and religion, and by 720 they had crossed into Europe and were in possession of Spain. For nearly the eight hundred years that followed, the Christian Spaniards fought to drive Mohammedanism from the peninsula, before they were successful.

The Conversion of the Malayans to Mohammedanism. — Not only did Mohammedanism move westward over Africa and Europe, it was carried eastward as well. Animated by their faith, the Arabs became the greatest sailors, explorers, merchants, and geographers of the age. They sailed from the Red Sea down the coast of Africa as far as Madagascar, and eastward to India, where they had settlements on both the Malabar and Coromandel coasts. Thence Arab missionaries brought their faith to Malaysia.

At that time the true Malays, the tribe from which the common term "Malayan" has been derived, were a

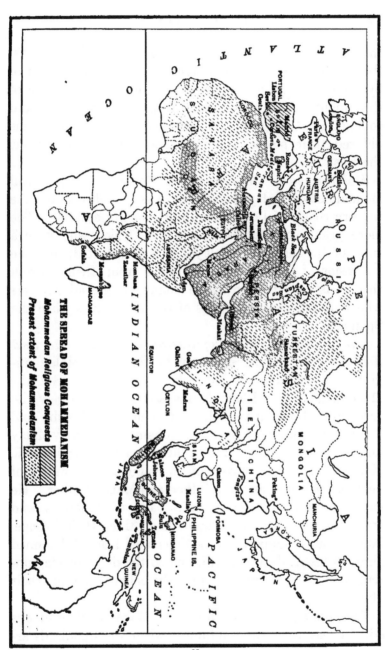

THE SPREAD OF MOHAMMEDANISM

Mohammedan Religious Conquests
Present extent of Mohammedanism

39

small people of Sumatra. At least as early as 1250 they were converted to Mohammedanism, brought to them by these Arabian missionaries, and under the impulse of this mighty faith they broke from their obscurity and commenced that great conquest and expansion that has diffused their power, language, and religion throughout the East Indies.

Mohammedan Settlement in Borneo. — A powerful Mohammedan Malay settlement was established on the western coasts of Borneo certainly as early as 1400. The more primitive inhabitants, like the Dyaks, who were a tribe of the primitive Malayans, were defeated, and the possession of the coast largely taken from them. From this coast of Borneo came many of the adventurers who were traversing the seas of the Philippines when the Spaniards arrived.

The Mohammedan Population of Mindanao and Jolo owes something certainly to this same Malay migration which founded the colony of Borneo. But the Maguindanao and Illano Moros seem to be largely descendants of primitive tribes, such as the Manobo and Tiruray, who were converted to Mohammedanism by Malay and Arab proselyters. The traditions of the Maguindanao Moros ascribe their conversion to Kabunsuan, a native of Johore, the son of an Arab father and Malay mother. He came to Maguindanao with a band of followers, and from him the datos of Maguindanao trace their lineage. Kabunsuan is supposed to be descended from Mohammed through his Arab father, Ali, and so the datos of Maguindanao to the present day proudly believe that in their veins flows the blood of the Prophet.

The Coming of the Spaniards. — Mohammedanism was still increasing in the Philippines when the Spaniards arrived. The Mohammedans already had a foothold on Manila Bay, and their gradual conquest of the archipelago was interrupted only by the coming of the Europeans. It is a strange historical occurrence that the Spaniards, having fought with the Mohammedans for nearly eight centuries for the possession of Spain, should have come westward around the globe to the Philippine Islands and there resumed the ancient conflict with them. Thus the Spaniards were the most determined opponents of Mohammedanism on both its western and eastern frontiers. · The'r ancient foes who crossed into Spain from Morocco had been always known as "Moros" or "Moors," and quite naturally they gave to these new Mohammedan enemies the same title, and Moros they are called to the present day.

Summary. — Such, then, are the elements which form the population of these islands, — a few thousands of the little Negritos; many wild mountain tribes of the primitive Malayans; a later immigration of Malayans of higher cultivation and possibilities than any that preceded them, who had been influenced by the Hinduism of Java and who have had in recent centuries an astonishing growth both in numbers and in culture; and last, the fierce Mohammedan sea-rovers, the true Malays.

CHAPTER III.

EUROPE AND THE FAR EAST ABOUT 1400 A.D.

The Mediæval Period in Europe. — *Length of the Middle Age.* — By the Middle Ages we mean the centuries between 500 and 1300 A.D. This period begins with the fall of the Roman Empire and the looting of the Imperial City by the rude German tribes, and ends with the rise of a new literature, a new way of looking at the world in general, and a passion for discovery of every kind.

These eight hundred years had been centuries of cruel struggle, intellectual darkness, and social depression, but also of great religious devotion. Edward Gibbon, one of the greatest historians, speaks of this period as " the triumph of barbarism and religion."

The population of Europe was largely changed, during the first few centuries of the Christian Era, as the Roman Empire, that greatest political institution of all history, slowly decayed. New peoples of German or Teutonic origin came, fighting their way into western Europe and settling wherever the land attracted them. Thus Spain and Italy received the Goths; France, the Burgundians and Franks; England, the Saxons and Angles or English.

These peoples were all fierce, warlike, free, unlettered barbarians. Fortunately, they were all converted to Christianity by Roman priests and missionaries. They embraced this faith with ardor, at the same time that other peoples and lands were being lost to Christendom. Thus it has resulted that the countries where Christianity arose and first established itself, are now no longer Christian, and this religion, which had an Asiatic and Semitic origin, has become the distinguishing faith of the people of western Europe. For centuries the countries of Europe were fiercely raided and disturbed by pillaging and murdering hordes; by the Huns, who followed in the Germans from the East ; by the Northmen, cruel pirating seamen from Scandinavia; and, as we have already seen, by the Mohammedans, or Saracens as they were called, who came into central Europe by way of Spain.

Character of the Life during this Period. — *Feudalism.* — Life was so beset with peril that independence or freedom became impossible, and there was developed a society which has lasted almost down to the present time, and which we call Feudalism. The free but weak man gave up his freedom and his lands to some stronger man, who became his lord. He swore obedience to this lord, while the lord engaged to furnish him protection and gave him back his lands to hold as a "fief," both sharing in the product. This lord swore allegiance to some still more powerful man, or "overlord," and became his "vassal," pledged to follow him to war with a certain number of armed men; and this overlord, on his part, owed allegiance to the prince, who was, perhaps, a duke or bishop (bishops at this time were also feudal lords), or to the king or emperor. Thus were men united into large groups or nations for help or protection. There was little understanding of love of country. Patriotism, as we feel it, was replaced by the passion of fidelity or allegiance to one's feudal superior.

Disadvantages of Feudalism. — The great curse of this system was that the feudal lords possessed the power to make war upon one another, and so continuous were

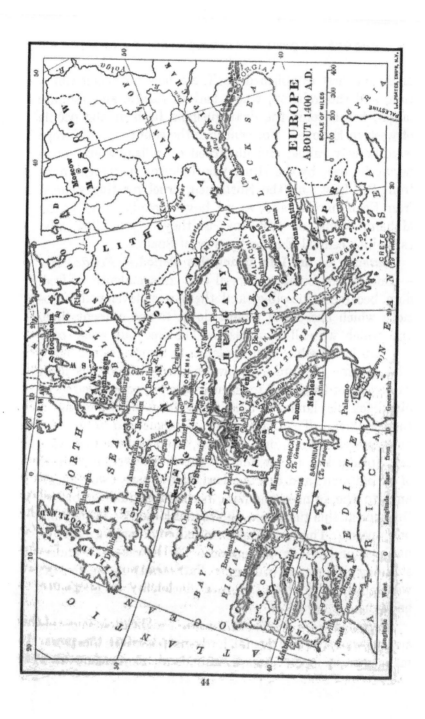

EUROPE
ABOUT 1400 A.D.

SCALE OF MILES
0   100   200   300   400

their jealousies and quarrelings that the land was never free from armed bands, who laid waste an opponent's country, killing the miserable serfs who tilled the soil, and destroying their homes and cattle.

There was little joy in life and no popular learning. If a man did not enjoy warfare, but one other life was open to him, and that was in the Church. War and religion were the pursuits of life, and it is no wonder that many of the noblest and best turned their backs upon a life that promised only fighting and bloodshed and, renouncing the world, became monks. Monasticism developed in Europe under such conditions as these, and so strong were the religious feelings of the age that at one time a third of the land of France was owned by the religious orders.

The Town. — The two typical institutions of the early Middle Age were the feudal castle, with its high stone walls and gloomy towers, with its fierce bands of warriors armed in mail and fighting on horseback with lance and sword, and the monastery, which represented inn, hospital, and school. Gradually, however, a third structure appeared. This was the town. And it is to these mediæval cities, with their busy trading life, their free citizenship, and their useful occupations, that the modern world owes much of its liberty and its intellectual light.

The Renaissance. — *Changes in Political Affairs.* — By 1400, however, the Middle Age had nearly passed and a new life had appeared, a new epoch was in progress, which is called the Renaissance, which means "rebirth." In political affairs the spirit of nationality had arisen, and feudalism was already declining. Men began to feel attachment to country, to king, and to fellow-citizens; and the national states, as we now know them, each with its naturally bounded territory, its common language, and its approximately common race, were appearing.

France and *England* were, of these states, the two most advanced politically just previous to the fifteenth century. At this distant time they were still engaged in a struggle which lasted quite a century and is known as the Hundred Years' War. In the end, England was forced to give up all her claims to territory on the continent, and the power of France was correspondingly increased. In France the monarchy (king and court) was becoming the supreme power in the land. The feudal nobles lost what power they had, while the common people gained nothing. In England, however, the foundations for a representative government had been laid. The powers of legislation and government were divided between the English king and a Parliament. The Parliament was first called in 1265 and consisted of two parts, — the Lords, representing the nobility; and the Commons, composed of persons chosen by the common people.

Germany was divided into a number of small principalities, — Saxony, Bavaria, Franconia, Bohemia, Austria, the Rhine principalities, and many others, — which united in a great assembly, or Diet, the head of which was some prince, chosen to be emperor.

Italy was also divided. In the north, in the valley of the Po, or Lombardy, were the duchy of Milan and the Republic of Venice; south, on the western coast, were the Tuscan states, including the splendid city of Florence. Thence, stretching north and south across the peninsula, were states of the church, whose ruler was the pope, for until less than fifty years ago the pope was not only the head of the church but also a temporal ruler. Embracing the southern part of the peninsula was the principality of Naples.

In the Spanish peninsula Christian states had arisen,
— in the west, Portugal, in the center and east, Castile,
Aragon, and Leon, from all of which the Mohammedans
had been expelled. But they still held the southern parts
of Spain, including the beautiful plain of Andalusia and
Grenada.

The Mohammedans, in the centuries of their life in
Spain, had developed an elegant and prosperous civilization. By means of irrigation and skillful planting, they
had converted southern Spain into a garden. They were
the most skillful agriculturists and breeders of horses and
sheep in Europe, and they carried to perfection many fine
arts, while knowledge and learning were nowhere further
advanced than here. Through contact with this remarkable people the Christian Spaniards gained much. Unfortunately, however, the spirit of religious intolerance was
so strong, and the hatred engendered by the centuries of
religious war was so violent, that in the end the Spaniard
became imbued with so fierce a fanaticism that he has
ever since appeared unable properly to appreciate or justly
to treat any who differed from him in religious belief.

The Conquests of the Mohammedans. — In the fifteenth century, religious toleration was but little known
in the world, and the people of the great Mohammedan
faith still threatened to overwhelm Christian Europe.
Since the first great conquests of Islam in the eighth century had been repulsed from central Europe, that faith had
shown a wonderful power of winning its way. In the
tenth century Asia Minor was invaded by hordes of Sel-
juks, or Turks, who poured down from central Asia in
conquering bands. These tribes had overthrown the
Arab's power in Mesopotamia and Asia Minor only to
become converts to his faith. With freshened zeal they

hurled themselves upon the old Christian empire, which
at Constantinople had survived the fall of the rest of the
Roman world.

The Crusades. — The Seljuk Turks had conquered most
of Asia Minor, Syria, and the Holy Land. A great fear
came over the people of Europe that the city of Constantinople would be captured and they, too, be overwhelmed
by these new Mohammedan enemies. The passionate
religious zeal of the Middle Age also roused the princes
and knights of Europe to try to wrest from the infidel the
Holy Land of Palestine, where were the birthplace of Christianity and the site of the Sepulcher of Christ. Palestine
was recovered and Christian states were established there,
which lasted for over a hundred and eighty years. Then
the Arab power revived and, operating from Egypt, finally
retook Jerusalem and expelled the Christian from the
Holy Land, to which he has never yet returned as a conqueror.

Effects of the Crusades. — These long, holy wars, or
"Crusades," had a profound effect upon Europe. The
rude Christian warrior from the west was astonished and
delighted with the splendid and luxurious life which he
met at Constantinople and the Arabian East. Even though
he was a prince, his life at home was barren of comforts
and beauty. Glass, linen, rugs, tapestries, silk, cotton,
spices, and sugar were some of the things which the
Franks and the Englishmen took home with them from
the Holy Land. Demand for these treasures of the East
became irresistible, and trade between western Europe
and the East grew rapidly.

The Commercial Cities of Italy. — The cities of Italy developed this commerce. They placed fleets upon the Mediterranean. They carried the crusaders out and brought

back the wares that Europe desired. In this way these cities grew and became very wealthy. On the west coast, where this trade began, were Amalfi, Pisa, Genoa, and Florence, and on the east, at the head of the Adriatic, was Venice. The rivalry between these cities of Italy was very fierce. They fought and plundered one another, each striving to win a monopoly for itself of this invaluable trade.

Venice, finally, was victorious. Her location was very favorable. From her docks the wares could be carried easily and by the shortest routes up the Po River and thence into France or northward over the Alps to the Danube. In Bavaria grew up in this trade the splendid German cities of Augsburg and Nuremberg, which passed these goods on to the cities of the Rhine, and so down this most beautiful river to the coast. Here the towns of Flanders and of the Low Countries, or Holland, received them and passed them on again to England and eastward to the countries of the Baltic.

Development of Modern Language. — Thus commerce and trade grew up in Europe, and, with trade and city life, greater intelligence, learning, and independence. Education became more common, and the universities of Europe were thronged. Latin in the Middle Age had been the only language that was written by the learned class. Now the modern languages of Europe took their form and began to be used for literary purposes. Italian was the first to be so used by the great Dante, and in the same half-century the English poet Chaucer sang in the homely English tongue, and soon in France, Germany, and Spain national literatures appeared. With this went greater freedom of expression. Authority began to have less weight.

Men began to inquire into causes and effects, to doubt

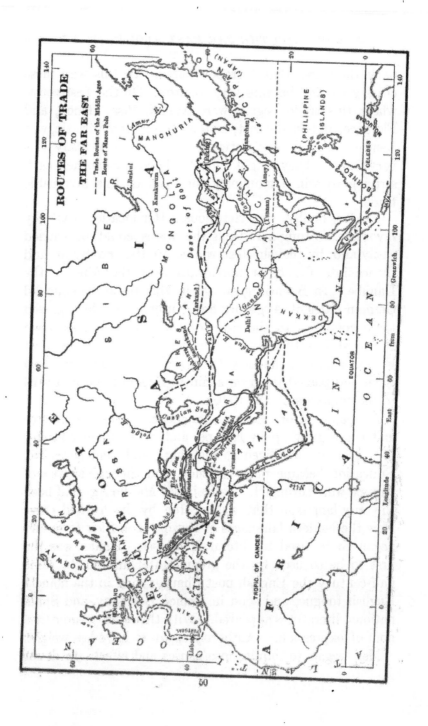

certain things, to seek themselves for the truth, and so the Renaissance came.   With it came a greater love for the beautiful, a greater joy in life, a fresh zest for the good of this world, a new passion for discovery, a thirst for adventure, and, it must also be confessed a new laxity of living and a new greed for gold.   Christian Europe was about to burst its narrow bounds.   It could not be repressed nor confined to its old limitations.   It could never turn backward.   Of all the great changes which have come over life and thought, probably none are greater than those which saw the transition from the mediæval to the modern world.

Trade with the East. — *Articles of Trade.* — Now we must go back for a moment and pursue an old inquiry further.   Whence came all these beautiful and inviting wares that had produced new tastes and passions in Europe?   The Italian traders drew them from the Levant, but the Levant had not produced them.   Neither pepper, spices, sugarcane, costly gems, nor rich silks, were produced on the shores of the Mediterranean.

Only the rich tropical countries of the East were capable of growing these rare plants, and up to that time of delivering to the delver many precious stones.   India, the rich Malaysian archipelago, the kingdom of China, — these are the lands and islands which from time immemorial have given up their treasures to be forwarded far and wide to amaze and delight the native of colder and less productive lands.

Routes of Trade to the Far East. — Three old sailing and caravan routes connect the Mediterranean with the Far East.   They are so old that we can not guess when men first used them.   They were old in the days of Solomon and indeed very ancient when Alexander the

Great conquered the East. One of these routes passed through the Black Sea, and across the Caspian Sea to Turkestan to those strange and romantic ancient cities, Bokhara and Samarkand. Thence it ran northeasterly across Asia, entering China from the north. Another crossed Syria and went down through Mesopotamia to the Indian Ocean. A third began in Egypt and went through the Red Sea, passing along the coast of Arabia to India.

All of these had been in use for centuries, but by the year 1400 two had been closed. A fresh immigration of Turks, the Ottomans, in the fourteenth century came down upon the scourged country of the Euphrates and Syria, and although these Turks also embraced Moham-medanism, their hostility closed the first two routes and commerce over them has never since been resumed.

Venetian Monopoly of Trade. — Thus all interest centered upon the southern route. By treaty with the sultan or ruler of Egypt, Venice secured a monopoly of the products which came over this route. Goods from the East now came in fleets up the Red Sea, went through the hands of the sultan of Egypt, who collected a duty for them, and then were passed on to the ships of the wealthy Venetian merchant princes, who carried them throughout Europe. Although the object of intense jeal-ousy, it seemed impossible to wrest this monopoly from Venice. Her fleet was the strongest on the Mediterranean, and her rule extended along the Adriatic to the Grecian islands. All eager minds were bent upon the trade with the East, but no way was known, save that which now Venice had gained.

Extent of Geographical Knowledge. — *The Maps of this Period.* — To realize how the problem looked to the sailor of Genoa or the merchant of Flanders at that time, we must understand how scanty and erroneous was the geographical knowledge of even the fifteenth century. It was believed that Jerusalem was the center of the world, a belief founded upon a biblical passage. The maps of this and earlier dates represent the earth in this way: In the center, Palestine, and beneath it the Mediterranean Sea, the only body of water which was well known; on the left side is Europe; on the right, Africa; and at the top, Asia — the last two continents very indefinitely mapped. Around the whole was supposed to flow an ocean, beyond the first few miles of which it was perilous to proceed lest the ship be carried over the edge of the earth or encounter other perils.

Ideas about the Earth. — The Greek philosophers before the time of Christ had discovered that the world is a globe, or ball, and had even computed rudely its circumference. But in the Middle Ages this knowledge had been disputed and contradicted by a geographer named Cosmas, who held that the world was a vast plane, twice as long as it was broad and surrounded by an ocean. This belief was generally adopted by churchmen, who were the only scholars of the Middle Ages, and came to be the universal belief of Christian Europe.

The Renaissance revived the knowledge of the writings of the old Greek geographers who had demonstrated the earth's shape to be round and had roughly calculated its size; but these writings did not have sufficient circulation in Europe to gain much acceptance among the Christian cosmographers. The Arabs, however, after conquering Egypt, Syria and northern Africa, translated into their own tongue the wisdom of the Greeks and became the best informed and most scientific geographers of the Middle Age, so that intercourse with the Arabs which

began with the Crusades helped to acquaint Europe somewhat with India and China.

The Far East. — *The Tartar Mongols.* — Then in the
thirteenth century all northern Asia and China fell under
the power of the Tartar Mongols. Russia was overrun by
them and western Europe threatened. At the Danube,
however, this tide of Asiatic conquest stopped, and then
a long period when Europe came into diplomatic and
commercial relations with these Mongols and through them
learned something of China.

Marco Polo Visits the Great Kaan. — Several Europeans visited the court of the Great Kaan, or Mongol
king, and of one of them, Marco Polo, we must speak n
particular. He was a Venetian, and when a young man
started in 1271 with his father and uncle on a visit to
the Great Kaan. They passed from Italy to Syria, across
to Bagdad, and so up to Turkestan, where they saw the
wonderful cities of this strange oasis, thence across the
Pamirs and the Desert of Gobi to Lake Baikal, where the
Kaan had his court. Here in the service of this prince
Marco Polo spent over seventeen years. So valuable indeed were his services that the Kaan would not permit
him to return. Year after year he remained in the East.
He traversed most of China, and was for a time "taotai,"
or magistrate, of the city of Yang Chan near the Yangtze
River. He saw the amazing wonders of the East. He
heard of "Zipangu," or Japan. He probably heard of
the Philippines.

Finally the opportunity came for the three Venetians
to return. The Great Kaan had a relative who was a
ruler of Persia, and ambassadors came from this ruler to
secure a Mongol princess for him to marry. The dangers
and hardships of the travel overland were considered too

difficult for the delicate princess, and it was decided to send her by water. Marco Polo and his father and uncle were commissioned to accompany the expedition to Persia.

History of Marco Polo's Travels. — They sailed from the port of Chin Cheu, probably near Amoy,[1] in the year 1292. They skirted the coasts of Cambodia and Siam and reached the eastern coasts of Sumatra, where they waited five months for the changing of the monsoon. Of the Malay people of Sumatra, as well as of these islands, their animals and productions, Marco Polo has left us most interesting and quite accurate accounts. The Malays on Sumatra were beginning to be converted to Mohammedanism, for Marco Polo says that many of them were "Saracens." He gained a good knowledge of the rich and mysterious Indian Isles, where the spices and flavorings grew. It was two years before the party, having crossed the Indian Ocean, reached Persia and the court of the Persian king. When they arrived they found that while they were making this long voyage the Persian king had died ; but they married the Mongol princess to his son, the young prince, who had succeeded him, and that did just as well.

From Persia the Venetians crossed to Syria and thence sailed to Italy, and at last reached home after an absence of twenty-six years. But Marco Polo's adventures did not end with his return to Venice. In a fierce sea fight between the Venetians and Genoese, he was made

---

[1] See Yule's *Marco Polo* for a discussion of this point and for the entire history of this great explorer, as well as a translation of his narrative. This book of Ser Marco Polo has been most critically edited with introduction and voluminous notes by the English scholar, Sir Henry Yule. In this edition the accounts of Marco Polo, covering so many countries and peoples of the Far East, can be studied.

a prisoner and confined in Genoa. Here a fellow captive wrote down from Marco's own words the story of his eastern adventures, and this book we have to-day. It is a record of adventure, travel, and description, so wonderful that for years it was doubted and its accuracy disbelieved. But since, in our own time, men have been able to traverse again the routes over which Marco Polo passed, fact after fact has been established, quite as he truthfully stated them centuries ago. To have been the first European to make this mighty circuit of travel is certainly a strong title to enduring fame.

Countries of the Far East. — *India.* — Let us now briefly look at the countries of the Far East, which by the year 1400 had come to exercise over the mind of the European so irresistible a fascination. First of all, India, as we have seen, had for centuries been the principal source of the western commerce. But long before the date we are considering, the scepter of India had fallen from the hand of the Hindu. From the seventh century, India was a prey to Mohammedan conquerors, who entered from the northwest into the valley of the Indus. At first these were Saracens or Arabs; later they were the same Mongol converts to Mohammedanism, whose attacks upon Europe we have already noticed.

In 1398 came the furious and bloody warrior, the greatest of all Mongols, — Timour, or Tamerlane. He founded, with capital at Delhi, the empire of the Great Mogul, whose rule over India was only broken by the white man. Eastward across the Ganges and in the Dekkan, or southern part of India, were states ruled over by Indian princes.

China. — We have seen how, at the time of Marco Polo, China also was ruled by the Tartar Mongols. The

Chinese have ever been subject to attack from the wandering horse-riding tribes of Siberia. Two hundred years before Christ one of the Chinese kings built the Great Wall that stretches across the northern frontier for one thousand three hundred miles, for a defense against northern foes. Through much of her history the Chinese have been ruled by aliens, as they are to-day. About 1368, however, the Chinese overthrew the Mongol rulers and established the Ming dynasty, the last Chinese house of emperors, who ruled China until 1644, when the Manchus, the present rulers, conquered the country.

China was great and prosperous under the Mings. Commerce flourished and the fleets of Chinese junks sailed to India, the Malay Islands, and to the Philippines for trade. The Grand Canal, which connects Peking with the Yangtze River basin and Hangchau, was completed. It was an age of fine productions of literature.

The Chinese seem to have been much less exclusive then than they are at the present time; much less a peculiar, isolated people than now. They did not then shave their heads nor wear a queue. These customs, as well as that hostility to foreign intercourse which they have to-day, has been forced upon China by the Manchus. China appeared at that time ready to assume a position of enormous influence among the peoples of the earth, — a position for which she was well fitted by the great industry of all classes and the high intellectual power of her learned men.

Japan. — Compared with China or India, or even some minor states, the development of Japan at this time was very backward. Her people were divided and there was constant civil war. The Japanese borrowed their civilization from the Chinese. From them they learned writing

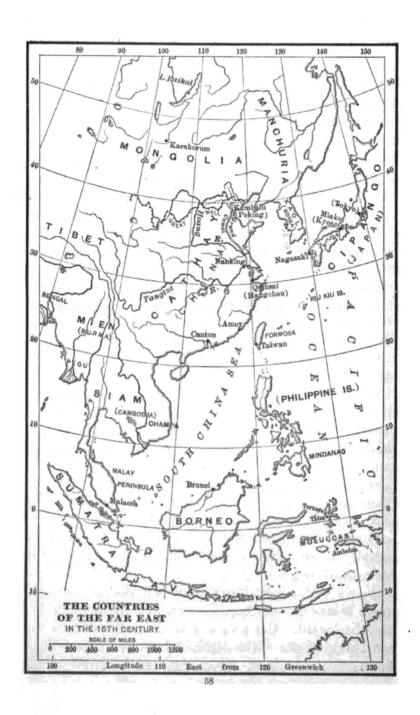

THE COUNTRIES
OF THE FAR EAST
IN THE 15TH CENTURY

SCALE OF MILES

0   200   400   600   800   1000 1200

and literature, and the Buddhist religion, which was introduced about 550 A.D. But in temperament they are a very different people, being spirited, warlike, and, until recent years, despising trading and commerce.

Since the beginning of her history, Japan has been an empire. The ruler, the Mikado, is believed to be of heavenly descent; but in the centuries we are discussing the government was controlled by powerful nobles, known as the Shogun, who kept the emperors in retirement in the palaces of Kyoto, and themselves directed the State. The greatest of these shoguns was Iyeyásu, who ruled Japan about 1600, soon after Manila was founded. They developed in Japan a species of feudalism, the great lords, or "daimios," owning allegiance to the shoguns, and about the daimios, as feudal retainers, bodies of samurai, who formed a partly noble class of their own. The samurai carried arms, fought at their lords' command, were students and literati, and among them developed that proud, loyal, and elevated code of morality known as "Búshido," which has done so much for the Japanese people. It is this samurai class who in modern times have effected the immense revolution in the condition and power of Japan.

The Malay Archipelago. — If now we look at the Malay Islands, we find, as we have already seen, that changes had been effected there. Hinduism had first elevated and civilized at least a portion of the race, and Mohammedanism and the daring seamanship of the Malay had united these islands under a common language and religion. There was, however, no political union. The Malay peninsula was divided. Java formed a central Malay power. Eastward among the beautiful Celebes and Moluccas, the true Spice Islands, were a multitude of small native rulers, rajas or datos, who surrounded themselves with retainers, kept rude courts, and gathered wealthy tributes of cinnamon, pepper, and cloves. The sultans of Ternate, Tidor, and Amboina were especially powerful, and the islands they ruled the most rich and productive.

Between all these islands there was a busy commerce. The Malay is an intrepid sailor, and an eager trader. Fleets of praos, laden with goods, passed with the changing monsoons from part to part, risking the perils of piracy, which have always troubled this archipelago. Borneo, while the largest of all these islands, was the least developed, and down to the present day has been hardly explored. The Philippines were also outside of most of this busy intercourse and had at that date few products to offer for trade. Their only connection with the rest of the Malay race was through the Mohammedan Malays of Jolo and Borneo. The fame of the Spice Islands had long filled Europe, but the existence of the Philippines was unknown.

Summary. — We have now reviewed the condition of Europe and of farther Asia as they were before the period of modern discovery and colonization opened. The East had reached a condition of quiet stability. Mohammedanism, though still spreading, did not promise to effect great social changes. The institutions of the East had become fixed in custom and her peoples neither made changes nor desired them. On the other hand western Europe had become aroused to an excess of ambition. New ideas, new discoveries and inventions were moving the nations to activity and change. That era of modern discovery and progress, of which we cannot yet perceive the end, had begun.

CHAPTER IV.

THE GREAT GEOGRAPHICAL DISCOVERIES.

An Eastern Passage to India. — *The Portuguese.* — We have seen in the last chapter how Venice held a monopoly of the only trading-route with the Far East. Some new way of reaching India must be sought, that would permit the traders of other Christian powers to reach the marts of the Orient without passing through Mohammedan lands. This surpassing achievement was accomplished by the Portuguese. So low at the present day has the power of Portugal fallen that few realize the daring and courage once displayed by her seamen and soldiers and the enormous colonial empire that she established.

Portugal freed her territory of the Mohammedan Moors nearly a century earlier than Spain; and the vigor and intelligence of a great king, John I., brought Portugal, about the year 1400, to an important place among the states of Europe. This king captured from the Moors the city of Ceuta, in Morocco; and this was the beginning of modern European colonial possessions, and the first bit of land outside of Europe to be held by a European power since the times of the Crusades. King John's youngest son was Prince Henry, famous in history under the title of "the Navigator." This young prince, with something of the same adventurous spirit that filled the Crusaders, was ardent to extend the power of his father's kingdom and to widen the sway of the religion which he devotedly professed. The power of the Mohammedans in the Mediterranean was too great for him hopefully to oppose and so he planned the conquest of the west coast of Africa, and its conversion to Christianity. With these ends in view, he established at Point Sagres, on the southwestern coast of Portugal, a naval academy and observatory. Here he brought together skilled navigators, charts, and geographies, and all scientific knowledge that would assist in his undertaking.[1]

He began to construct ships larger and better than any in use. To us they would doubtless seem very clumsy and small, but this was the beginning of ocean ship-building. The compass and the astrolabe, or sextant, the little instrument with which, by calculating the height of the sun above the horizon, we can tell distance from the equator, were just coming into use. These, as well as every other practicable device for navigation known at that time, were supplied to these ships.

Exploration of the African Coast. — Thus equipped and ably manned, the little fleets began the exploration of the African coast, cautiously feeling their way southward and ever returning with reports of progress made. Year after year this work went on. In 1419 the Madeira Islands were rediscovered and colonized by Portuguese settlers. The growing of sugarcane was begun, and vines were brought from Burgundy and planted there. The

---

[1] See the noted work *The Life of Prince Henry of Portugal, surnamed the Navigator, and its Results,* by Richard Henry Major, London, 1868. Many of the views of Mr. Major upon the importance of Prince Henry's work and especially its early aims, have been contradicted in more recent writings. The importance of the Sagres Observatory is belittled. Doubts are expressed as to the farsightedness of Prince Henry's plans, and the best opinion of to-day holds that he did not hope to discover a new route to India by way of Africa, but sought simply the conquest of the " Guinea," which was known to the Europeans through the Arab Geographers, who called it " Bilad Ghana " or " Land of Wealth." The students, if possible, should read the essay of Mr. E. J. Payne, *The Age of Discovery,* in the *Cambridge Modern History,* Vol I.

wine of the Madeiras has been famous to this day. Then were discovered the Canaries and in 1444 the Azores. The southward exploration of the coast of the mainland steadily continued until in 1445 the Portuguese reached the mouth of the Senegal River.   Up to this point the African shore had not yielded much of interest to the Portuguese explorer or trader.   Below Morocco the great Sahara Desert reaches to the sea and renders barren the coast for hundreds of miles.

South of the mouth of the Senegal and comprising the whole Guinea coast, Africa is tropical, well watered, and populous. This is the home of the true African Negro. Here, for almost the first time, since the beginning of the Middle Ages, Christian Europe came in contact with a race of ruder culture and different color than its own. This coast was found to be worth exploiting; for it yielded, besides various desirable resinous gums, three articles which have distinguished the exploitation of Africa, namely, gold, ivory, and slaves.

Beginning of Negro Slavery in Europe. — At this point begins the horrible and revolting story of European Negro slavery. The ancient world had practiced this ownership of human chattels, and the Roman Empire had declined under a burden of half the population sunk in bondage. To the enormous detriment and suffering of mankind, Mohammed had tolerated the institution, and slavery is permitted by the Koran. But it is the glory of the mediæval church that it abolished human slavery from Christian Europe. However dreary and unjust feudalism may have been, it knew nothing of that institution which degrades men and women to the level of cattle and remorselessly sells the husband from his family, the mother from her child.

Slaves in Portugal. — The arrival of the Portuguese upon the coast of Guinea now revived not the bondage of one white man to another, but that of the black to the white. The first slaves carried to Portugal were regarded simply as objects of peculiar interest, captives to represent to the court the population of those shores which had been added to the Portuguese dominion. But southern Portugal, from which the Moors had been expelled, had suffered from a lack of laborers, and it was found profitable to introduce Negroes to work these fields.

Arguments to Justify Slavery. — So arose the institution of Negro slavery, which a century later upon the shores of the New World was to develop into so tremendous and terrible a thing. Curiously enough, religion was evoked to justify this enslavement of the Africans. The Church taught that these people, being heathen, were fortunate to be captured by Christians, that they might thereby be brought to baptism and conversion; for it is better for the body to perish than for the soul to be cast into hell. At a later age, when the falsity of this teaching had been realized, men still sought to justify the institution by arguing that the Almighty had created the African of a lower state especially that he might serve the superior race.

The coast of Guinea continued to be the resort of slavers down to the middle of the last century, and such scenes of cruelty, wickedness, and debauchery have occurred along its shores as can scarcely be paralleled in brutality in the history of any people.

The Portuguese can hardly be said to have colonized the coast in the sense of raising up there a Portuguese population. As he approached the equator the white man found that, in spite of his superior strength, he could not permanently people the tropics.   Diseases new to his experience attacked him.   His energy declined.   If he brought his family with him, his children were few or feeble and shortly his race had died out.

The settlements of the Portuguese were largely for the purposes of trade.   At Sierra Leone, Kamerun, or Loango, they built forts and established garrisons, mounting pieces of artillery that gave them advantage over the attacks of the natives, and erecting warehouses and the loathsome "barracoon," where the slaves were confined to await shipment.   Such decadent little settlements still linger along the African coast, although the slave-trade happily has ended.

The Successful Voyage of Vasco da Gama. — Throughout the century Prince Henry's policy of exploration was continued.   Slowly the middle coast of Africa became known.   At last in 1486, Bartholomew Diaz rounded the extremity of the continent.   He named it the Cape of Storms; but the Portuguese king, with more prophetic sight, renamed it the Cape of Good Hope.   It was ten years, however, before the Portuguese could send another expedition.   Then Vasco da Gama rounded the cape again, followed up the eastern coast until the Arab trading-stations were reached.   Then he struck across the sea, landed at the Malabar coast of India, and in 1498 arrived at Calcutta.   The end dreamed of by all of Europe had been achieved.   A sea-route to the Far East had been discovered.

Results of Da Gama's Voyage. — The importance of this performance was instantly recognized in Europe. Venice was ruined.   "It was a terrible day," said a contemporary writer, "when the word reached Venice.   Bells were rung, men wept in the streets, and even the bravest were silent." The Arabs and the native rulers made a desperate effort to expel the Portuguese from the Indian Ocean, but their opponents were too powerful. In the course of twenty years Portugal had founded an empire that had its forts and trading-marts from the coast of Arabia to Malaysia. Zanzibar, Aden, Oman, Goa, Calicut, and Madras were all Portuguese stations, fortified and secured. In the Malay peninsula was founded the colony of Malacca. It retained its importance and power until in the last century, when it dwindled before the competition of Singapore.

The work of building up this great domain was largely that of one man, the intrepid Albuquerque. Think what his task was! He was thousands of miles from home and supplies, he had only such forces and munitions as he could bring with him in his little ships, and opposed to him were millions of inhabitants and a multitude of Mohammedan princes. Yet this great captain built up an Indian empire. Portugal at one bound became the greatest trading and colonizing power in the world. Her sources of wealth appeared fabulous, and, like Venice, she made every effort to secure her monopoly. The fleets of other nations were warned that they could not make use of the Cape of Good Hope route, on penalty of being captured or destroyed.

Reaching India by Sailing West. — *The Earth as a Sphere.* — Meanwhile, just as Portugal was carrying to completion her project of reaching India by sailing *east*, Europe was electrified by the supposed successful attempt of reaching India by sailing directly *west*, across the Atlantic. This was the plan daringly attempted in 1492 by Christopher Columbus. Columbus was an Italian sailor and cosmographer of Genoa. The idea of sailing west to

India did not originate with him, but his is the immortal glory of having persistently sought the means and put the idea into execution.

The Portuguese discoveries along the African coast gradually revealed the extension of this continent and the presence of people beyond the equator, and the possibility of passing safely through the tropics. This knowledge was a great stimulus to the peoples of Europe. The geographical theory of the Greeks, that the world is round, was revived. The geographers, however, in making their calculations of the earth's circumference, had fallen into an error of some thousands of miles; that is, instead of finding that it is fully twelve thousand miles from Europe around to the East Indies, they had supposed it about four thousand, or even less. Marco Polo too had exaggerated the distance he had traveled and from his accounts men had been led to believe that China, Japan, and the Spice Islands lie much further to the east than they actually do.

By sailing west across one wide ocean, with no intervening lands, it was thought that one could arrive at the island-world off the continent of Asia. This was the theory that was revived in Italy and which clung in men's minds for years and years, even after America was discovered.

An Italian, named Toscanelli, drew a map showing how this voyage could be made, and sent Columbus a copy. By sailing first to the Azores, a considerable portion of the journey would be passed, with a convenient resting-stage. Then about thirty-five days' favorable sailing would bring one to the islands of "Cipango," or Japan, which Marco Polo had said lay off the continent of Asia. From here the passage could readily be pursued to Cathay and India.

The Voyage of Christopher Columbus. — The romantic and inspiring story of Columbus is told in many books, — his poverty, his genius, his long and discouraging pursuit of the means to carry out his plan. He first applied to Portugal; but, as we have seen, this country had been pursuing another plan steadily for a century, and, now that success appeared almost at hand, naturally the Portuguese king would not turn aside to favor Columbus's plan.

For years Columbus labored to interest the Spanish court. A great event had happened in Spanish history. Ferdinand, king of Aragon, had wedded Isabella of Castile, and this marriage united these two kingdoms into the modern country of Spain. Soon the smaller states except Portugal were added, and the war for the expulsion of the Moors was prosecuted with new vigor. In 1492, Grenada, the last splendid stronghold of the Mohammedans in the peninsula, surrendered, and in the same year Isabella furnished Columbus with the ships for his voyage of discovery.

Columbus sailed from Palos, August 3, 1492, reached the Canaries August 24, and sailed westward on September 6. Day after day, pushed by the strong winds, called the "trades," they went forward. Many doubts and fears beset the crews, but Columbus was stout-hearted. At the end of thirty-four days from the Canaries, on October 12, they sighted land. It was one of the groups of beautiful islands lying between the two continents of America. But Columbus thought that he had reached the East Indies that really lay many thousands of miles farther west. Columbus sailed among the islands of the archipelago, discovered Cuba and Hispaniola (Haiti), and then returned to convulse Europe with excitement over the new-found way

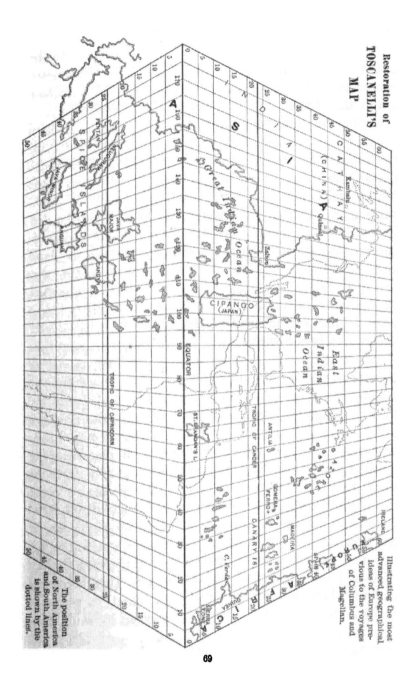

Restoration of
TOSCANELLI'S
MAP

Illustrating the most
advanced geographical
ideas of Europe pre-
vious to the voyages
of Columbus and
Magellan.

The position
of North America
and South America
is shown by the
dotted lines.

69

to the East. He had not found the rich Spice Islands, the peninsula of India, Cathay or Japan, but every one believed that these must be close to the islands on which Columbus had landed.

The tall, straight-haired, copper-colored natives, whom Columbus met on the islands, he naturally called "Indians"; and this name they still bear. Afterwards the islands were called the "West Indies." Columbus made three more voyages for Spain. On the fourth, in 1498, he touched on the coast of South America. Here he discovered the great Orinoco River. Because of its large size, he must have realized that a large body of land opposed the passage to the Orient. He died in 1506, disappointed at his failure to find India, but never knowing what he had found, nor that the history of a new hemisphere had begun with him.

The Voyage of the Cabots. — In the same year that Columbus discovered the Orinoco, Sebastian Cabot, of Italian parentage, like Columbus, secured ships from the king of England, hoping to reach China and Japan by sailing west on a northern route. What he did discover was a rugged and uninviting coast, with stormy headlands, cold climate, and gloomy forests of pine reaching down to the sandy shores. For nine hundred miles he sailed southward, but everywhere this unprofitable coast closed the passage to China. It was the coast of Labrador and the United States. Yet for years and years it was not known that a continent three thousand miles wide and the greatest of all oceans lay between Cathay and the shore visited by Cabot's ships. This land was thought to be a long peninsula, an island, or series of islands, belonging to Asia. No one supposed or could suppose that there was a continent here.

Naming the New World. — But in a few years Europe did realize that a new continent had been discovered in South America. If you will look at your maps, you will see that South America lies far to the eastward of North America and in Brazil approaches very close to Africa. This Brazilian coast was visited by a Portuguese fleet on the African route in 1499, and two years later an Italian fleet traversed the coast from the Orinoco to the harbor of Rio Janeiro. Their voyage was a veritable revelation. They entered the mighty current of the Amazon, the greatest river of the earth. They saw the wondrous tropical forests, full of monkeys, great snakes, and stranger animals. They dealt and fought with the wild and ferocious inhabitants, whose ways startled and appalled the European. All that they saw filled them with greatest wonder. This evidently was not Asia, nor was it the Indies. Here, in fact, was a new continent, a veritable "Mundus Novus."

The pilot of this expedition was an Italian, named Amerigo Vespucci. On the return this man wrote a very interesting letter or little pamphlet, describing this new world, which was widely read, and brought the writer fame. A few years later a German cosmographer, in preparing a new edition of Ptolemy's geography, proposed to give to this new continent the name of the man who had made known its wonders in Europe. So it was called "America." Long after, when the northern shores were also proved to be those of a continent, this great land was named "North America." No injustice was intended to Columbus when America was so named. It was not then supposed that Columbus had discovered a continent. The people then believed that Columbus had found a new route to India and had discovered some new islands that lay off the coast of Asia.

Spain Takes Possession of the New Lands. — Of these newly found islands and whatever wealth they might be found to contain, Spain claimed the possession by right of discovery. And of the European nations, it was Spain which first began the exploration and colonization of America. Spain was now free from her long Mohammedan wars, and the nation was being united under Ferdinand and Isabella. The Spaniards were brave, adventurous, and too proud to engage in commerce or agriculture, but ready enough to risk life and treasure in quest of riches abroad. The Spaniards were devotedly religious, and the Church encouraged conquest, that missionary work might be extended. So Spain began her career that was soon to make her the foremost power of Europe and one of the greatest colonial empires the world has seen. It is amazing what the Spaniards accomplished in the fifty years following Columbus's first voyage.

Hispaniola was made the center from which the Spaniards extended their explorations to the continents of both North and South America. On these islands of the West Indies they found a great tribe of Indians, — the Caribs. They were fierce and cruel. The Spaniards waged a warfare of extermination against them, killing many, and enslaving others for work in the mines. The Indian proved unable to exist as a slave. And his sufferings drew the attention of a Spanish priest, Las Casas, who by vigorous efforts at the court succeeded in having Indian slavery abolished and African slavery introduced to take its place. This remedy was in the end worse than the disease, for it gave an immense impetus to the African slave-trade and peopled America with a race of Africans in bondage.

Other Spanish Explorations and Discoveries. — Meanwhile, the Spanish soldier, with incredible energy, courage,

and daring, pushed his conquests. In 1513, Florida was
discovered, and in the same year Balboa crossed the narrow isthmus of Panama and saw the Pacific Ocean. Contrary to what is often supposed, he did not dream of its
vast extent, but supposed it to be a narrow body of water
lying between Panama and the Asian islands. He named
it the "South Sea," a name that survived after its true
character was revealed by Magellan. Then followed the
two most romantic and surprising conquests of colonial
history, — that of Mexico by Cortes in 1521, and of Peru
by Pizarro in 1533–34. These great countries were inhabited by Indians, the most advanced and cultured on
the American continents. And here the Spaniards found
enormous treasures of gold and silver. Then, the discovery of the mines of Bogota opened the greatest source
of the precious metal that Europe had ever known. Spaniards flocked to the New World, and in New Spain, as
Mexico was called, was established a great vice-royalty.
Year after year enormous wealth was poured into Spain
from these American possessions.

Emperor Charles V. — Meanwhile great political power
had been added to Spain in Europe. In 1520 the throne
of Spain fell to a young man, Charles, the grandson of
Ferdinand and Isabella. His mother was Juana, the
Spanish princess, and his father was Philip the Handsome, of Burgundy. Philip the Handsome was the son of
Maximilian, the Archduke of Austria. Now it curiously
happened that the thrones of each of these three countries was left without other heirs than Charles, and in
1520 he was King of Spain, Archduke of Austria, and
Duke of Burgundy and the Low Countries, including the
rich commercial cities of Holland and Belgium. In addition to all this, the German princes elected him German

emperor, and although he was King Charles the First of
Spain, he is better known in history as Emperor Charles
the Fifth.[1]

He was then an untried boy of twenty years, and no
one expected to find in him a man of resolute energy, cold
persistence, and great executive ability.   But so it proved,
and this was the man that made of Spain the greatest
power of the time. He was in constant warfare. He
fought four wars with King Francis I. of France, five
wars with the Turks, both in the Danube valley and in
Africa, and an unending succession of contests with the
Protestant princes of Germany.   For Charles, besides many
other important changes, saw the rise of Protestantism,
and the revolt of Germany, Switzerland, and England
from Catholicism.   The first event in his emperorship
was the assembling of the famous German Diet at Worms,
where was tried and condemned the real founder of the
Protestant religion, Martin Luther.

The Voyage of Hernando Magellan. — In the mean time
a way had at last been found to reach the Orient from
Europe by sailing west. This discovery, the greatest voyage ever made by man, was accomplished, in 1521, by the
fleet of Hernando Magellan. Magellan was a Portuguese,
who had been in the East with Albuquerque. He had
fought with the Malays in Malacca, and had helped to
establish the Portuguese power in India.

On his return to Portugal, the injustice of the court
drove him from his native country, and he entered the
service of Spain. Charles the Fifth commissioned him
to attempt a voyage of discovery down the coast of South

---

[1] The classical work on this famous ruler is Robertson's *Life of
Charles the Fifth*, but the student should consult if possible more
recent works.

America, with the hope of finding a passage to the East. This was Magellan's great hope and faith, — that south of the new continent of America must lie a passage westward, by which ships could sail to China. As long as Portugal was able to keep closed the African route to all other ships than her own, the discovery of some other way was imperative.

On the 20th of September, 1519, Magellan's fleet of five ships set sail from Seville, which was the great Spanish shipping-port for the dispatch of the colonial fleets. On December 13 they reached the coast of Brazil and then coasted southward. They traded with the natives, and at the mouth of the Rio de la Plata stayed some days to fish.

The weather grew rapidly colder and more stormy as they went farther south, and Magellan decided to stop and winter in the Bay of San Julian. Here the cold of the winter, the storms, and the lack of food caused a conspiracy among his captains to mutiny and return to Spain. Magellan acted with swift and terrible energy. He went himself on board one of the mutinous vessels, killed the chief conspirator with his own hand, executed another, and then "marooned," or left to their fate on the shore, a friar and one other, who were leaders in the plot.

The Straits of Magellan. — The fleet sailed southward again in August but it was not until November 1, 1520, that Magellan entered the long and stormy straits that bear his name and which connect the Atlantic and Pacific oceans. South of them were great bleak islands, cold and desolate. They were inhabited by Indians, who are probably the lowest and most wretched savages on the earth. They live on fish and mussels. As they go at all times naked, they carry with them in their

boats brands and coals of fire.   Seeing the numerous lights
on the shore, Magellan named these islands Tierra del
Fuego (the Land of Fire).   For twenty days the ships
struggled with the contrary and shifting winds that prevail in this channel, during which time one ship deserted
and returned to Spain.   Then the remaining four ships
passed out onto the boundless waters of the Pacific.

Westward on the Pacific Ocean. — But we must not
make the mistake of supposing that Magellan and his followers imagined that a great ocean confronted them.
They expected that simply sailing northward to the latitude of the Spice Islands would bring them to these desired places.   This they did, and then turned westward,
expecting each day to find the Indies; but no land appeared.   The days lengthened into weeks, the weeks into
months, and still they went forward, carried by the trade
winds over a sea so smooth and free from tempests that
Magellan named it the "Pacific."

But they suffered horribly from lack of food, even
eating in their starvation the leather slings on the masts.
It was a terrible trial of their courage.   Twenty of their
number died.   The South Pacific is studded with islands,
but curiously their route lay just too far north to behold
them.   From November 28, when they emerged from the
Straits of Magellan, until March 7, when they reached
the Ladrones, they encountered only two islands, and these
were small uninhabited rocks, without water or food, which
in their bitter disappointment they named las Desven-
turadas (the Unfortunate Islands).

The Ladrone Islands. — Their relief must have been
inexpressible when, on coming up to land on March the
7th, they found inhabitants and food, yams, cocoanuts,
and rice.   At these islands the Spaniards first saw the

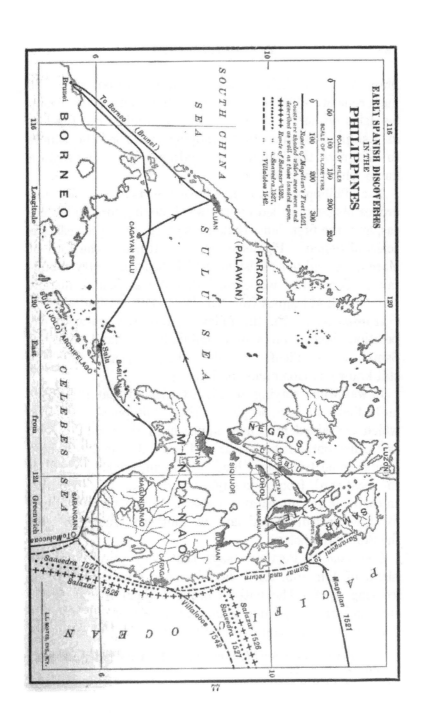

EARLY SPANISH DISCOVERIES
IN THE
PHILIPPINES

SCALE OF MILES

SCALE OF KILOMETERS

Coasts are shaded which were seen and described as well as those landed upon.

━━━━━ Route of Magellan's Fleet 1521.
+++++ " " Saavedra 1527.
••••••• " " " 1528.
– – – – " " Villalobos 1542.

prao, with its light outrigger, and pointed sail. So numerous were these craft that they named the group las Islas de las Velas (the Islands of Sails); but the loss of a ship's boat and other annoying thefts led the sailors to designate the islands Los Ladrones (the Thieves), a name which they still retain.

The Philippine Islands.— *Samar.* — Leaving the Ladrones Magellan sailed on westward looking for the Moluccas, and the first land that he sighted was the eastern coast of Samar. Pigafetta says: '' Saturday, the 16th of March, we sighted an island which has very lofty mountains. Soon after we learned that it was Zamal, distant three hundred leagues from the islands of the Ladrones."[1]

Homonhón.— On the following day the sea-worn expedition, landed on a little uninhabited island south of Samar which Pigafetta called Humunu, and which is still known as Homonhón or Jomonjól.

It was while staying at this little island that the Spaniards first saw the people of the Philippines. A prao which contained nine men approached their ship. They saw other boats fishing near and learned that all of these people came from the island of Suluan, which lies off to the eastward from Jomonjól about twenty kilometres. In their life and appearance these fishing people were much like the present Samal laut of southern Mindanao and the Sulu Archipelago.

Limasaua. — Pigafetta says that they stayed on the island of Jomonjól eight days but had great difficulty in securing food. The natives brought them a few cocoanuts and oranges, palm wine, and a chicken or two, but this was all that could be spared, so, on the 25th, the

---

[1] *Primer Viaje alrededor del Mundo*, Spanish translation by Amoretti, Madrid, 1899, page 27.

Spaniards sailed again, and near the south end of Leyte landed on the little island of Limasaua. Here there was a village, where they met two chieftains, whom Pigafetta calls "kings," and whose names were Raja Calambú and Raja Ciagu. These two chieftains were visiting Limasaua and had their residences one at Butúan and one at Cagayan on the island of Mindanao. Some histories have stated that the Spaniards accompanied one of these chieftains to Butúan, but this does not appear to have been the case.

On the island of Limasaua the natives had dogs, cats, hogs, goats, and fowls. They were cultivating rice, maize, breadfruit, and had also cocoanuts, oranges, bananas, citron, and ginger. Pigafetta tells how he visited one of the chieftains at his home on the shore. The house was built as Filipino houses are today, raised on posts and thatched. Pigafetta thought it looked "like a haystack."

It had been the day of San Lazarus when the Spaniards first reached these islands, so that Magellan gave to the group the name of the Archipelago of Saint Lazarus, the name under which the Philippines were frequently described in the early writings, although another title, Islas del Poniente or Islands of the West, was more common up to the time when the title Filipinas became fixed.

Cebu. — Magellan's people were now getting desperately in need of food, and the population on Limasaua had very inadequate supplies; consequently the natives directed him to the island of Cebu, and provided him with guides.

Leaving Limasaua the fleet sailed for Cebu, passing several large islands, among them Bohol, and reaching Cebu harbor on Sunday, the 7th of April. A junk from Siam was anchored at Cebu when Magellan's ships arrived there; and this, together with the knowledge that the Filipinos showed of the surrounding countries, including China on the one side and the Moluccas on the other, is additional evidence of the extensive trade relations at the time of the discovery.

Cebu seems to have been a large town and it is reported that more than two thousand warriors with their lances appeared to resist the landing of the Spaniards, but assurances of friendliness finally won the Filipinos, and Magellan formed a compact with the dato of Cebu, whose name was Hamalbar.

The Blood Compact. — The dato invited Magellan to seal this compact in accordance with a curious custom of the Filipinos. Each chief wounded himself in the breast and from the wound each sucked and drank the other's blood. It is not certain whether Magellan participated in this "blood compact," as it has been called; but later it was observed many times in the Spanish settlement of the islands, especially by Legaspi.

The natives were much struck by the service of the mass, which the Spaniards celebrated on their landing, and after some encouragement desired to be admitted to the Spaniards' religion. More than eight hundred were baptized, including Hamalbar. The Spaniards established a kind of "factory" or trading-post on Cebu, and for some time a profitable trade was engaged in. The Filipinos well understood trading, had scales, weights, and measures, and were fair dealers.

Death of Magellan.— And now follows the great tragedy of the expedition. The dato of Cebu, or the "Christian king," as Pigafetta called their new ally, was at war with the islanders of Mactán. Magellan, eager to assist one who had adopted the Christian faith, landed on Mactán with fifty men and in the battle that ensued was killed by an arrow through the leg and spear-thrust through the breast. So died the one who was unquestionably the greatest explorer and most daring adventurer of all time. "Thus," says Pigafetta, "perished our guide, our light, and our support." It was the crowning disaster of the expedition.

The Fleet Visits Other Islands. — After Magellan's death, the natives of Cebu rose and killed the newly

Magellan Monument, Manila.

elected leader, Serrano, and the fleet in fear lifted its anchors and sailed southward from the Bisayas. They had lost thirty-five men and their numbers were reduced to one hundred and fifteen. One of the ships was burned, there being too few men surviving to handle three vessels. After touching at western Mindanao, they sailed westward, and saw the small group of Cagayan Sulu. The few inhabitants they learned were Moros, exiled from Borneo. They landed on Paragua, called Puluan (hence Palawan), where they observed the sport of cock-fighting, indulged in by the natives.

From here, still searching for the Moluccas, they were guided to Borneo, the present city of Brunei. Here was the powerful Mohammedan colony, whose adventurers were already in communication with Luzon and had established a colony on the site of Manila. The city was divided into two sections, that of the Mohammedan Malays, the conquerors, and that of the Dyaks, the primitive population of the island. Pigafetta exclaims over the riches and power of this Mohammedan city. It contained twenty-five thousand families, the houses built for most part on piles over the water. The king's house was of stone, and beside it was a great brick fort, with over sixty brass and iron cannon. Here the Spaniards saw elephants and camels, and there was a rich trade in ginger, camphor, gums, and in pearls from Sulu.

Hostilities cut short their stay here and they sailed eastward along the north coast of Borneo through the Sulu Archipelago, where their cupidity was excited by the pearl fisheries, and on to Maguindanao. Here they took some prisoners, who piloted them south to the Moluccas, and finally, on November 8, they anchored at Tidor. These Molucca islands, at this time, were at the height of the Malayan power. The ruler, or raja of Tidor was Almanzar, of Ternate Corala; the "king" of Gilolo was Yusef. With all these rulers the Spaniards exchanged presents, and the rajas are said by the Spaniards to have sworn perpetual amnesty to the Spaniards and acknowledged themselves vassals of the king. In exchange for cloths, the Spaniards laid in a rich cargo of cloves, sandalwood, ginger, cinnamon, and gold. They established here a trading-post and hoped to hold these islands against the Portuguese.

The Return to Spain. — It was decided to send one ship, the "Victoria," to Spain by way of the Portuguese route and the Cape of Good Hope, while the other would return to America. Accordingly the "Victoria," with a little crew of sixty men, thirteen of them natives, under the command of Juan Sebastian del Cano, set sail. The passage was unknown to the Spaniards and full of perils. They sailed to Timor and thence out into the Indian Ocean. They rounded Africa, sailing as far south as 42 degrees. Then they went northward, in constant peril of capture by some Portuguese fleet, encountering storms and with scarcity of food. Their distress must have been extreme, for on this final passage twenty-one of their small number died.

At Cape Verdi they entered the Portuguese port for supplies, trusting that at so northern a point their real voyage would not be suspected. But some one of the party, who went ashore for food, in an hour of intoxication boasted of the wonderful journey they had performed and showed some of the products of the Spice Islands. Immediately the Portuguese governor gave orders for the seizure of the Spanish vessel and El Cano, learning of his danger, left his men, who had gone on shore, raised sail, and put out for Spain.

On the 6th of September, 1522, they arrived at San Lucar, at the mouth of the Guadalquivir River, on which is situated Seville, one ship out of the five, and eighteen men out of the company of 234, who had set sail almost three full years before. Spain welcomed her worn and tired seamen with splendid acclaim. To El Cano was given a title of nobility and the famous coat-of-arms, showing the sprays of clove, cinnamon, and nutmeg, and the effigy of the globe with the motto, the proudest and worthiest ever displayed on any adventurer's shield, "Hic primus circum dedit me."

The First Circumnavigation of the Earth.—Thus with enormous suffering and loss of life was accomplished the first circumnavigation of the earth. It proved that Asia could be reached, although by a long and circuitous route, by sailing westward from Europe. It made known to Europe that the greatest of all oceans lies between the New World and Asia, and it showed that the earth is incomparably larger than had been believed and supposed. It was the greatest voyage of discovery that has ever been accomplished, and greater than can ever be performed again.

New Lands Divided between Spain and Portugal. — By this discovery of the Philippines and a new way to the Spice Islands, Spain became engaged in a long dispute with Portugal. At the beginning of the modern age, there was in Europe no system of rules by which to regulate conduct between states. That system of regulations and customs which we call International Law, and by which states at the present time are guided in their dealings, had not arisen. During the middle age, disputes between sovereigns were frequently settled by reference to the emperor or to the pope, and the latter had frequently asserted his right to determine all such questions as might arise. The pope had also claimed to have the right of disposing of all heathen and newly discovered lands and peoples.

So, after the discovery of the East Indies by Portugal and of the West Indies by Spain, Pope Alexander VI., divided the new lands between them. He declared that

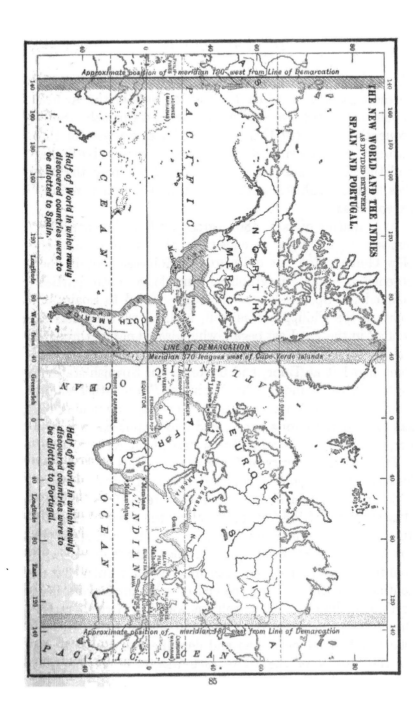

THE NEW WORLD AND THE INDIES
AS DIVIDED BETWEEN
SPAIN AND PORTUGAL.

Approximate position of meridian 180° west from Line of Demarcation

Half of World in which newly discovered countries were to be allotted to Spain.

LINE OF DEMARCATION
Meridian 370 leagues west of Cape Verde Islands

Half of World in which newly discovered countries were to be allotted to Portugal.

Approximate position of meridian 180° east from Line of Demarcation

PACIFIC OCEAN

ATLANTIC OCEAN

INDIAN OCEAN

NORTH AMERICA

SOUTH AMERICA

EUROPE

all newly discovered countries halfway around the earth to the east of a meridian 100 leagues west of the Azores should be Portuguese, and all to the west Spanish. Subsequently he shifted this line to 270 leagues west of the Azores. This division, it was supposed, would give India and the Malay islands to Portugal, and to Spain the Indies that Columbus had discovered, and the New World, except Brazil.

As a matter of fact, 180 degrees west of the meridian last set by the pope extended to the western part of New Guinea, and not quite to the Moluccas; but in the absence of exact geographical knowledge both parties claimed the Spice Islands. Portugal denied to Spain all right to the Philippines as well, and, as we shall see, a conflict in the Far East began, which lasted nearly through the century. Portugal captured the traders, whom El Cano had left at Tidor, and broke up the Spanish station in the Spice Islands. The "Trinidad," the other ship, which was intended to return to America, was unable to sail against the strong winds, and had to put back to Tidor, after cruising through the waters about New Guinea.

Effect of the Century of Discoveries. — This circumnavigation of the globe completed a period of discovery which had begun a hundred years before with the timid, slow attempts of the Portuguese along the coast of Africa. In these years a new era had opened. At its beginning the European knew little of any peoples outside of his own countries, and he held not one mile of land outside the continent of Europe. At the end of a hundred years the earth had become fairly well known, the African race, the Malay peoples, the American Indians, and the Pacific islanders had all been seen and described, and from now on the history of the white race was to be connected with that of these other races. The age of colonization, of world-wide trade and intercourse, had begun. The white man, who had heretofore been narrowly pressed in upon Europe, threatened again and again with conquest by the Mohammedan, was now to cover the seas with his fleets and all lands with his power.

CHAPTER V.

THE FILIPINO PEOPLE BEFORE THE ARRIVAL OF THE SPANIARDS.

Position of Tribes. — On the arrival of the Spaniards, the population of the Philippines seems to have been distributed by tribes in much the same manner as at present. Then, as now, the Bisaya occupied the central islands of the archipelago and some of the northern coast of Mindanao. The Bicol, Tagálog, and Pampango were in the same parts of Luzon as we find them to-day. The Ilocano occupied the coastal plain facing the China Sea, but since the arrival of the Spaniards they have expanded considerably and their settlements are now numerous in Pangasinan, Nueva Vizcaya, and the valley of the Cagayan.

The Number of People. — These tribes which to-day number nearly 7,000,000 souls, at the time of Magellan's discovery were, probably, not more than 500,000. The first enumeration of the population made by the Spaniards in 1591, and which included practically all of these tribes, gives a population of less than 700,000. (See Chapter VIII., *The Philippines Three Hundred Years Ago.*)

There are other facts too that show us how sparse the population must have been. The Spanish expeditions found many coasts and islands in the Bisayan group without inhabitants. Occasionally a sail or a canoe would be seen, and then these would disappear in some small "estero" or mangrove swamp and the land seem as unpopulated as before. At certain points, like Limasaua, Butúan, and Bohol, the natives were more numerous, and Cebu was a large and thriving community; but

88

the Spaniards had nearly everywhere to search for settled places and cultivated lands.

The sparsity of population is also well indicated by the great scarcity of food. The Spaniards had much difficulty in securing sufficient provisions. A small amount of rice, a pig and a few chickens, were obtainable here and there, but the Filipinos had no large supplies. After the settlement of Manila was made, a large part of the food of the city was drawn from China. The very ease with which the Spaniards marched where they willed and reduced the Filipinos to obedience shows that the latter were weak in numbers. Laguna and the Camarines seem to have been the most populous portions of the archipelago. All of these things and others show that the Filipinos were but a small fraction of their present number.

On the other hand, the Negritos seem to have been more numerous, or at least more in evidence. They were immediately noticed on the island of Negros, where at the present they are few and confined to the interior; and in the vicinity of Manila and in Batangas, where they are no longer found, they were mingling with the Tagálog population.

Conditions of Culture. — The culture of the various tribes, which is now quite the same throughout the archipelago, presented some differences. In the southern Bisayas, where the Spaniards first entered the archipelago, there seem to have been two kinds of natives: the hill dwellers, who lived in the interior of the islands in small numbers, who wore garments of tree bark and who sometimes built their houses in the trees; and the sea dwellers, who were very much like the present day Moro tribes south of Mindanao, who are known as the Sámal, and who built their villages over the sea or on the shore and lived much in boats. These were probably later arrivals than the forest people. From both of these elements the Bisaya Filipinos are descended, but while the coast people have been entirely absorbed, some of the hill-folk are still pagan and uncivilized, and must be very much as they were when the Spaniards first came.

The highest grade of culture was in the settlements where there was regular trade with Borneo, Siam, and China, and especially about Manila, where many Mohammedan Malays had colonies.

Languages of the Malayan Peoples. — With the exception of the Negrito, all the languages of the Philippines belong to one great family, which has been called the "Malayo-Polynesian." All are believed to be derived from one very ancient mother-tongue. It is astonishing how widely this Malayo-Polynesian speech has spread. Farthest east in the Pacific there is the Polynesian, then in the groups of small islands, known as Micronesian; then Melanesian or Papuan; the Malayan throughout the East Indian archipelago, and to the north the languages of the Philippines. But this is not all; for far westward on the coast of Africa is the island of Madagascar, many of whose languages have no connection with African but belong to the Malayo-Polynesian family.[1]

The Tagálog Language. — It should be a matter of great interest to Filipinos that the great scientist, Baron

---

[1] The discovery of this famous relationship is attributed to the Spanish Jesuit Abbé, Lorenzo Hervas, whose notable *Catalogo de las Lenguas de las Naciones conocidas* was published in 1800–05; but the similarity of Malay and Polynesian had been earlier shown by naturalists who accompanied the second voyage of the famous Englishman, Captain Cook (1772–75). The full proof, and the relation also of Malagasy, the language of Madagascar, was given in 1838 by the work of the great German philologist, Baron William von Humboldt.

William von Humboldt, considered the Tagálog to be the richest and most perfect of all the languages of the Malayo-Polynesian family, and perhaps the type of them all. "It possesses," he said, "all the forms collectively of which particular ones are found singly in other dialects; and it has preserved them all with very trifling exceptions unbroken, and in entire harmony and symmetry." The Spanish friars, on their arrival in the Philippines, devoted themselves at once to learning the native dialects and to the preparation of prayers and catechisms in these native tongues. They were very successful in their studies. Father Chirino tells us of one Jesuit who learned sufficient Tagálog in seventy days to preach and hear confession. In this way the Bisayan, the Tagálog, and the Ilocano were soon mastered.

In the light of the opinion of Von Humboldt, it is interesting to find these early Spaniards pronouncing the Tagálog the most difficult and the most admirable. "Of all of them," says Padre Chirino, "the one which most pleased me and filled me with admiration was the Tagálog. Because, as I said to the first archbishop, and afterwards to other serious persons, both there and here, I found in it four qualities of the four best languages of the world: Hebrew, Greek, Latin, and Spanish; of the Hebrew, the mysteries and obscurities; of the Greek, the articles and the precision not only of the appellative but also of the proper nouns; of the Latin, the wealth and elegance; and of the Spanish, the good breeding, politeness, and courtesy." [1]

An Early Connection with the Hindus. — The Malayan languages contain also a considerable proportion of words borrowed from the Sanskrit, and in this the Tagálog,

---

[1] *Relacion de las Islas Filipinas*, 2d ed., p. 52.

Bisayan, and Ilocano are included. Whether these words were passed along from one Malayan group to another, or whether they were introduced by the actual presence and power of the Hindu in this archipelago, may be fair ground for debate; but the case for the latter position has been so well and brilliantly put by Dr. Pardo de Tavera that his conclusions are here given in his own words. "The words which Tagálog borrowed," he says, "are those which signify intellectual acts, moral conceptions, emotions, superstitions, names of deities, of planets, of numerals of high number, of botany, of war and its results and consequences, and finally of titles and dignities, some animals, instruments of industry, and the names of money."

From the evidence of these works, Dr. Pardo argues for a period in the early history of the Filipinos, not merely of commercial intercourse, like that of the Chinese, but of Hindu political and social domination. "I do not believe," he says, "and I base my opinion on the same words that I have brought together in this vocabulary, that the Hindus were here simply as merchants, but that they dominated different parts of the archipelago, where to-day are spoken the most cultured languages, — the Tagálo, the Visayan, the Pampanga, and the Ilocano; and that the higher culture of these languages comes precisely from the influence of the Hindu race over the Filipino."

The Hindus in the Philippines. — "It is impossible to believe that the Hindus, if they came only as merchants, however great their number, would have impressed themselves in such a way as to give to these islanders the number and the kind of words which they did give. These names of dignitaries, of caciques, of high functionaries of the court, of noble ladies, indicate that all of these high positions with names of Sanskrit origin were occupied at one time by men who spoke that language. The words of a similar origin for objects of war, fortresses, and battle-songs, for designating objects of religious belief, for superstitions, emotions, feelings, industrial and farming activities, show us clearly that the warfare, religion, literature, industry, and agriculture were at one time in the hands of the Hindus, and that this race was effectively dominant in the Philippines." [1]

Systems of Writing among the Filipinos. — When the Spaniards arrived in the Philippines, the Filipinos were using systems of writing borrowed from Hindu or Javanese sources. This matter is so interesting that one can not do better than to quote in full Padre Chirino's account, as he is the first of the Spanish writers to mention it and as his notice is quite complete.

"So given are these islanders to reading and writing that there is hardly a man, and much less a woman, that does not read and write in letters peculiar to the island of Manila, very different from those of China, Japan, and of India, as will be seen from the following alphabet.

"The vowels are three; but they serve for five, and are,

| a | e, i | o, u |

The consonants are no more than twelve, and they serve to write both consonant and vowel, in this form. The letter alone, without any point either above or below, sounds with *a*.

---

[1] Another possible explanation of the many Sanskrit terms which are found in the Philippine languages, is that the period of contact between Filipinos and Hindus occurred not in the Philippines but in Java and Sumatra, whence the ancestors of the Filipinos came.

Ba	ca	da	ga	ha	la
ma	na	pa	sa	ta	ya

Placing the point above, each one sounds with *e* or with *i*.

Bi	qui	di	gui	hi	li
be	que	de	gue	he	le
mi	ni	pi	si	ti	yi
me	ne	pe	se	te	ye

Placing the point below, it sounds with *o* or with *u*.

bo	co	do	go	ho	lo
bu	cu	du	gu	hu	lu
mo	no	po	so	to	yo
mu	nu	pu	su	tu	yu

For instance, in order to say ' cama,' the two letters alone suffice.

$$\mathcal{I} \quad \mathcal{U}$$

ca - ma

If to the $\mathcal{I}$ there is placed a point above, it will say

$$\overset{\text{\tiny ?}}{\mathcal{I}} \quad \mathcal{U}$$

que - ma

If it is given to both below, it will say

$$\underset{\text{\tiny ?}}{\mathcal{I}} \quad \underset{\text{\tiny ..}}{\mathcal{U}}$$

co - mo

The final consonants are supplied or understood in all cases, and so to say 'cantar,' they write

$$\mathcal{I} \quad \mathcal{C}$$

ca - ta

barba,

$$\mathcal{O} \quad \mathcal{O}\cdot$$

ba - ba

But with all, and that without many evasions, they make themselves understood, and they themselves understand marvellously. And the reader supplies, with much skill and ease, the consonants that are lacking. They have learned from us to write running the lines from the left hand to the right, but formerly they only wrote from above downwards, placing the first line (if I remember rightly) at the left hand, and continuing with the others to the right, the opposite of the Chinese and Japanese. . . . They write upon canes or on leaves of a palm, using for a pen a point of iron. Nowadays in writing not only their own but also our letters, they use a feather very well cut, and paper like ourselves.

They have learned our language and pronunciation, and write as well as we do, and even better; for they are so bright that they learn everything with the greatest ease. I have brought with me handwriting with very good and correct lettering.   In Tigbauan, I had in school a very small child, who in three months' time learned, by copying from well-written letters that I set him, to write enough better than I, and transcribed for me writings of importance very faithfully, and without errors or mistakes.   But enough of languages and letters; now let us return to our occupation with human souls." [1]

Sanskrit Source of the Filipino Alphabet.— Besides the Tagálog, the Bisaya, Pampango, Pangasinan, and Ilocano had alphabets, or more properly syllabaries similar to this one.   Dr. Pardo de Tavera has gathered many data concerning them, and shows that they were undoubtedly received by the Filipinos from a ·Sanskrit source.

Early Filipino Writings. — The Filipinos used this writing for setting down their poems and songs, which were their only literature.   None of this, however, has come down to us, and the Filipinos soon adopted the Spanish alphabet, forming the syllables necessary to write their language from these letters.   As all these have phonetic values, it is still very easy for a Filipino to learn to pronounce and so read his own tongue.   These old characters lingered for a couple of centuries, in certain places. Padre Totanes [2] tells us that it was rare in 1705 to find a person who could use them ; but the Tagbanua, a pagan

----

[1] *Relacion de las Islas Filipinas*, 2d ed., pp. 58, 59, chap. XVII.

[2] *Arte de la Lengua Tagala.*

people on the island of Paragua, use a similar syllabary to this day. Besides poems, they had songs which they sang as they rowed their canoes, as they pounded the rice from its husk, and as they gathered for feast or entertainment; and especially there were songs for the dead. In these songs, says Chirino, they recounted the deeds of their ancestors or of their deities.

Chinese in the Philippines.— *Early Trade.* — Very different from the Hindu was the early influence of the Chinese. There is no evidence that, previous to the Spanish conquest, the Chinese settled or colonized in these islands at all; and yet three hundred years before the arrival of Magellan their trading-fleets were coming here regularly and several of the islands were well known to them. One evidence of this prehistoric trade is in the ancient Chinese jars and pottery which have been exhumed in the vicinity of Manila, but the Chinese writings themselves furnish us even better proof. About the beginning of the thirteenth century, though not earlier than 1205, a Chinese author named Chao Ju-kua wrote a work upon the maritime commerce of the Chinese people. One chapter of his work is devoted to the Philippines, which he calls the country of Mayi.[1] According to this record it is indicated that the Chinese were familiar with the islands of the archipelago seven hundred years ago.[2]

---

[1] This name is derived, in the opinion of Professor Blumentritt, from Bayi, or Bay, meaning Laguna de Bay. Professor Meyer, in his *Distribution of the Negritos,* suggests an identification from this Chinese record, of the islands of Mindanao, Palawan (called Pa-lao-yu) and Panay, Negros, Cebu, Leyte, Samar, Bohol, and Luzon.

[2] Through the courtesy of Professor Zulueta, of the Manila Liceo, permission was given to use from Chao Ju-kua's work these quotations, translated from the Chinese manuscript by Professor Blumentritt. The English translation is by Mr. P. L. Stangl.

Chinese Description of the People. — " The country of Mayi," says this interesting classic, " is situated to the north of Poni (Burney, or Borneo). About a thousand families inhabit the banks of a very winding stream. The natives clothe themselves in sheets of cloth resembling bed sheets, or cover their bodies with sarongs. (The sarong is the gay colored, typical garment of the Malay.) Scattered through the extensive forests are copper Buddha images, but no one knows how they got there.[1]

Filipino Iron Treasure Box.

" When the merchant (Chinese) ships arrive at this port they anchor in front of an open place . . . which serves as a market, where they trade in the produce of the country. When a ship enters this port, the captain makes presents of white umbrellas (to the mandarins). The merchants are obliged to pay this tribute in order to obtain the good will of these lords." The products of the country are stated to be yellow wax, cotton, pearls, shells, betel nuts, and yuta cloth, which was perhaps one of the several cloths still woven of abacá, or piña. The articles imported by the Chinese were " porcelain, trade gold, objects of lead, glass beads of all colors, iron cooking-pans, and iron needles."

The Negritos. — Very curious is the accurate mention in this Chinese writing, of the Negritos, the first of all

---

[1] " This would confirm," says Professor Blumentritt, " Dr. Pardo de Tavera's view that in ancient times the Philippines were under the influence of Buddhism from India."

accounts to be made of the little blacks. "In the interior of the valleys lives a race called Hai-tan (Aeta). They are of low stature, have round eyes of a yellow color, curly hair, and their teeth are easily seen between their lips. (That is, probably, not darkened by betel-chewing or artificial stains.) They build their nests in the treetops and in each nest lives a family, which only consists of from three to five persons. They travel about in the densest thickets of the forests, and, without being seen themselves, shoot their arrows at the passers-by; for this reason they are much feared. If the trader (Chinese) throws them a small porcelain bowl, they will stoop down to catch it and then run away with it, shouting joyfully."

Increase in Chinese Trade.—These junks also visited the more central islands, but here traffic was conducted on the ships, the Chinese on arrival announcing themselves by beating gongs and the Filipinos coming out to them in their light boats. Among other things here offered by the natives for trade are mentioned "strange cloth," perhaps cinamay or jusi, and fine mats.

This Chinese trade continued probably quite steadily until the arrival of the Spaniards. Then it received an enormous increase through the demand for Chinese food-products and wares made by the Spaniards, and because of the value of the Mexican silver which the Spaniards offered in exchange.

Trade with the Moro Malays of the South. — The spread of Mohammedanism and especially the foundation of the colony of Borneo brought the Philippines into important commercial relations with the Malays of the south. Previous to the arrival of the Spaniards these relations seem to have been friendly and peaceful. The Mohammedan

Malays sent their praos northward for purposes of trade, and they were also settling in the north Philippines as they had in Mindanao.

When Legaspi's fleet, soon after its arrival, lay near the island of Bohol, the " Maestro de Campo " had a hard fight with a Moro vessel which had come up for trade, and took six prisoners. One of them, whom they call the "pilot," was closely interrogated by the Adelantado and some interesting information obtained, which is recorded by Padre San Augustin.[1] Legaspi had a Malay slave interpreter with him and San Augustin says that Padre Urdaneta "knew well the Malayan language." The pilot said that "those of Borneo brought for trade with the Filipinos, copper and tin, which was brought to Borneo from China, porcelain, dishes, and bells made in their fashion, very different from those that the Christians use, and benzoin, and colored blankets from India, and cooking-pans made in China, and that they also brought iron lances very well tempered, and knives and other articles of barter, and that in exchange for them they took away from the islands gold, slaves, wax, and a kind of small seashell which they call 'sijueyes,' and which passes for money in the kingdom of Siam and other places; and also they carry off some white cloths, of which there is a great quantity in the islands."

Butúan, on the north coast of Mindanao, seems to have been quite a trading-place resorted to by vessels from all quarters. This country, like many other parts of the Philippines, has produced from time immemorial small quantities of gold, and all the early voyagers speak of the gold earrings and ornaments of the natives. Butúan also produced sugarcane and was a trading-port for

[1] *Conquista de las Islas Filipinas*, p. 95.

slaves. This unfortunate traffic in human life seems to have been not unusual, and was doubtless stimulated by the commerce with Borneo. Junks from Siam trading with Cebu were also encountered by the Spaniards.

Result of this Intercourse and Commerce. — This intercourse and traffic had acquainted the Filipinos with many of the accessories of civilized life long before the arrival of the Spaniards. Their chiefs and datos dressed in silks, and maintained some splendor of surroundings; nearly the whole population of the tribes of the coast wrote and

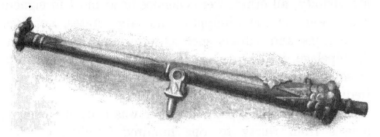

Filipino Portable Iron Cannon.

communicated by means of a syllabary; vessels from Luzon traded as far south as Mindanao and Borneo, although the products of Asia proper came through the fleets of foreigners; and perhaps what indicates more clearly than anything else the advance the Filipinos were making through their communication with outside people is their use of firearms. Of this point there is no question. Everywhere in the vicinity of Manila, on Lubang, in Pampanga, at Cainta and Laguna de Bay, the Spaniards encountered forts mounting small cannon, or "lantakas." [1] The Filipinos seem to have understood, more-

---

[1] *Relacion de la Conquista de la Isla de Luzón*, 1572; in Retana, *Archivo del Bibliófilo Filipino*, vol.' I.

over, the arts of casting cannon and of making powder.
The first gun-factory established by the Spaniards was in
charge of a Filipino from Pampanga.

Early Political and Social Life. — *The Barangay.* —
The weakest side of the culture of the early Filipinos was
their political and social organization, and they were weak
here in precisely the same way that the now uncivilized
peoples of northern Luzon are still weak. Their state did
not embrace the whole tribe or nation; it included simply
the community. Outside of the settlers in one immediate vicinity, all others were enemies or at most foreigners.
There were in the Philippines no large states, nor even
great rajas and sultans such as were found in the Malay
Archipelago, but instead on every island were a multitude
of small communities, each independent of the other and
frequently waging war.

The unit of their political order was a little cluster of
houses from thirty to one hundred families, called a
"barangay," and which still exists in the Philippines as
the "barrio." At the head of each barangay was a chief
known as the "dato," a word no longer used in the
northern Philippines, though it persists among the Moros
of Mindanao. The powers of these datos within their
small areas appear to have been great, and they were
treated with utmost respect by the people.

The barangays were grouped together in tiny federa-
tions including about as much territory as the present
towns, whose affairs were conducted by the chiefs or
datos, although sometimes they seem to have all been in
obedience to a single chief, known in some places as the
"hari," at other times by the Hindu word "raja," or the
Mohammedan term "sultan." Sometimes the power of
one of these rajas seems to have extended over the

whole of a small island, but usually their "kingdoms" embraced only a few miles.

Changes Made by the Spaniards. — The Spaniards, in enforcing their authority through the islands, took away the real power from the datos, grouping the barangays into towns, or "pueblos," but making the datos "cabezas de barrio," or "gobernadorcillos." Something of the old distinction between the dato, or "principal," and the common man may be still represented in the "gente illustrada," or the more wealthy, educated, and influential class found in each town, and the "gente baja," or the poor and uneducated.

Classes of Filipinos under the Datos. — Beneath the datos, according to Chirino and Morga, there were three classes of Filipinos; the free persons, or "maharlica," who paid no tribute to the dato, but who accompanied him to war, rowed his boat when he went on a journey, and attended him in his house. This class is called by Morga "timauas." [1]

Then there was a very large class, who appear to have been freedmen or liberated slaves, who had acquired their own homes and lived with their families, but who owed to dato or maharlica heavy debts of service; to sow and harvest in his ricefields, to tend his fish-traps, to row his canoe, to build his house, to attend him when he had guests, and to perform any other duties that the chief might command. These semi-free were called "aliping namamahay," and their condition of bondage descended to their children.

Beneath these existed a class of slaves. These were the "siguiguiliris," and they were numerous. Their slavery

---

[1] *Sucesos de las Filipinas*, p. 297.

arose in several ways. Some were those who as children had been captured in war and their lives spared. Some became slaves by selling their freedom in times of hunger. But most of them became slaves through debt, which descended from father to son. The sum of five or six pesos was enough in some cases to deprive a man of his freedom.

These slaves were absolutely owned by their lord, who could theoretically sell them like cattle; but, in spite of its bad possibilities, this Filipino slavery was ordinarily not of a cruel or distressing nature. The slaves frequently associated on kindly relations with their masters and were not overworked. This form of slavery still persists in the Philippines among the Moros of Mindanao and Jolo. Children of slaves inherited their parents' slavery. If one parent was free and the other slave, the first, third, and fifth children were free and the second, fourth, and sixth slaves. This whole matter of inheritance of slavery was curiously worked out in minute details.

Life in the Barangay. — Community feeling was very strong within the barangay. A man could not leave his own barangay for life in another without the consent of the community and the payment of money. If a man of one barrio married a woman of another, their children were divided between the two barangays. The barangay was responsible for the good conduct of its members, and if one of them suffered an injury from a man outside, the whole barangay had to be appeased. Disputes and wrongs between members of the same barangay were referred to a number of old men, who decided the matter in accordance with the customs of the tribe, which were handed down by tradition.[1]

---

[1] These data are largely taken from the account of the customs of the Tagálog prepared by Friar Juan de Plasencia, in 1589, at the

The Religion of the Filipinos. — The Filipinos on the arrival of the Spaniards were fetish-worshipers, but they had one spirit whom they believed was the greatest of all and the creator or maker of things. The Tagálog called this deity Bathala,[1] the Bisaya, Laon, and the Ilocano, Kabunian. They also worshiped the spirits of their ancestors, which were represented by small images called "anitos." Fetishes, which are any objects believed to possess miraculous power, were common among the people, and idols or images were worshiped. Pigafetta describes some idols which he saw in Cebu, and Chirino tells us that, within the memory of Filipinos whom he knew, they had idols of stone, wood, bone, or the tooth of a crocodile, and that there were some of gold.

They also reverenced animals and birds, especially the crocodile, the raven, and a mythical bird of blue or yellow color, whch was called by the name of their deity Bathala.[2] They had no temples or public places of worship, but each one had his anitos in his own house and performed his sacrifices and acts of worship there. As sacrifices they killed pigs or chickens, and made such occasions times of feasting, song, and drunkenness. The life of the .

---

request of Dr. Santiago de Vera, the governor and president of the Audiencia. Although there are references to it by the early historians of the Philippines, this little code did not see the light until a few years ago, when a manuscript copy was discovered in the convent of the Franciscans at Manila, by Dr. Pardo de Tavera, and was by him published. It treats of slave-holding, penalties for crime, inheritances, adoption, dowry, and marriage. (*Las Costumbres de los Tagálog en Filipinas, segun el Padre Plasencia,* by T. H. Pardo de Tavera. Madrid, 1892.)

[1] See on this matter *Diccionario Mitologico de Filipinas,* by Blumentritt; Retana, *Archivo del Bibliófilo Filipino,* vol. II.

[2] This word is of Sanskrit origin and is common throughout Malaysia.

Filipino was undoubtedly filled with superstitious fears and imaginings.

The Mohammedan Malays. — The Mohammedans outside of southern Mindanao and Jolo, had settled in the vicinity of Manila Bay and on Mindoro, Lubang, and adjacent coasts of Luzon. The spread of Mohammedanism was stopped by the Spaniards, although it is narrated that for a long time many of those living on the shores of Manila Bay refused to eat pork, which is forbidden by the Koran, and practiced the rite of circumcision. As late as 1583, Bishop Salazar, in writing to the king of affairs in the Philippines, says the Moros had preached the law of Mohammed to great numbers in these islands and by this preaching many of the Gentiles had become Mohammedans; and further he adds, "Those who have received this foul law guard it with much persistence and there is great difficulty in making them abandon it; and with cause too, for the reasons they give, to our shame and confusion, are that they were better treated by the preachers of Mohammed than they have been by the preachers of Christ." [1]

Material Progress of the Filipinos. — The material surroundings of the Filipino before the arrival of the Spaniards were in nearly every way quite as they are to-day. The "center of population" of each town to-day, with its great church, tribunal, stores and houses of stone and wood, is certainly in marked contrast; but the appearance of a barrio a little distance from the center is to-day probably much as it was then. Then, as now, the bulk of the people lived in humble houses of bam-

---

[1] *Relacion de las Cosas de las Filipinas hecha por Sr. Domingo de Salazar, Primer obispo de dichas islas,* 1583; in Retana, *Archivo,* vol. III.

boo and nipa raised on piles above the dampness of the soil; then, as now, the food was largely rice and the excellent fish which abound in river and sea. There were on the water the same familiar bancas and fish corrals, and on land the rice fields and cocoanut groves. The Filipinos had then most of the present domesticated animals, — dogs, cats, goats, chickens, and pigs, — and perhaps in Luzon the domesticated buffalo, although this animal was widely introduced into the Philippines from China after the Spanish conquest. Horses came with the Spaniards and their numbers were increased by the bringing in of Chinese mares, whose importation is frequently mentioned.

The Spaniards introduced also the cultivation of tobacco, coffee, and cacao, and perhaps also the native corn of America, the maize, although Pigafetta says they found it already growing in the Bisayas.

The Filipino has been affected by these centuries of Spanish sovereignty far less on his material side than he has on his spiritual, and it is mainly in the deepening and elevating of his emotional and mental life and not in the bettering of his material condition that advance has been made.

CHAPTER VI.

THE SPANISH SOLDIER AND THE SPANISH MISSIONARY.   ·

History of the Philippines as a Part of the History of the Spanish Colonies. — We have already seen how the Philippines were discovered by Magellan in his search for the Spice Islands. Brilliant and romantic as is the story of that voyage, it brought no immediate reward to Spain. Portugal remained in her enjoyment of the Eastern trade and nearly half a century elapsed before Spain obtained a settlement in these islands. But if for a time he neglected the Far East, the Spaniard from the Peninsula threw himself with almost incredible energy and devotion into the material and spiritual conquest of America. All the greatest achievements of the Spanish soldier and the Spanish missionary had been secured within fifty years from the day when Columbus sighted the West Indies.

In order to understand the history of the Philippines, we must not forget that these islands formed a part of this great colonial empire and were under the same administration; that for over two centuries the Philippines were reached through Mexico and to a certain extent governed by Mexico; that the same governors, judges, and soldiers held office in both hemispheres, passing from America to the Philippines and being promoted from the Islands to the higher official positions of Mexico and Peru. So to understand the rule of Spain in the Philippines, we must study the great administrative machinery and the great body of laws which she developed for the government of the Indies.[1]

Character of the Spanish Explorers. — The conquests themselves were largely effected through the enterprise and wealth of private individuals; but these men held commissions from the Spanish crown, their actions were subject to strict royal control, and a large proportion of the profits and plunder of their expeditions were paid to the royal treasury. Upon some of these conquerors the crown bestowed the proud title of "adelantado." The Spanish nobility threw themselves into these hazardous undertakings with the courage and fixed determination born of their long struggle with the Moors. Out of the soul-trying circumstances of Western conquest many obscure men rose, through their brilliant qualities of spirit, to positions of eminence and power; but the exalted offices of viceroy and governor were reserved for the titled favorites of the king.

The Royal Audiencia. — Very early the Spanish court, in order to protect its own authority, found it necessary to succeed the ambitious and adventurous conqueror by a ruler in close relationship with and absolute dependence on the royal will. Thus in Mexico, Cortes the conqueror was removed and replaced by the viceroy Mendoza, who established upon the conquests of the former the great Spanish colony of New Spain, to this day the most successful of all the states planted by Spain in America.

To limit the power of the governor or viceroy, as well

---

[1] The foundation and character of this great colonial administration have been admirably described by the Honorable Bernard Moses, United States Philippine Commissioner and the first Secretary of Public Instruction, in his work, *The Establishment of Spanish Rule in America.*

as to act as a supreme court for the settlement of actions
and legal questions, Spain created the "Royal Audiencia."
This was a body of men of noble rank and learned in the
law, sent out from Spain to form in each country a colonial court; but their powers were not alone judicial;
they were also administrative. In the absence of the
governor they assumed his duties.

Treatment of the Natives by the Spanish. — In his treatment of the natives, whose lands he captured, the Spanish king attempted three things, — first, to secure to the
colonist and to the crown the advantages of his labor,
second, to convert the Indians to the Christian religion as
maintained by the Roman Catholic Church, and third, to
protect them from cruelty and inhumanity. Edict after
edict, law after law, issued from the Spanish throne with
these ends in view. As they stand upon the greatest of
colonial law-books, the *Recopilacion de Leyes de las Indias*,
they display an admirable sensitiveness to the needs of
the Indian and an appreciation of the dangers to which
he was subjected; but in the actual practice these beneficent provisions were largely useless.

The first and third of Spain's purposes in her treatment
of the native proved incompatible. History has shown
that liberty and enlightenment can not be taken from a
race with one hand and protection given it with the other.
All classes of Spain's colonial government were frankly in
pursuit of wealth. Greed filled them all, and was the
mainspring of every discovery and every settlement. The
king wanted revenue for his treasury; the noble and the
soldier, booty for their private purse; the friar, wealth for
his order; the bishop, power for his church. All this
wealth had to come out of the native toiler on the lands
which the Spanish conqueror had seized; and while noble

motives were probably never absent and at certain times prevailed, yet in the main the native of America and of the Philippines was a sufferer under the hand and power of the Spaniard.

"The Encomenderos."—Spain's system of controlling the lives and the labor of the Indians was based to a certain extent on the feudal system, still surviving in the Peninsula at the time of her colonial conquests. The captains and soldiers and priests of her successful conquests had assigned to them great estates or fruitful lands with their native inhabitants, which they managed and ruled for their own profit. Such estates were called first "repartimientos." But very soon it became the practice, in America, to grant large numbers of Indians to the service of a Spaniard, who had over them the power of a master and who enjoyed the profits of their labor. In return he was supposed to provide for the conversion of the Indians and their religious instruction. Such a grant of Indians was called an "encomienda." The "encomendero" was not absolute lord of the lives and properties of the Indians, for elaborate laws were framed for the latter's protection. Yet the granting of subjects without the land on which they lived made possible their transfer and sale from one encomendero to another, and in this way thousands of Indians of America were made practically slaves, and were forced into labor in the mines.

As we have already seen, the whole system was attacked by the Dominican priest, Las Casas, a truly noble character in the history of American colonization, and various efforts were made in America to limit the encomiendas and to prevent their introduction into Mexico and Peru ; but the great power of the encomendero in America, together with the influence of the Church, which held extensive encomiendas, had been sufficient to extend the institution, even against Las Casas' impassioned remonstrances. Its abolition in Mexico was decreed in 1544, but "commissioners representing the municipality of Mexico and the religious orders were sent to Spain to ask the king to revoke at least those parts of the 'New Laws' which threatened the interests of the settlers. By a royal decree of October 20, 1545, the desired revocation was granted. This action filled the Spanish settlers with joy and the enslaved Indians with despair." [1]

Thus was the institution early established as a part of the colonial system and came with the conquerors to the Philippines.

Restrictions on Colonization and Commerce. — For the management of all colonial affairs the king created a great board, or bureau, known as the "Council of the Indies," which sat in Madrid and whose members were among the highest officials of Spain. The Spanish government exercised the closest supervision over all colonial matters, and colonization was never free. All persons, wares, and ships, passing from Spain to any of her colonial possessions, were obliged to pass through Seville, and this one port alone.

This wealthy ancient city, situated on the river Guadalquivir in southwestern Spain, was the gateway to the Spanish Empire. From this port went forth the mailed soldier, the robed friar, the adventurous noble, and the brave and highborn Spanish ladies, who accompanied their husbands to such great distances over the sea. And back to this port were brought the gold of Peru, the silver of Mexico, and the silks and embroideries of China, dispatched through the Philippines.

---

[1] Moses: *Establishment of Spanish Rule in America*, p. 12.

It must be observed that all intercourse between Spain and her colonies was rigidly controlled by the government. Spain sought to create and maintain an exclusive monopoly of her colonial trade. To enforce and direct this monopoly, there was at Seville the Commercial House, or "Casa de Contratacion." No one could sail from Spain to a colonial possession without a permit and after government registration. No one could send out goods or import them except through the Commercial House and upon the payment of extraordinary imposts. Trade was absolutely forbidden to any except Spaniards. And by her forts and fleets Spain strove to isolate her colonies from the approach of Portuguese, Dutch, or English, whose ships, no less daringly manned than those of Spain herself, were beginning to traverse the seas in search of the plunder and spoils of foreign conquest and trade.

Summary of the Colonial Policy of Spain. — Spain sought foreign colonies, first, for the spoils of accumulated wealth that could be seized and carried away at once, and, secondly, for the income that could be procured through the labor of the inhabitants of the lands she gained. In framing her government and administration of her colonies, she sought primarily the political enlightenment and welfare neither of the Spanish colonist nor the native race, but the glory, power, and patronage of the crown. The commercial and trade regulations were devised, not to develop the resources and increase the prosperity of the colonies, but to add wealth to the Peninsula. Yet the purposes of Spain were far from being wholly selfish. With zeal and success she sought the conversion of the heathen natives, whom she subjected, and in this showed a humanitarian interest in advance of the Dutch and English, who rivaled her in colonial empire.

The colonial ideals under which the policy of Spain was framed were those of the times. In the centuries that have succeeded, public wisdom and conscience on these matters have immeasurably improved. Nations no longer make conquests frankly to exploit them, but the public opinion of the world demands that the welfare of the colonial subject be sought and that he be protected from official greed. There is great advance still to be made. It can hardly be said that the world yet recognizes that a stronger people should assist a weaker without assurance of material reward, but this is the direction in which the most enlightened feeling is advancing. Every undertaking of the white race, which has such aims in view, is an experiment worthy of the most profound interest and most solicitous sympathy.

Result of the Voyage of Magellan and El Cano. — The mind of the Spanish adventurer was greatly excited by the results of Sebastian del Cano's voyage. Here was the opportunity for rich trade and great profit. Numerous plans were laid before the king, one of them for the building of an Indian trading-fleet and an annual voyage to the Moluccas to gather a great harvest of spices.

Portugal protested against this move until the question of her claim to the Moluccas, under the division of Pope Alexander, could be settled. The exact longitude of Ternate west from the line 370 leagues beyond the Verde Islands was not well known. Spaniards argued that it was less than 180 degrees, and, therefore, in spite of Portugal's earlier discovery, belonged to them. The pilot, Medina, for example, explained to Charles V. that from the meridian 370 degrees west of San Anton (the most westerly island of the Verde group) to the city of Mexico was 59 degrees, from Mexico to Navidad, 9 degrees, and from this port to Cebu, 100 degrees, a total of only 168 degrees, leaving a margin of 12 degrees; therefore by the pope's decision the Indies, Moluccas, Borneo, Gilolo, and the Philippines were Spain's.[1] A great council of embassadors and cosmographers was held at Badajoz in 1524, but reached no agreement. Spain announced her resolution to occupy the Moluccas, and Portugal threatened with death the Spanish adventurers who should be found there.

The First Expedition to the Philippines. — Spain acted immediately upon her determination, and in 1525 dispatched an expedition under Jofre de Loaisa to reap the fruits of Magellan's discoveries.[2] The captain of one vessel was Sebastian del Cano, who completed the voyage of Magellan. On his ship sailed Andres de Urdaneta, who later became an Augustian friar and accompanied the expedition of Legaspi that finally effected the settlement of the Philippines. Not without great hardship and losses did the fleet pass the Straits of Magellan and enter the Pacific Ocean. In mid-ocean Loaisa died, and four days later the heroic Sebastian del Cano. Following a route somewhat similar to that óf Magellan, the fleet reached first the Ladrone Islands and later the coast of Mindanao. From here they attempted to sail to Cebu, but the strong northeast monsoon drove them southward to the Moluccas, and they landed on Tidor the last day of the year 1526.

---

[1] *Demarcación del Maluco, hecha por el maestro Medina,* in *Documentos inéditos,* vol. V., p. 552.

[2] This and subsequent voyages are given in the *Documentos inéditos,* vol. V., and a graphic account is in Argensola's *Conquista de las Islas Molucas.* They are also well narrated in English by Burney, *Discoveries in the South Sea,* vol. I., chapters V., XII., and XIV.

The Failure of the Expedition. — The Portuguese were at this moment fighting to reduce the native rajas of these islands to subjection. They regarded the Spaniards as enemies, and each party of Europeans was shortly engaged in fighting and in inciting the natives against the other. The condition of the Spaniards became desperate in the extreme, and indicates at what cost of life the conquests of the sixteenth century were made. Their ships had become so battered by storm as to be no longer seaworthy. The two officers, who had successively followed Loaisa and El Cano in command, had likewise perished. Of the 450 men who had sailed from Spain, but 120 now survived. These, under the leadership of Hernando de la Torre, threw up a fort on the island of Tidor, unable to go farther or to retire, and awaited hoped-for succor from Spain.

Relief came, not from the Peninsula, but from Mexico. Under the instructions of the Spanish king, in October, 1527, Cortes dispatched from Mexico a small expedition in charge of D. Alvaro de Saavedra. Swept rapidly by the equatorial trades, in a few months Saavedra had traversed the Carolines, reprovisioned on Mindanao, and reached the survivors on Tidor. Twice they attempted to return to New Spain, but strong trade winds blow without cessation north and south on either side of the equator for the space of more than twelve hundred miles, and the northern latitude of calms and prevailing westerly winds were not yet known.

Twice Saavedra beat his way eastward among the strange islands of Papua and Melanesia, only to be at last driven back upon Tidor and there to die. The survivors were forced to abandon the Moluccas. By surrendering to the Portuguese they were assisted to return to Europe by way of Malacca, Ceylon, and Africa, and they arrived at Lisbon in 1536, the survivors of Loaisa's expedition, having been gone from Spain eleven years.

The efforts of the Spanish crown to obtain possession of the Spice Islands, the Celebes and Moluccas, with their coveted products of nutmeg, cinnamon, and pepper, were for the time being ended. By the Treaty of Zaragoza (1529) the Emperor, Charles V., for the sum of three hundred and fifty thousand gold ducats, renounced all claim to the Moluccas. For thirteen years the provisions of this treaty were respected by the Spaniards, and then another attempt was made to obtain a foothold in the East Indies.

The Second Expedition to the Philippines. — The facts that disaster had overwhelmed so many, that two oceans must be crossed, and that no sailing-route from Asia back to America was known, did not deter the Spaniards from their perilous conquests; and in 1542 another expedition sailed from Mexico, under command of Lopez de Villalobos, to explore the Philippines and if possible to reach China.

Across the Pacific they made a safe and pleasant voyage. In the warm waters of the Pacific they sailed among those wonderful coral atolls, rings of low shore, decked with palms, grouped in beautiful archipelagoes, whose appearance has never failed to delight the navigator, and whose composition is one of the most interesting subjects known to students of the earth's structure and history. Some of these coral islands Villalobos took possession of in the name of Spain. These were perhaps the Pelew Islands or the Carolines.

At last Villalobos reached the east coast of Mindanao, but after some deaths and sickness they sailed again and were carried south by the monsoon to the little island of Sarangani, south of the southern peninsula of Mindanao. The natives were hostile, but the Spaniards drove them from their stronghold and made some captures of musk, amber, oil, and gold-dust. In need of provisions, they planted the maize, or Indian corn, the wonderful cereal of America, which yields so bounteously, and so soon after planting. Food was greatly needed by the Spaniards and was very difficult to obtain.

The Naming of the Islands. — Villalobos equipped a small vessel and sent it northward to try to reach Cebu. This vessel reached the coast of Samar. Villalobos gave to the island the name of Filipina, in honor of the Spanish Infante, or heir apparent, Philip, who was soon to succeed his father Charles V. as King Philip the Second of Spain. Later in his correspondence with the Portuguese Villalobos speaks of the archipelago as Las Filipinas. Although for many years the title of the Islas del Poniente continued in use, Villalobos' name of Filipinas gradually gained place and has lived.

The End of the Expedition. — While on Sarangani demands were made by the Portuguese, who claimed that Mindanao belonged with the Celebes, that the Spaniards should leave. Driven from Mindanao by lack of food and hostility of the natives, Villalobos was blown southward by storms to Gilolo. Here, after long negotiations, the Portuguese compelled him to surrender. The survivors of the expedition dispersed, some remaining in the Indies, and some eventually reaching Spain; but Villalobos, overwhelmed by discouragement, died on the island of Amboyna. The priest who ministered to him in his last hours was the famous Jesuit missionary to the Indies, Saint Francis Xavier.

Twenty-three years were to elapse after the sailing of Villalobos' fleet before another Spanish expedition should reach the Philippines. The year 1565 dates the permanent occupation of the archipelago by the Spanish.

Increase in Political Power of the Church. — Under Philip the Second, the champion of ecclesiasticism, the Spanish crown cemented the union of the monarchy with the church and devoted the resources of the empire, not only to colonial acquisition, but to combating the Protestant revolution on the one hand and heathenism on the other. The Spanish king effected so close a union of the church and state in Spain, that from this time on churchmen rose higher and higher in the Spanish councils, and profoundly influenced the policy and fate of the nation. The policy of Philip the Second, however, brought upon Spain the revolt of the Dutch Lowlands and the wars with England, and her struggle with these two nations drained her resources both on land and sea, and occasioned a physical and moral decline. But while Spain was constantly losing power and prestige in Europe, the king was extending his colonial domain, lending royal aid to the ambitious adventurer and to the ardent missionary friar. Spain's object being to christianize as well as to conquer, the missionary became a very important figure in the history of every colonial enterprise, and these great orders to whom missions were intrusted thus became the central institutions in the history of the Philippines.

The Rise of Monasticism. — Monasticism was introduced into Europe from the East at the very commencement of the Middle Ages. The fundamental idea of the old monasticism was retirement from human society in the belief that the world was bad and could not be bettered, and that men could lead holier lives and better please God by forsaking secular employments and family relations, and devoting all their attention to purifying their characters. The first monastic order in Europe were the Benedictines, organized in the seventh century, whose rule and organization were the pattern for those that followed.

The clergy of the church were divided thus into two groups, — first, the parish priests, or ministers, who lived among the people over whom they exercised the care of souls, and who, because they were of the people themselves and lived their lives in association with the community, were known as the "secular clergy," and second, the monks, or "regular clergy," were so called because they lived under the "rule" of their order.

In the early part of the thirteenth century monasticism, which had waned somewhat during the preceding two centuries, received a new impetus and inspiration from the organization of new orders known as brethren or "Friars." The idea underlying their organization was noble, and above that of the old monasticism; for it was the idea of service, of ministry both to the hearts and bodies of depressed and suffering men.

The Dominicans. — The Order of Dominicans was organized by Saint Dominic, an Italian, about 1215. The primary object of its members was to defend the doctrines of the Church and, by teaching and preaching, destroy the doubts and protests which in the thirteenth century were beginning to disturb the claims of the Catholic Church and the Papacy. The Dominican friars did not live in communities, but traveled about, humbly clad, preaching in the villages and towns, and seeking to expose and punish the heretic. The mediæval universities, through their study of philosophy and the Roman law, were producing a class of men disposed to hold opinions contrary to the teachings of the Church. The Dominicans realized the importance of these great centers of instruction and entered them as teachers and masters, and by the beginning of the fifteenth century had made them strongholds of conservatism and orthodoxy.

. *The Franciscans.* — A few years after this organization, the Order of Franciscans was founded by Saint Francis of Assisi, of Spain. The aims of this order were not only to preach and administer the sacraments, but to nurse the sick, provide for the destitute, and alleviate the dreadful misery which affected whole classes in the Middle Ages. They took vows of absolute poverty, and so humble was the garb prescribed by their rule that they went barefooted from place to place.

The Augustinian Order was founded by Pope Alexander IV., in 1265, and still other orders came later.

The Degeneration of the Orders. — Without doubt the early ministrations of these friars were productive of great good both on the religious and humanitarian sides. But, as the orders became wealthy, the friars lost their spirituality and their lives grew vicious. By the beginning of the sixteenth century the administration of the Church throughout Europe had become so corrupt, the economic burden of the religious orders so great, and religious teaching and belief so material, that the best and noblest minds in all countries were agitating for reform.

The Reformation. — In addition to changes in church administration, many Christians were demanding a greater freedom of religious thinking and radical changes in the Church doctrine which had taken form in the Middle Ages. Thus, while all the best minds in the Church were united in seeking a reformation of character and of administration, great differences arose between them as to the possibility of change in Church doctrines. These differences accordingly separated them into two parties, the Papacy adhering strongly to the doctrine as it was then accepted, while various leaders in the north of Europe, including Martin Luther in Germany, Swingli in Switzerland, and John Calvin in France and Geneva, broke with the authority of the Pope and declared for a liberation of the individual conscience.

Upon the side of the Papacy, the Emperor Charles the Fifth threw the weight of the Spanish monarchy, and to enforce the Papal authority he attacked the German princes by force of arms. The result was a great revolt from the Roman Catholic Church, which spread all over northern Germany, a large portion of Switzerland, the lowlands of the Rhine, and England, and which included a numerous and very influential element among the French people. These countries, with the exception of France, have remained Protestant to the present day; and the great expansion of the English people in America and the East has established Protestantism in all parts of the world.

Effects of the Reformation in the Roman Catholic Church. — The reform movement, which lasted through the century, brought about a great improvement in the Roman Catholic Church. Many, who remained devoted to Roman Catholic orthodoxy, were zealous for administrative reform. A great assembly of Churchmen, the Council of Trent, for years devoted itself to legislation to correct abuses. The Inquisition was revived and put into force against Protestants, especially in the dominions of Spain, and the religious orders were reformed and stimulated to new sacrifices and great undertakings.

But greater, perhaps, than any of these agencies in reestablishing the power of the Pope and reviving the life of the Roman Catholic Church was the organization of a new order, the "Society of Jesus." The founder was a Spaniard, Ignatius Loyola. The Jesuits devoted themselves especially to education and missionary activity. Their schools soon covered Europe, while their mission stations were to be found in both North and South America, India, the East Indies, China, and Japan.

The Spanish Missionary. — The Roman Catholic Church, having lost a large part of Europe, thus strove to make up the loss by gaining converts in heathen lands. Spain, being the power most rapidly advancing her conquests abroad, was the source of the most tireless missionary effort. (From the time of Columbus, every fleet that sailed to gain plunder and lands for the Spanish kingdom carried bands of friars and churchmen to convert to Christianity the heathen peoples whom the sword of the soldier should reduce to obedience.

"The Laws of the Indies" gave special power and prominence to the priest. In these early days of Spain's colonial empire many priests were men of piety, learning, and unselfish devotion. Their efforts softened somewhat the violence and brutality that often marred the Spanish treatment of the native, and they became the civilizing agents among the peoples whom the Spanish soldiers had conquered.

In Paraguay, California, and the Philippines the power and importance of the Spanish missionary outweighed that of the soldier or governor in the settlement of those countries and the control of the native inhabitants. Churchmen, full of the missionary spirit, pressed upon the king the duties of the crown in advancing the cross, and more than one country was opened to Spanish settlement through the enthusiasm of the priest.

CONQUEST AND SETTLEMENT
BY THE SPANIARDS
IN THE
PHILIPPINES, 1565-1590

SCALE OF MILES
0   50   100   150   200   250

SCALE OF KILOMETRES
0   100   200   300

CHAPTER VII.

PERIOD OF CONQUEST AND SETTLEMENT, 1565–1600.

Cause of Settlement and Conquest of the Philippines. — The previous Spanish expeditions whose misfortunes have been narrated, seemed to have proved to the Court of Spain that they could not drive the Portuguese from the Moluccas. But to the east of the Moluccas lay great unexplored archipelagoes, which might lie within the Spanish demarcation and which might yield spices and other valuable articles of trade; and as the Portuguese had made no effective occupation of the Philippines, the minds of Spanish conquerors turned to this group also as a coveted field of conquest, even though it was pretty well understood that they lay in the latitude of the Moluccas, and so were denied by treaty to Spain.

In 1559 the Spanish king, Felipe II., commanded the viceroy of Mexico to undertake again the discovery of the islands lying "toward the Moluccas," but the rights of Portugal to islands within her demarcation were to be respected. Five years passed before ships and equipments could be prepared, and during these years the objects of the expedition received considerable discussion and underwent some change.

The king invited Andres de Urdaneta, who years before had been a captain in the expedition of Loaisa, to accompany the expedition as a guide and director. Urdaneta, after his return from the previous expedition, had renounced military life and had become an Augustinian friar. He was known to be a man of wise judgment, with good knowledge of cosmography, and as a missionary he was able to give to the expedition that religious strength which characterized all Spanish undertakings.

It was Urdaneta's plan to colonize, not the Philippines, but New Guinea; but the Audiencia of Mexico, which had charge of fitting out the expedition, charged it in minute instructions to reach and if possible colonize the Philippines, to trade for spices and to discover the return sailing route back across the Pacific to New Spain. The natives of the islands were to be converted to Christianity, and missionaries were to accompany the expedition. In the quaint language of Fray Gaspar de San Augustin, there were sent "holy guides to unfurl and wave the banners of Christ, even to the remotest portions of the islands, and to drive the devil from the tyrannical possession, which he had held for so many ages, usurping to himself the adoration of those peoples." [1]

The Third Expedition to the Philippines. — The expedition sailed from the port of Natividad, Mexico, November 21, 1564, under the command of Miguel Lopez de Legaspi. The ships followed for a part of the way a course further south than was necessary, and touched at some inhabited islands of Micronesia. About the 22d of January they reached the Ladrones and had some trouble with the natives. They reached the southern end of Samar about February the 13th. Possession of Samar was taken by Legaspi in the name of the king, and small parties were sent both north and south to look for villages of the Filipinos.

A few days later they rounded the southern part of Samar, crossed the strait to the coast of southern Leyte,

---

[1] Fray Gaspar de San Agustin: *Conquista de las Islas Filipinas,* lib. I., c. 13.

and the field-marshal, Goyti, discovered the town of Cabalian, and on the 5th of March the fleet sailed to this town. Provisions were scarce on the Spanish vessels, and great difficulty was experienced in getting food from the few natives met in boats or in the small settlements discovered.

Legaspi at Bohol. — About the middle of March the fleet arrived at Bohol, doubtless the southern or eastern shore. While near here Goyti in a small boat captured a Moro prao from Borneo and after a hard fight brought back the Moros as prisoners to Legaspi. There proved to be quite a trade existing between the Moros from Borneo and the natives of Bohol and Mindanao.

Legaspi.

Here on Bohol they were able to make friendly terms with the natives, and with Sicatuna, the dato of Bohol, Legaspi performed the ceremony of blood covenant. The Spanish leader and the Filipino chief each made a small cut in his own arm or breast and drank the blood of the other. According to Gaspar de San Augustin, the blood was mixed with a little wine or water and drunk from a goblet.[1] This custom was the most sacred bond of friendship among the Filipinos, and friendship so pledged was usually kept with great fidelity.

Legaspi in Cebu. — On the 27th of April, 1565, Legaspi's fleet reached Cebu. Here, in this beautiful strait

The Blood Compact.

and fine anchoring-ground, Magellan's ships had lingered until the death of their leader forty-four years before. A splendid native settlement lined the shore, so Father Chirino tells us, for a distance of more than a league. The natives of Cebu were fearful and greatly agitated,

---

[1] One of the best paintings of the Filipino artist Juan Luna, which hangs in the Ayuntamiento in Manila, represents Legaspi in the act of the " Pacto de Sangre " with this Filipino chieftain.

and seemed determined to resist the landing of the Spaniards. But at the first discharge of the guns of the ships, the natives abandoned the shore, and, setting fire to the town, retreated into the jungles and hills. Without loss of life the Spaniards landed, and occupied the harbor and town.

Finding of "the Holy Child of Cebu." — The Spanish soldiers found in one of the houses of the natives a small wooden image of the Child Jesus. A similar image, Pigafetta tells us, he had himself given to a native while in the island with Magellan. It had been preserved by the natives and was regarded by them as an object of veneration. To the pious

The Holy Child (Santo Niño) of Cebu.

Spaniards the discovery of this sacred object was hailed as an event of great good fortune. It was taken by the monks, and carried to a shrine especially erected for it. It still rests in the church of the Augustinians, an object of great devotion.

Settlement Made at Cebu. — In honor of this image this first settlement of the Spaniards in the Philippines received the name of "City of the Most Holy Name of Jesus." Here Legaspi established himself, and, by great tact and skill, gradually won the confidence and friendship of the inhabitants. A formal peace was at last concluded in which the dato, Tupas, recognized the sovereignty of Spain; and the people of Cebu and the Spaniards bound themselves to assist each other against the enemies of either.

They had some difficulty in understanding one another, but the Spaniards had with them a Mohammedan Malay of Borneo, called Cid-Hamal, who had been taken from the East Indies to the Peninsula and thence to Mexico and Legaspi's expedition. The languages of Malaysia and the Philippines are so closely related that this man was able to interpret. Almost immediately, however, the missionaries began the study of the native dialect, and Padre Chirino tells us that Friar Martin Herrada made here the first Filipino vocabulary, and was soon preaching the Gospel to the natives in their own language.

The great difficulty experienced by Legaspi was to procure sufficient food for his expedition. At different times he sent a ship to the nearest islands, and twice his ship went south to Mindanao to procure a cargo of cinnamon to be sent back to New Spain.

Thus month by month the Spaniards gained acquaintance with the beautiful island sea of the archipelago, with its green islands and brilliant sheets of water, its safe harbors and picturesque settlements.

The Bisayans. — In 1569, Legaspi discovered the great island of Panay. Here they were fortunate in securing a great abundance of supplies and the friendship of the natives, who received them well. These beautiful central islands of the Philippines are inhabited by Bisaya. The

Spaniards found this tribe tattooing their bodies with ornamental designs, a practice widespread throughout Oceanica, and which still is common among the tribes of northern Luzon. This practice caused the Spaniards to give to the Bisayas the title of "Islas de los Pintados" (the Islands of the Painted).

Discovery of the Northern Return Route across the Pacific. — Before the arrival of the expedition in the Philippines, the captain of one of Legaspi's ships, inspired by ungenerous ambition and the hopes of getting a reward, outsailed the rest of the fleet. Having arrived first in the islands, he started at once upon the return voyage. Unlike preceding captains who had tried to return to New Spain by sailing eastward from the islands against both wind and ocean current, this captain sailed northward beyond the trades into the more favorable westerly winds, and found his way back to America and New Spain.

Soon after arriving in the Philippines, Legaspi's instructions required him to dispatch at least one vessel on the return voyage to New Spain. Accordingly on June 1st the San Pablo set sail, carrying about two hundred men, including Urdenata and another friar. This vessel also followed the northern route across the Pacific, and after a voyage of great hardship, occupying three and a half months, it reached the coast of North America at California and followed it southward to Acapulco.

The discovery made by these captains of a favorable route for vessels returning from the islands to New Spain safe from capture by the Portuguese, completed the plans of the Spanish for the occupation of the Philippines. In 1567 another vessel was dispatched by Legaspi and made this voyage successfully.

The sailing of these vessels left Legaspi in Cebu with a colony of only one hundred and fifty Spaniards, poorly provided with resources, to commence the conquest of the Philippines. But he won the friendship and respect of the inhabitants, and in 1568 two galleons with reinforcements arrived from Acapulco. From this time on nearly yearly communication was maintained, fresh troops with munitions and supplies arriving with each expedition.

The First Expedition against the Moro Pirates. — *Pirates of Mindoro.* — The Spaniards found the Straits of San Bernardino and the Mindoro Sea swarming with the fleets of Mohammedan Malays from Borneo and the Jolo Archipelago. To a race living so continuously upon the water, piracy has always possessed irresistible attractions. In the days of Legaspi, the island of Mindoro had been partially settled by Malays from the south, and many of these settlements were devoted to piracy, preying especially upon the towns on the north coast of Panay. In January, 1570, Legaspi dispatched his grandson, Juan de Salcedo, to punish these marauders.[1]

Capture of Pirate Strongholds. — Salcedo had a force of forty Spaniards and a large number of Bisaya. He landed on the western coast of Mindoro and took the pirate town of Mamburao. The main stronghold of the Moros he found to be on the small island of Lubang, northwest of Mindanao. Here they had three strong forts with high walls, on which were mounted small brass cannon, or "lantakas." Two of these forts were surrounded by moats. There were several days of fighting before Lubang was conquered. The possession of Lubang brought

---

[1] There is an old account of this interesting expedition by one who participated. (*Relacion de la Conquista de la Isla de Luzon*, Manila, 1572; Retana, *Archivo del Bibliofilo Filipino*, vol. IV.)

the Spaniards almost to the entrance of Manila Bay. Meanwhile, a captain, Enriquez de Guzman, had discovered Masbate, Burias, and Ticao, and had landed on Luzon in the neighborhood of Albay, called then, "Italon."

Conquest of the Moro City of Manila. — *Expedition from Panay.* — Reports had come to Legaspi of an important Mohammedan settlement named "May-nila," on the shore of a great bay, and a Mohammedan chieftain, called Maomat, was procured to guide the Spaniards on their conquest of this region.[1] For this purpose Legaspi

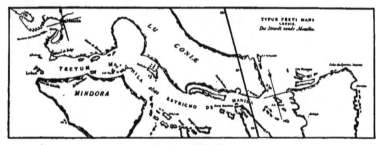

Straits of Manila.

sent his field-marshal, Martin de Goiti, with Salcedo, one hundred and twenty Spanish soldiers, and fourteen or fifteen boats filled with Bisayan allies. They left Panay early in May, and, after stopping at Mindoro, came to anchor in Manila Bay, off the mouth of the Pasig River.

The Mohammedan City. — On the south bank of the river was the fortified town of the Mohammedan chieftain, Raja Soliman; on the north bank was the town of Tondo, under the Raja Alcandora, or Lacandola. Morga[2] tells us that these Mohammedan settlers from the island

---

[1] Morga: *Sucesos de las Islas Filipinas,* 2d ed., p. 10.

[2] *Sucesos, de las Islas Filipinas.* P. 316.

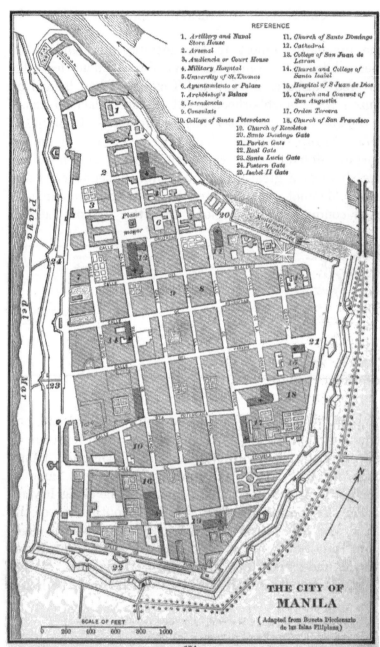

REFERENCE

1. Artillery and Naval Store House
2. Arsenal
3. Audiencia or Court House
4. Military Hospital
5. University of St. Thomas
6. Ayuntamiento or Palace
7. Archbishop's Palace
8. Intendencia
9. Consulate
10. College of Santa Potenciana
11. Church of Santo Domingo
12. Cathedral
13. College of San Juan de Letran
14. Church and College of Santa Isabel
15. Hospital of S Juan de Dios
16. Church and Convent of San Augustin
17. Orden Tercera
18. Church of San Francisco
19. Church of Recoletos
20. Santo Domingo Gate
21. Parian Gate
22. Real Gate
23. Santa Lucia Gate
24. Postern Gate
25. Isabel II Gate

Playa del Mar

Plaza mayor

SCALE OF FEET
0   200   400   600   800   1000

THE CITY OF
MANILA

(Adapted from Buzeta Diccionario
de las Islas Filipinas)

of Borneo had commenced to arrive on the island only a few years before the coming of the Spaniards. They had settled and married among the Filipino population already occupying Manila Bay, and had introduced some of the forms and practices of the Mohammedan religion. The city of Manila was defended by a fort, apparently on the exact sight of the present fort of Santiago. It was built of the trunks of palms, and had embrasures where were mounted a considerable number of cannon, or lantakas.

Capture of the City. — The natives received the foreigners at first with a show of friendliness, but after they had landed on the banks of the Pasig, Soliman, with a large force, assaulted them. The impetuous Spaniards charged, and carried the fortifications, and the natives fled, setting fire to their settlement. When the fight was over the Spaniards found among the dead the body of a Portuguese artillerist, who had directed the defense. Doubtless he was one who had deserted from the Portuguese garrison far south in the Indian archipelago to cast in his fortunes with the Malays. It being the commencement of the season of rains and typhoons, the Spaniards decided to defer the occupation of Manila, and, after exploring Cavite harbor, they returned to Panay.

A year was spent in strengthening their hold on the Bisayas and in arranging for their conquest of Luzon. On Masbate was placed a friar and six soldiers, so small was the number that could be spared.

Founding of the Spanish City of Manila. — With a force of 280 men Legaspi returned in the spring of 1571 to the conquest of Luzon. It was a bloodless victory. The Filipino rajas declared themselves vassals of the Spanish king, and in the months of May and June the Spaniards established themselves in the present site of the city.

At once Legaspi gave orders for the reconstruction of the fort, the building of a palace, a convent for the Augustinian monks, a church, and 150 houses. The boundaries of this city followed closely the outlines of the Tagálog city "Maynila," and it seems probable that the location of buildings then established have been adhered to until the present time. This settlement appeared so desirable to Legaspi that he at once designated it as the capital of the archipelago. Almost immediately he organized its governing assembly, or ayuntamiento.

The First Battle on Manila Bay. — In spite of their ready submission, the rajas, Soliman and Lacandola, did not yield their sovereignty without a struggle. They were able to secure assistance in the Tagálog and Pampanga settlements of Macabebe and Hagonoy. A great fleet of forty war-praos gathered in palm-lined estuaries on the north shore of Manila Bay, and came sweeping down the shallow coast to drive the Spaniards from the island. Against them were sent Goiti and fifty men. The protective mail armor, the heavy swords and lances, the horrible firearms, coupled with the persistent courage and fierce resolution of the Spanish soldier of the sixteenth century, swept back this native armament. The chieftain Soliman was killed.

The Conquest of Central Luzon. — Goiti continued his marching and conquering northward until nearly the whole great plain of central Luzon, that stretches from Manila Bay to the Gulf of Lingayen, lay submissive before him. A little later the raja Lacandola died, having accepted Christian baptism, and the only powerful resistance on the island of Luzon was ended.

Goiti was sent back to the Bisayas, and the command of the army of Luzon fell to Salcedo, the brilliant and

daring grandson of Legaspi, at this time only twenty-two
years of age. This young knight led his command up the
Pasig River. Cainta and Taytay, at that time important Tagálog towns, were conquered, and then the country south of Laguna de Bay. The town of Cainta was
fortified and defended by small cannon, and although
Salcedo spent three days in negotiations, it was only
taken by storm, in which four hundred Filipino men and
women perished.[1] From here Salcedo marched over the
mountains to the Pacific coast and south into the Camarines, where he discovered the gold mines of Paracale and
Mamburao.

At about this time the Spaniards conquered the Cuyos
and Calamianes islands and the northern part of Paragua.

Exploration of the Coast of Northern Luzon. — In 1572,
Salcedo, with a force of only forty-five men, sailed northward from Manila, landed in Zambales and Pangasinan,
and on the long and rich Ilocos coast effected a permanent
submission of the inhabitants. He also visited the coast
farther north, where the great and fertile valley of the
Cagayan, the largest river of the archipelago, reaches to
the sea. From here he continued his adventurous journey
down the Pacific coast of Luzon to the island of Polillo,
and returned by way of Laguna de Bay to Manila.

Death of Legaspi. — He arrived in September, 1572, to
find that his grandfather and commander, Legaspi, had
died a month before (August 20, 1572). After seven
years of labor the conqueror of difficulties was dead, but
almost the entire archipelago had been added to the crown
of Spain. Three hundred years of Spanish dominion secured little more territory than that traversed and pacified

---

[1] *Conquista de la Isla de Luzon*, p. 24.

by the conquerors of these early years. In spite of their slender forces, the daring of the Spaniards induced them to follow a policy of widely extending their power, effecting settlements, and enforcing submission wherever rich coasts and the gathering of population attracted them.

Legaspi Monument, Luneta.

Within a single year's time most of the coast country of Luzon had been traversed, important positions seized, and the inhabitants portioned out in encomiendas. On the death of Legaspi, the command fell to Guido de Lavezares.

Reasons for this Easy Conquest of the Philippines. — The explanation of how so small a number of Europeans could so rapidly and successfully reduce to subjection the inhabitants of a territory like the Philippines, separated into so many different islands, is to be found in several things.

First. — The expedition had a great leader, one of those knights combining sagacity with resolution, who glorify the brief period when Spanish prestige was highest. No policy could ever be successful in the Philippines which did not depend for its strength upon giving a measure of satisfaction to the Filipino people. Legaspi did this. He appears to have won the native datos, treating them with consideration, and holding out to them the expectations of a better and more prosperous era, which the sovereignty of the Spaniard would bring. Almost from the beginning, the natives of an island already reduced flocked to his standard to assist in the conquest of another. The small forces of the Spanish soldiers were augmented by hundreds of Filipino allies.

Second. — Another reason is found in the wonderful courage and great fighting power of the Spanish soldier. Each man, splendidly armored and weaponed, deadly with either sword or spear, carrying in addition the arquebus, the most efficient firearm of the time, was equal in combat to many natives who might press upon him with their naked bodies and inferior weapons.

Third. — Legaspi was extremely fortunate in his captains, who included such old campaigners as the field-marshal Martin de Goiti, who had been to the Philippines before with Villalobos, and such gallant youths as Salcedo, one of the most attractive military figures in all Spanish history.

Fourth. — In considering this Spanish conquest, we must understand that the islands were far more sparsely inhabited than they are to-day. The Bisayan islands, the rich Camarines, the island of Luzon, had, in Legaspi's time, only a small fraction of their present great populations. This population was not only small, but it was also extremely disunited. Not only were the great tribes separated by the differences of language, but, as we have already seen, each tiny community was practically independent, and the power of a dato very limited. There were no great princes, with large forces of fighting retainers whom they could call to arms, such as the Portuguese had encountered among the Malays south in the Moluccas.

Fifth. — But certainly one of the greatest factors in the yielding of the Filipino to the Spaniard was the preaching of the missionary friars. No man is so strong with an unenlightened and barbarous race as he who claims power from God. And the preaching of the Catholic faith, with its impressive and dramatic services, its holy sacraments, its power to arrest the attention and to admit at once the rude mind into the circle of its ministry, won the heart of the Filipino. Without doubt he was ready and eager for a loftier and truer religious belief and ceremonial. There was no powerful native priesthood to oppose the introduction of Christianity. The preaching of the faith and the baptism of converts proceeded almost as rapidly as the marching of Salcedo's soldiers.

The Dangers of the Spanish Occupation. — Such conditions assured the success of the Spanish occupation, provided the small colony could be protected from outside attacks. But even from the beginning the position of this little band of conquerors was perilous. Their numbers were small and of necessity much scattered, and their only source of succor lay thousands of miles away, across the greatest body of water on the earth, in a land itself a colony newly wrested from the hand of the Indian. Across the narrow waters of the China Sea, only a few days' distant, even in the slow-sailing junks, lay the teeming shores of the most populous country in the world, in those days not averse to foreign conquest.

Attempt of the Chinese under Limahong to Capture Manila. — *Activity of the Southern Chinese.* — It was from the Chinese that the first heavy blow fell. The southeastern coast of China, comprising the provinces of

Kwangtung and Fukien, has always exhibited a restlessness and passion for emigration not displayed by other parts of the country. From these two provinces, through the ports of Amoy and Canton, have gone those Chinese traders and coolies to be found in every part of the East and many other countries of the world. Two hundred years before the arrival of the Spaniards, Chinese junks traversed the straits and seas and visited regularly the coast of Mindanao.

Limahong's Expedition to the Philippines.— This coast of China has always been notorious for its piracy. The distance of the capital at Peking and the weakness of the provincial viceroys have made impossible its suppression. It was one of these bold filibusters of the China Sea, called Limahong, who two years after the death of Legaspi attempted the conquest of the Philippines. The stronghold of this corsair was the island of Pehon, where he fortified himself and developed his power.

Here, reports of the prosperous condition of Manila reached him, and he prepared a fleet of sixty-two war-junks, with four thousand soldiers and sailors. The accounts even state that a large number of women and artisans were taken on board to form the nucleus of the settlement, as soon as the Spaniards should be destroyed. In the latter part of November, 1574, this powerful fleet came sweeping down the western coast of Luzon and on the 29th gathered in the little harbor of Mariveles, at the entrance to Manila Bay. Eight miles south of Manila is the town of Parañaque, on an estuary which affords a good landing-place for boats entering from the bay. Here on the night following, Limahong put ashore six hundred men, under one of his generals, Sioco, who was a Japanese.

The Attack upon Manila. — From here they marched

rapidly up the beach · and fell furiously upon the city. Almost their first victim was the field-marshal Goiti. The fort of Manila was at this date a weak affair, without ditches or escarpment, and it was here that the struggle took place. The Spaniards, although greatly outnumbered, were able to drive back the Chinese; but they themselves lost heavily. Limahong now sent ashore heavy reinforcements, and prepared to overwhelm the garrison. The Spaniards were saved from defeat by the timely arrival of Salcedo with fifty musketeers. From his station at Vigan he had seen the sails of Limahong's fleet, cruising southward along the Luzon coast, and, suspecting that so great an expedition could have no other purpose than the capture of Manila, he embarked in seven small boats, and reached the city in six days, just in time to participate in the furious battle between the Spaniards and the entire forces of the Chinese pirate. The result was the complete defeat of the Chinese, who were driven back upon their boats at Parañaque.

The Result of Limahong's Expedition. — Although defeated in his attack on Manila, Limahong was yet determined on a settlement in Luzon, and, sailing northward, he landed in Pangasinan and began constructing fortifications at the mouth of the river Lingayen. The Spaniards did not wait for him to strengthen himself and to dispute with them afresh for the possession of the island, but organized in March an expedition of two hundred and fifty Spaniards and fifteen hundred Filipinos under Salcedo. They landed suddenly in the Gulf of Lingayen, burned the entire fleet of the Chinese, and scattered a part of the forces in the surrounding mountains. The rest, though hemmed in by the Spaniards, were able to construct small boats, in which they escaped from the islands.

Thus ended this formidable attack, which threatened for a time to overthrow the power of Spain in the East. It was the beginning, however, of important relations with China. Before Limahong's escape a junk arrived from the viceroy of Fukien, petitioning for the delivery of the Chinese pirate. Two Augustinian friars accompanied his junk back to China, eager for such great fields of missionary conquest. They carried letters from Lavezares inviting Chinese friendship and intercourse.

Beginning of a New Period of Conquest. — In the spring of 1576, Salcedo died at Vigan, at the age of twenty-seven. With his death may be said to close the first period of the history in the Philippines, — that of the Conquest, extending from 1565 to 1576. For the next twenty-five years the ambitions of the Spaniards were not content with the exploration of this archipelago, but there were greater and more striking conquests, to which the minds of both soldier and priest aspired.

Despite the settlement with Portugal, the rich Spice Islands to the south still attracted them, and there were soon revealed the fertile coasts of Siam and Cambodia, the great empire of China, the beautiful island of Formosa, and the Japanese archipelago. These, with their great populations and wealth, were more alluring fields than the poor and sparsely populated coasts of the Philippines. So, for the next quarter of a century, the policy of the Spaniards in the Philippines was not so much to develop these islands themselves, as to make them a center for the commercial and spiritual conquest of the Orient.[1]

---

[1] See the letter of Bishop Salazar to the king, explaining his motives in coming to the Philippines. Retana, *Biblioteca Filipina*, vol. I.; *Relacion*, 1583, p. 4.

A Treaty with the Chinese. — The new governor arrived in the Islands in August, 1575. He was Dr. Francisco La-Sande. In October there returned the ambassadors who had been sent to China by Lavezares. The viceroy of Fukien had received them with much ceremony. He had not permitted the friars to remain, but had forwarded the governor's letter to the Chinese emperor. In February following came a Chinese embassy, granting a port of the empire with which the Spaniards could trade. This port, probably, was Amoy, which continued to be the chief port of communication with China to the present day.

It was undoubtedly commerce and not the missionaries that the Chinese desired. Two Augustinians attempted to return with this embassy to China, but the Chinese on leaving the harbor of Manila landed on the coast of Zambales, where they whipped the missionaries, killed their servants and interpreter, and left the friars bound to trees, whence they were rescued by a small party of Spaniards who happened to pass that way.

Sir Francis Drake's Noted Voyage. — The year 1577 is notable for the appearance in the East of the great English sea-captain, freebooter, and naval hero, Francis Drake. England and Spain, at this moment, while not actually at war, were rapidly approaching the conflict which made them for centuries traditional enemies. Spain was the champion of Roman ecclesiasticism. Her king, Philip the Second, was not only a cruel bigot, but a politician of sweeping ambition. His schemes included the conquest of France and England, the extermination of Protestantism, and the subjection of Europe to his own and the Roman authority.

The English people scented the danger from afar, and

while the two courts nominally maintained peace, the daring seamen of British Devon were quietly putting to sea in their swift and terrible vessels, for the crippling of the Spanish power. The history of naval warfare records no more reckless adventures than those of the English mariners during this period. Audacity could not rise higher.

Drake's is the most famous and romantic figure of them all. In the year 1577, he sailed from England with the avowed purpose of sweeping the Spanish Main. He passed the Straits of Magellan, and came up the western coast of South America, despoiling the Spanish shipping from Valparaiso to Panama. Thence he came on across the Pacific, touched the coast of Mindanao, and turned south to the Moluccas.

The Portuguese had nominally annexed the Moluccas in 1522, but at the time of Drake's visit they had been driven from Ternate, though still holding Tidor. Drake entered into friendly relations with the sultan of Ternate, and secured a cargo of cloves. From here he sailed boldly homeward, daring the Portuguese fleets, as he had defied the Spanish, and by way of Good Hope returned to England, his fleet the first after Magellan's to circumnavigate the globe.

A Spanish Expedition to Borneo. — The appearance of Drake in the Moluccas roused La-Sande to ambitious action. The attraction of the southern archipelagoes was overpowering, and at this moment the opportunity seemed to open to the governor to force southward his power. One of the Malay kings of Borneo, Sirela, arrived in Manila, petitioning aid against his brother, and promising to acknowledge the sovereignty of the king of Spain over the island of Borneo. La-Sande went in person to restore this chieftain to power. He had a fleet of galleys and. frigates, and, according to Padre Gaspar de San Augustin, more than fifteen hundred Filipino bowmen from Pangasinan, Cagayan, and the Bisayas accompanied the expedition. He landed on the coast of Borneo, destroyed the fleet of praos and the city of the usurper, and endeavored to secure Sirela in his principality. Sickness among his fleet and the lack of provisions forced him to return to Manila.

The First Attack upon the Moros of Jolo. — On his return he sent an officer against the island of Jolo. This officer forced the Joloanos to recognize his power, and from there he passed to the island of Mindanao, where he further enforced obedience upon the natives. This was the beginning of the Spanish expeditions against the Moros, which had the effect of arousing in these Mohammedan pirates such terrible retaliatory vengeance. Under La-Sande the conquest of the Camarines was completed by Captain Juan Chavés and the city of Nueva Caceres founded.

The Appointment of Governor Ronquillo. — It was the uniform policy of the Spanish government to limit the term of office of the governor to a short period of years. This was one of the futile provisions by which Spain attempted to control both the ambition and the avarice of her colonial captains. But Don Gonzalo Ronquillo had granted to him the governorship of the Philippines for life, on the condition of his raising and equipping a force of six hundred in Spain, largely at his own expense, for the better protection and pacification of the archipelago. This Ronquillo did, bringing his expedition by way of Panama. He arrived in April, 1580, and although he died at the end of three years, his rule came at an important time.

The Spanish and the Portuguese Colonies Combined. —
In 1580, Philip II. conquered and annexed to Spain the
kingdom of Portugal, and with Portugal came necessarily
to the Spanish crown those rich eastern colonies which
the valor of Da Gama and Albuquerque had won. Portugal rewon her independence in 1640, but for years Manila
was the capital of a colonial empire, extending from Goa
in India to Formosa.

Events of Ronquillo's Rule. — Ronquillo, under orders
from the crown, entered into correspondence with the
captain of the Portuguese fortress on the island of Tidor,
and the captain of Tidor petitioned Ronquillo for assistance in reconquering the tempting island of Ternate.
Ronquillo sent south a considerable expedition, but after
arriving in the Moluccas the disease of beri-beri in the
Spanish camp defeated the undertaking. Ronquillo also
sent a small armada to the coasts of Borneo and Malacca,
where a limited amount of pepper was obtained.

The few years of Ronquillo's reign were in other ways
important. A colony of Spaniards was established at
Oton, on the island of Panay, which was given the name
of Arêvalo (Iloilo). And under Ronquillo was pacified
for the first time the great valley of the Cagayan. At the
mouth of the river a Japanese adventurer, Tayfusa, or
Tayzufu, had established himself and was attempting the
subjugation of this important part of northern Luzon.
Ronquillo sent against him Captain Carreon, who expelled
the intruder and established on the present site of Lao-lo
the city of Nueva Segovia. Two friars accompanied this
expedition and the occupation of this valley by the Spaniards was made permanent.

The First Conflicts between the Church and the State. —
In March, 1581, there arrived the first Bishop of Manila,

Domingo de Salazar. Almost immediately began those conflicts between the spiritual and civil authorities, and between bishop and the regular orders, which have filled to such an extent the history of the islands. The bishop was one of those authoritative, ambitious, and arrogant characters, so typical in the history of the Church. It was largely due to his protests against the autocratic power of the governor that the king was induced to appoint the first Audiencia. The character and power of these courts have already been explained. The president and judges arrived the year following the death of Ronquillo, and the

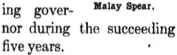

president, Dr. Santiago de Vera, became acting governor during the succeeding five years.

Malay Spear.

Malay Shield.

In 1587, the first Dominicans, fifteen in number, arrived, and founded their celebrated mission, La Provincia del Santisimo Rosario.

Increasing Strength of the Malays. — De Vera continued the policy of his predecessors and another fruitless attack was made on Ternate in 1585. The power of the Malay people was increasing, while that of the Europeans was decreasing. The sultans had expelled their foreign masters, and neither Spaniard nor Portuguese were able to effect the conquest of the Moluccas. There were uprisings of the natives in Manila and in Cagayan and Ilocos.

The Decree of 1589. — Affairs in the Islands did not yet, however, suit Bishop Salazar, and as the representative of both governor and bishop, the Jesuit, Alonso Sanchez, was dispatched in 1586 to lay the needs of the colony before the king. Philip was apparently impressed with the necessity of putting the government of the Islands upon a better adminstrative basis. To this end he published the important decree of 1589.

The governor now became a paid officer of the crown, at a salary of ten thousand ducats. For the proper protection of the colony and the conquest of the Moluccas, a regular force of four hundred soldiers accompanied the governor. His powers were extended to those of an actual viceregent of the king, and the Audiencia was abolished.

Malay Shield.

The man selected to occupy this important post was Don Gomez Perez Dasmariñas, who arrived with the new constitution in May, 1590. So great was the chagrin of the bishop at the abolition of the Audiencia and the increase of the governor's power, that he himself set out for Spain to lay his wishes before the court.

The Missionary Efforts of the Friars. — Twenty-four

Franciscans came with Dasmariñas and the presence of the three orders necessitated the partition of the Islands among them. The keenest rivalry and jealousy existed among them over the prosecution of missions in still more foreign lands. To the missionaries of this age it seemed a possible thing to convert the great and conservative nations of China and Japan to the Western religion.

In the month of Dasmariñas' arrival, a company of Dominicans attempted to found a mission in China, and, an embassy coming from Japan to demand vassalage from the Philippines, four of the newly arrived Franciscans accompanied the Japanese on their return.

A year later, in 1592, another embassy from the king of Cambodia arrived, bringing gifts that included two elephants, and petitioning for succor against the king of Siam. This was the beginning of an alliance between Cambodia and the Philippines which lasted for many years, and which occasioned frequent military aid and many efforts to convert that country.

Death of Dasmariñas. — But the center of Dasmariñas' ambitions was the effective conquest of the East Indies and the extension of Spanish power and his own rule through the Moluccas. With this end in view, for three years he made preparations. For months the shores were lined with the yards of the shipbuilders, and the great forests of Bulacan fell before the axes of the Indians. More than two hundred vessels, "galeras," "galeotas," and "virrayes," were built, and assembled at Cavite.

In the fall of 1593, the expedition, consisting of over nine hundred Spaniards, Filipino bowmen and rowers, was ready. Many of the Filipinos, procured to row these boats, were said to have been slaves, purchased through the Indian chiefs by the Spanish encomenderos. The governor sent forward this great fleet under the command of his son, Don Luis, and in the month of October he himself set sail in a galley with Chinese rowers. But on the night of the second day, while off the island of Maricaban, the Chinese oarsmen rose against the Spaniards, of whom there were about forty on the ship, and killed almost the entire number, including the governor. They then escaped in the boat to the Ilocos coast and thence to China.

The murder of this active and illustrious general was a determining blow to the ambitious projects for the conquest of the East Indies. Among other papers which Dasmariñas brought from Spain was a royal cedula giving him power to nominate his successor, who proved to be his son, Don Luis, who after some difficulty succeeded temporarily to his father's position.

Arrival of the Jesuits. — In June, 1595, there arrived Don Antonio de Morga, who had been appointed assessor and lieutenant-governor of the Islands, to succeed Don Luis. With Morga came the first Jesuit missionaries. He was also the bearer of an order granting to the Jesuits the exclusive privilege of conducting missions in China and Japan. The other orders were forbidden to pass outside the Islands.

An attempt to Colonize Mindanao. — In the year 1596, the Captain Rodriguez de Figueroa received the title of governor of Mindanao, with exclusive right to colonize the island for "the space of two lives." He left Iloilo in April with 214 Spaniards, two Jesuit priests, and many natives. They landed in the Rio Grande of Mindanao, where the defiant dato, Silonga, fortified himself and resisted them. Almost immediately Figueroa rashly ventured on shore and was killed by Moros. Reinforcements were sent under Don Juan Ronquillo, who, after nearly bringing the datos to submission, abandoned all he had gained. The Spaniards burned their forts on the Rio Grande and retired to Caldera, near Zamboanga, where they built a presidio.

Death of Franciscans in Japan. — The new governor, Don Francisco Tello de Guzman, arrived on June 1, 1596. He had previously been treasurer of the Casa de Contratacion in Seville. Soon after his arrival an important and serious tragedy occurred in Japan. The ship for Acapulco went ashore on the Japanese coast and its rich cargo was seized by the feudal prince where the vessel sought assistance. The Franciscans had already missions in these islands, and a quarrel existed between them and the Portuguese Jesuits over this missionary field. The latter succeeded in prejudicing the Japanese court against the Franciscans, and when they injudiciously pressed for the return of the property of the wrecked galleon, "San Felipe," the emperor, greedy for the rich plunder, and exasperated by their preaching, met their petitions with the sentence of death. They were horribly crucified at the port of Nagasaki, February 5, 1597. This emperor was the proud and cruel ruler, Taycosama. He was planning the conquest of the Philippines themselves, when death ended his plans.

The First Archbishop in the Philippines. — Meanwhile the efforts of Salazar at the Spanish court had effected further important changes for the Islands. The reëstablishment of the Royal Audiencia was ordered, and his own position was elevated to that of archbishop, with the three episcopal sees of Ilocos, Cebu, and the Camarines. He did not live to assume this office, and the first archbishop of the Philippines was Ignacio Santibañez, who also died three months after his arrival, on May 28, 1598.

Reëstablishment of the Audiencia. — The Audiencia was reëstablished with great pomp and ceremony. The royal seal was borne on a magnificently caparisoned horse to the cathedral, where a Te Deum was chanted, and then to the Casas Reales, where was inaugurated the famous court that continued without interruption down to the end of Spanish rule. Dr. Morga was one of the first oidores, and the earliest judicial record which can now be found in the archives of this court is a sentence bearing his signature.

The Rise of Moro Piracy. — The last years of De Guzman's governorship were filled with troubles ominous for the future of the Islands. The presidio of Caldera was destroyed by the Moros. Following this victory, in the year 1599, the Moros of Jolo and Maguindanao equipped a piratical fleet of fifty caracoas, and swept the coasts of the Bisayas. Cebu, Negros, and Panay were ravaged, their towns burned, and their inhabitants carried off as slaves.

The following year saw the return of a larger and still more dreadful expedition. The people of Panay abandoned their towns and fled into the mountains, under the belief that these terrible attacks had been inspired by the Spaniards. To check these pirates, Juan Gallinato, with a force of two hundred Spaniards, was sent against Jolo, but, like so many expeditions that followed his, he accomplished nothing. The inability of the Spaniards was now revealed and the era of Moro piracy had begun. "From this time until the present day" (about the year 1800), wrote Zuñiga, "these Moros have not ceased to infest our colonies; innumerable are the Indians they have captured, the towns they have looted, the rancherias they have destroyed, the vessels they have taken. It seems as if God has preserved them for vengeance on the Spaniards that they have not been able to subject them in two hundred years, in spite of the expeditions sent against them, the armaments sent almost very year to pursue them.   In a very little while we conquered all the islands of the Philippines; but the little island of Jolo, a part of Mindanao,

Moro Prao.

and other islands near by we have not been able to subjugate to this day." [1]

Battle at Mariveles with the Dutch. — In October, 1600, two Dutch vessels appeared in the Islands; it was the famous expedition of the Dutch admiral, Van Noort. They had come through the Straits of Magellan, on a voyage around the world.   The Dutch were in great need of provisions.   As they were in their great enemy's colony, they captured and sunk several boats, Spanish and Chi-

[1] Zuñiga: *Historia de Filipinas*, pp. 195, 196.

nese, bound for Manila with rice, poultry, palm-wine, and other stores of food. At Mariveles, a Japanese vessel from Japan was overhauled. Meanwhile in Manila great excitement and activity prevailed. The Spaniards fitted up two galleons and the "Oidor" Morga himself took command with a large crew of fighting men.

On November 14, they attacked the Dutch, whose crews were greatly reduced to only eighty men on both ships. The vessel commanded by Morga ran down the flagship of Van Noort, and for hours the ships lay side by side while a hand-to-hand fight raged on the deck and in the hold. The ships taking fire, Morga disengaged his ship, which was so badly shattered that it sank, with great loss of life; but Morga and some others reached the little island of Fórtuna. Van Noort was able to extinguish the fire on his vessel, and escape from the Islands. He eventually reached Holland. His smaller vessel was captured with its crew of twenty-five men, who were all hung at Cavite.[1]

Other Troubles of the Spanish. — In the year 1600, two ships sailed for Acapulco, but one went down off the Catanduanes and the other was shipwrecked on the Ladrones. "On top of all other misfortunes, Manila suffered, in the last months of this government, a terrible earthquake, which destroyed many houses and the church of the Jesuits."[2]

The Moros, the Dutch, anxieties and losses by sea, the visitations of God,—how much of the history of the seventeenth century in the Philippines is filled with these four things!

---

[1] Both Van Noort and Morga have left us accounts of this sea-fight, the former in his journal, *Description of the Failsome Voyage Made Round the World*, and the latter in his famous, *Sucesos de las Islas Filipinas*.

[2] Montero y Vidal: *Historia de Filipinas*, vol. I., p. 199.

CHAPTER VIII.

THE PHILIPPINES THREE HUNDRED YEARS AGO.

Condition of the Archipelago at the Beginning of the Seventeenth Century. — *The Spanish Rule Completely Established.* — At the close of the sixteenth century the Spaniards had been in possession of the Philippines for a generation. In these thirty-five years the most striking of all the results of the long period of Spanish occupation were accomplished. The work of these first soldiers and missionaries established the limits and character of Spanish rule as it was to remain for 250 years. Into this first third of a century the Spaniard crowded all his heroic feats of arms, exploration, and conversion. Thereafter, down to 1850, new fields were explored, and only a few new tribes Christianized.

The survey of the archipelago given by Morga soon after 1600 reads like a narrative of approximately modern conditions. It reveals to us how great had been the activities of the early Spaniard and how small the achievements of his countrymen after the seventeenth century began. All of the large islands, except Paragua and the Moro country, were, in that day, under encomiendas, their inhabitants paying tributes and for the most part professing the Catholic faith.

The smaller groups and islets were almost as thoroughly exploited. Even of the little Catanduanes, lying off the Pacific coast of Luzon, Morga could say, "They are well populated with natives, — a good race, all encomended to Spaniards, with doctrine and churches, and an alcalde-mayor, who does justice among them."

He says of the Babuyanes at the extreme north of the archipelago, "They are not encomended, nor is tribute collected among them, nor are there Spaniards among them, because they are of little reason and politeness, and there have neither been Christians made among them nor have they justices." They continued in this condition until a few years before the end of Spanish rule. In 1591, however, the Babuyanes had been given in encomienda to Esteban de la Serna and Francisco Castillo. They are put as having two thousand inhabitants and five hundred "tributantes," but all unsubdued ("todos alçados").

On some islands the hold of the Spaniards was more extensive in Morga's day than at a later time. Then the island of Mindoro was regarded as important, and in the early years and decades of Spanish power appears to have been populous along the coasts. Later it was desolated by the Moro pirates and long remained wild and almost uninhabited except by a shifting population from the mainland of Luzon.

The Encomiendas. — The first vessels that followed the expedition of Legaspi had brought orders from the king that the Islands should be settled, and divided in encomiendas to those who had conquered and won them.[1] On this instruction, Legaspi had given the Filipinos in encomienda to his captains and soldiers as fast as the conquest proceeded.

We are fortunate to have a review of these encomiendas, made in 1591, about twenty-five years after the system was introduced into the Islands.[2] There were then 267

---

[1] *Relacion de la Conquista de Luzon*, 1572, p. 15.

[2] *Relacion de las Encomiendas, existentes en Filipinas*, Retana, *Archivo del Bibliófilo Filipino*, vol. IV.

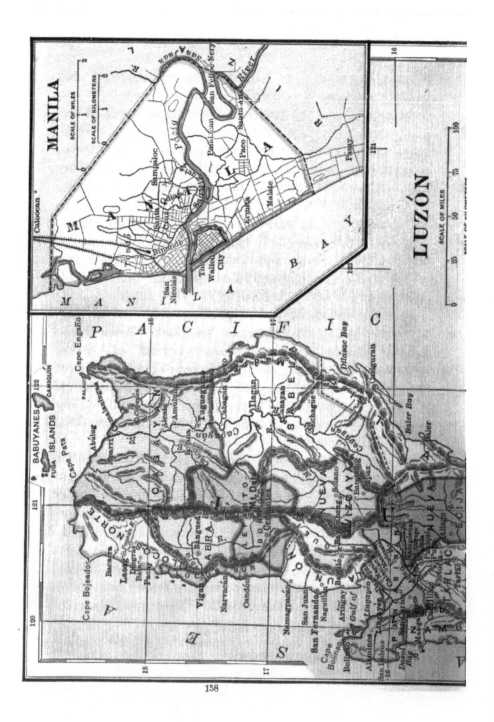

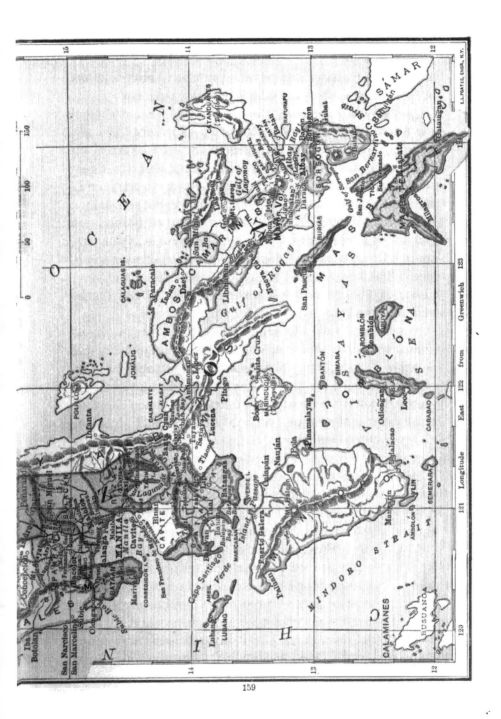

encomiendas in the Philippines, of which thirty-one were of the king, and the remainder of private persons.

Population under the Encomiendas. — From the enu-. meration of these encomiendas, we learn that the most populous parts of the archipelago were La Laguna, with 24,000 tributantes and 97,000 inhabitants, and the Camarines, which included all the Bicol territory, and the Catanduanes, where there were 21,670 tributantes and a population of over 86,000. In the vicinity of Manila and Tondo, which included Cavite and Marigondon, the south shore of the bay, and Pasig and Taguig, there were collected 9,410 tributes, and the population was estimated at about 30,000. In Ilocos were reported 17,130 tributes and 78,520 souls.

The entire valley of the Cagayan had been divided among the soldiers of the command which had effected the conquest. In the list of encomiendas a few can be recognized, such as Yguig and Tuguegarao, but most of the names are not to be found on maps of to-day. Most of the inhabitants were reported to be "rebellious" (alçados), and some were apparently the same wild tribes which still occupy all of this water-shed, except the very. banks of the river; but none the less had the Spaniards divided them off into "repartimentos." One soldier had even taken as an encomienda the inhabitants of the upper waters of the river, a region which is called in the *Relacion* "Pugao," with little doubt the habitat of the same Igorrote tribe as the Ipugao, who still dwell in these mountains. The upper valley of the Magat, or Nueva Vizcaya, does not appear to have been occupied and probably was not until the missions of the eighteenth century.

The population among the Bisayan islands was quite surprisingly small, considering its present proportions.

Masbate, for example, had but 1,600 souls; Burias, a like number; the whole central group, leaving out Panay, only 15,833 tributes, or about 35,000 souls. There was a single encomienda in Butúan, Mindanao, and another on the Caraga coast. There were a thousand tributes collected in the encomienda of Cuyo, and fifteen hundred in Calamianes, which, says the *Relacion,* included "los negrillos," probably the mixed Negrito population of northern Palawan.

The entire population under encomiendas is set down as 166,903 tributes, or 667,612 souls. This is, so far as known, the earliest enumeration of the population of the Philippines. Barring the Igorrotes of northern Luzon and the Moros and other tribes of Mindanao, it is a fair estimate of the number of the Filipino people three hundred years ago.

It will be noticed that the numbers assigned to single encomenderos in the Philippines were large. In America the number was limited. As early as 1512, King Ferdinand had forbidden any single person, of whatever rank or grade, to hold more than three hundred Indians on one island.[1] But in the Philippines, a thousand or twelve hundred "tributantes" were frequently held by a single Spaniard.

Condition of the Filipinos under the Encomiendas.— Frequent Revolts. —That the Filipinos on many of these islands bitterly resented their condition is evidenced by the frequent uprisings and rebellions. The encomenderos were often extortionate and cruel, and absolutely heedless of the restrictions and obligations imposed upon them by the Laws of the Indies. Occasionally a new governor,

---

[1] *Ordenanzas . . . para la Reparticion de los Indios de la Isla Española,* in *Documentos Ineditas,* vol. I., p. 236.

under the first impulse of instructions from Mexico or Spain, did something to correct abuses. Revolts were almost continuous during the year 1583, and the condition of the natives very bad, many encomenderos regarding them and treating them almost as slaves, and keeping them at labor to the destruction of their own crops and the misery of their families. Gov. Santiago de Vera reached the Islands the following year and made a characteristic attempt to improve the system, which is thus related by Zuñiga: —

"As soon as he had taken possession of the government, he studied to put into effect the orders which he brought from the king, to punish certain encomenderos, who had abused the favor they had received in being given encomiendas, whereby he deposed Bartolomé de Ledesma, encomendero of Abuyo (Leyte), and others of those most culpable, and punished the others in proportion to the offenses which they had committed, and which had been proven.

"In the following year of 1585, he sent Juan de Morones and Pablo de Lima, with a well equipped squadron, to the Moluccas, which adventure was as unfortunate as those that had preceded it, and they returned to Manila without having been able to take the fortress of Ternate. The governor felt it very deeply that the expedition had failed, and wished to send another armada in accordance with the orders which the king had given him; but he could not execute this because the troops from New Spain did not arrive, and because of the Indians, who lost no occasion which presented itself to shake off the yoke of the Spaniards.

"The Pampangos and many inhabitants of Manila confederated with the Moros of Borneo, who had come for trade, and plotted to enter the city by night, set it on fire, and, in the confusion of the conflagration, slay all the Spaniards. This conspiracy was discovered through an Indian woman, who was married to a Spanish soldier, and measures to meet the conspiracy were taken, before the mine exploded, many being seized and suffering exemplary punishment.

" The islands of Samar, Ybabao, and Leyte were also in disturbance, and the encomendero of Dagami, pueblo of Leyte, was in peril of losing his life, because the Indians were incensed by his thievings in the collection of tribute, which was paid in wax, and which he compelled them to have weighed with a steelyard which he had made double the legal amount, and wanted to kill him. They would have done so if he had not escaped into the mountains and afterwards passed by a banca to the island of Cebu. The governor sent Captain Lorenzo de la Mota to pacify these disturbances; he made some punishments, and with these everything quieted down." [1]

Three years later, however, the natives of Leyte were again in revolt. In 1589 Cagayan rose and killed many Spaniards. The revolt seems to have spread from here to the town of Dingras, Ilocos, where the natives rose against the collectors of tribute, and slew six Spaniards of the pueblo of Fernandina. (Zuñiga, *Historia de Filipinas*, p. 165.) [2]

Effects of the Spanish Government. — The Spanish occupation had brought ruin and misery to some parts of

---

[1] *Historia de Filipinas*, p. 157, et sq.

[2] Among other documents, which throw a most unfavorable light upon the condition of the Filipinos under the encomiendas, is the letter to the king from Domingo de Salazar, the first bishop of the Philippines, which describes the conditions about 1583.

the country. Salazar describes with bitterness the evil condition of the Filipinos. In the rich fields of Bulacan and Pampanga, great gangs of laborers had been impressed, felling the forests for the construction of the Spanish fleets and manning these fleets at the oars, on voyages which took them for four and six months from their homes. The governor, Don Gonzalez de Ronquillo, had forced many Indians of Pampanga into the mines of Ilocos, taking them from the sowing of their rice. Many had died in the mines and the rest returned so enfeebled that they could not plant. Hunger and famine had descended upon Pampanga, and on the encomienda of Guido de Lavazares over a thousand had died from starvation.[1]

The Taxes. — The taxes were another source of abuse. Theoretically, the tax upon Indians was limited to the "tributo," the sum of eight reales (about one dollar) yearly from the heads of all families, payable either in gold or in produce of the district. But in fixing the prices of these commodities there was much extortion, the encomenderos delaying the collection of the tribute until the season of scarcity, when prices were high, but insisting then on the same amount as at harvest-time.

The principal, who occupied the place of the former dato, or "maharlica," like the gobernadorcillo of recent times, was responsible for the collecting of the tribute, and his lot seems to have been a hard one. "If they do not give as much as they ask, or do not pay for as many Indians as they say there are, they abuse the poor principal, or throw him into the pillory (cepo de cabeza), because all the encomenderos, when they go to make collections, take their pillories with them, and there they keep

---

[1] Domingo de Salazar, *Relacion de las Cosas de las Filipinas*, 1583, p. 5, in Retana Archives, vol. 3.

him and torment him, until forced to give all they ask. They are even said to take the wife and daughter of the principal, when he can not be found. Many are the principales who have died under these torments, according to reports."

Salazar further states that he has known natives to be sold into slavery, in default of tribute. Neither did they impose upon adults alone, but "they collect tribute from infants, the aged and the slaves, and many do not marry because of the tribute, and others slay their children." [1]

Scarcity of Food. — Salazar further charges that the alcaldes mayores (the alcaldes of provinces), sixteen in number, were all corrupt, and, though their salaries were small, they accumulated fortunes. For further enumeration of economic ills, Salazar details how prices had evilly increased. In the first years of Spanish occupation, food was abundant. There was no lack of rice, beans, chickens, pigs, venison, buffalo, fish, cocoanuts, bananas, and other fruits, wine and honey; and a little money bought much. A hundred gantas (about three hundred pints) of rice could then be bought for a toston (a Portuguese coin, worth about a half-peso), eight to sixteen fowls for a like amount, a fat pig for from four to six reales. In the year of his writing (about 1583), products were scarce and prices exorbitant. Rice had doubled, chickens were worth a real, a good pig six to eight pesos. Population had decreased, and whole towns were deserted, their inhabitants having fled into the hills.

General Improvement under Spanish Rule. — This is one side of the picture. It probably is overdrawn by the bishop, who was jealous of the civil authority and who began the first of those continuous clashes between the

---

[1] *Relacion*, pp. 13, 14.

church and political power in the Philippines. Doubtless if we could see the whole character of Spanish rule
in these decades, we should see that the actual condition
of the Filipino had improved and his grade of culture
had arisen. No one can estimate the actual good that
comes to a people in being brought under the power of a
government able to maintain peace and dispense justice.
Taxation is sometimes grievous, corruption without excuse; but almost anything is better than anarchy.

Before the coming of the Spaniards, it seems unques-
tionable that the Filipinos suffered greatly under two terrible grievances that inflict barbarous society, — in the first
place, warfare, with its murder, pillage, and destruction,
not merely between tribe and tribe, but between town
and town, such as even now prevails in the wild
mountains of northern Luzon, among the primitive Malayan tribes; and in the second place, the weak and poor
man was at the mercy of the strong and rich.

The establishment of Spanish sovereignty had certainly
mitigated, if it did not wholly remedy, these conditions.
" All of these provinces," Morga could write, "are pacified
and are governed from Manila, having alcaldes mayores,
corregidors, and lieutenants, each one of whom governs in
his district or province and dispenses justice. The chieftains (principales), who formerly held the other natives in
subjection, no longer have power over them in the manner
which they tyrannically employed, which is not the least
benefit these natives have received in escaping from such
slavery." [1]

Old Social Order of the Filipinos but Little Disturbed. —
Some governors seem to have done their utmost to improve the condition of the people and to govern them

---

[1] *Sucesos de las Filipinas,* p. 334.

well. Santiago de Vera, as we have seen, even went so
far as to commission the worthy priest, Padre Juan
de Plasencia, to investigate the customs and social organization of the Filipinos, and to prepare an account of
their laws, that they might be more suitably governed.
This brief code — for so it is — was distributed to
alcaldes, judges, and encomenderos, with orders to pattern their decisions in accordance with Filipino custom.[1]

In ordering local affairs, the Spaniards to some extent
left the old social order of the Filipinos undisturbed.
The several social classes were gradually suppressed, and
at the head of each barrio, or small settlement, was
appointed a head, or cabeza de barangay. As these
barangayes were grouped into pueblos, or towns, the
former datos were appointed captains and gobernadorcillos.

The Payment of Tribute. — The tribute was introduced
in 1570.[2] It was supposed to be eight reales or a peso of
silver for each family. Children under sixteen and those
over sixty were exempt. In 1590 the amount was raised
to ten reales. To this was added a real for the church,
known as "sanctorum," and, on the organization of the
towns, a real for the caja de communidad or municipal
treasury. Under the encomiendas the tribute was paid
to the encomenderos, except on the royal encomiendas;
but after two or three generations, as the encomiendas
were suppressed, these collections went directly to the
insular treasury. There was, in addition to the tribute,
a compulsory service of labor on roads, bridges, and

---

[1] *Las Costumbres de los Tagáloes en Filipinas segun el Padre Plasencia.* Madrid, 1892.

[2] Blumentritt: *Organization Communale des Indigines des Philippines, traduis de l'Allemand,* par A. Hugot. 1881.

public works, known as the "corvee," a feudal term, or
perhaps more generally as the "polos y servicios." Those
discharging this enforced labor were called "polistas."

Conversion of the Filipinos to Christianity. — The population had been very rapidly Christianized. All accounts
agree that almost no difficulty was encountered in baptizing the more advanced tribes. "There is not in these
islands a province," says Morga, "which resists conversion and does not desire it." [1] Indeed, the Islands seem
to have been ripe for the preaching of a higher faith,
either Christian or Mohammedan. For a time these two
great religions struggled together in the vicinity of Manila,[2] but at the end of three decades Spanish power
and religion were alike established. Conversion was
delayed ordinarily only by the lack of sufficient numbers
of priests. We have seen that this conversion of the
people was the work of the missionary friars. In 1591
there were 140 in the Islands, but the *Relacion* de Encomiendas calls for 160 more to properly supply the peoples
which had been laid under tribute.

Coming of the Friars. — The Augustinians had been the
first to come, accompanying Legaspi. Then came the
barefooted friars of the Order of Saint Francis. The first
Jesuits, padres Antonio Sedeño and Alonzo Sanchez, came
with the first bishop of the Islands, Domingo de Salazar,
in 1580. They came apparently without resources. Even
their garments brought from Mexico had rotted on the
voyage. They found a little, poor, narrow house in a
suburb of Manila, called Laguio (probably Concepcion).
"So poorly furnished was it," says Chirino, "that the
same chest which held their books was the table on which

---

[1] *Sucesos de las Filipinas*, p. 332.
[2] See Salazar's relation on this point.

they ate. Their food for many days was rice, cooked in water, without salt or oil or fish or meat or even an egg, or anything else except that sometimes as a regalo they enjoyed some salt sardines." [1] After the Jesuits, came, as we have seen, the friars of the Dominican order, and lastly the Recollects, or unshod Augustinians.

Division of the Archipelago among the Religious Orders. — The archipelago was districted among these missionary bands. The Augustinians had many parishes in the Bisayas, on the Ilocano coast, some in Pangasinan, and all of those in Pampanga. The Dominicans had parts of Pangasinan and all of the valley of Cagayan. The Franciscans controlled the Camarines and nearly all of southern Luzon, and the region of Laguna de Bay. All of these orders had convents and monasteries both in the city of Manila and in the country round about. The imposing churches of brick and stone, which now characterize nearly every pueblo, had not in those early decades been erected; but Morga tells us that "the churches and monasteries were of wood, and well built, with furniture and beautiful ornaments, complete service, crosses, candlesticks, and chalices of silver and gold." [2]

The First Schools. — Even in these early years there seem to have been some attempts at the education of the natives. The friars had schools in reading and writing for boys, who were also taught to serve in the church, to sing, to play the organ, the harp, guitar, and other instruments. We must remember, however, that the Filipino before the arrival of the Spaniard had a written language, and even in pre-Spanish times there must have been instruction given to the child. The type of humble school,

---

[1] Chirino: *Relacion*, pp. 19, 20.
[2] Morga, p. 329.

that is found to-day in remote barrios, conducted by an old man or woman, on the floor or in the yard of a home, where the ordinary family occupations are proceeding, probably does not owe its origin to the Spaniards, but dates from a period before their arrival. The higher education established by the Spaniards appears to have been exclusively for the children of Spaniards. In 1601 the Jesuits, pioneers of the Roman Catholic orders in education, established the College of San José.

Establishment of Hospitals. — The city early had notable foundations of charity. The high mortality which visited the Spaniards in these islands and the frequency of diseases early called for the establishment of institutions for the orphan and the invalid. In Morga's time there were the orphanages of San Andres and Santa Potenciana. There was the Royal Hospital, in charge of three Franciscans, which burned in the conflagration of 1603, but was reconstructed. There was also a Hospital of Mercy, in charge of Sisters of Charity from Lisbon and the Portuguese possessions of India.

Close by the Monastery of Saint Francis stood then, where it stands to-day, the hospital for natives, San Juan de Dios. It was of royal patronage, but founded by a friar of the Franciscan order, Juan Clemente. "Here," says Morga, "are cured a great number of natives of all kinds of sicknesses, with much charity and care. It has a good house and offices of stone, and is administered by the barefooted religious of Saint Francis. Three priests are there and four lay-brethren of exemplary life, who, with the doctors, surgeons, and apothecaries, are so dexterous and skilled that they work with their hands marvelous cures, both in medicine and surgery." [1]

---
[1] *Sucesos de las Filipians,* p. 323.

Mortality among the Spaniards. — Mortality in the Philippines in these years of conquest was frightfully high. The waste of life in her colonial adventures, indeed, drained Spain of her best and most vigorous manhood. In the famous old English collection of voyages, published by Hakluyt in 1598, there is printed a captured Spanish letter of the famous sea-captain, Sebastian Biscaino, on the Philippine trade. Biscaino grieves over the loss of life which had accompanied the conquest of the Philippines, and the treacherous climate of the tropics. "The country is very unwholesome for us Spaniards. For within these 20 years, of 14,000 which have gone to the Philippines, there are 13,000 of them dead, and not past 1,000 of them left alive." [1]

The Spanish Population. — The Spanish population of the Islands was always small, — at the beginning of the seventeenth century certainly not more than two thousand, and probably less later in the century. Morga divides them into five classes: the prelates and ecclesiastics; the encomenderos, colonizers, and conquerors; soldiers and officers of war and marine; merchants and men of business; and the officers of his Majesty's government. "Very few are living now," he says, "of those first conquistadores who won the land and effected the conquest with the Adelantado Miguel Lopez de Legaspi." [2]

The Largest Cities. — Most of this Spanish population dwelt in Manila or in the five other cities which the Span-

---

[1] *The Principal Navigations, Voiages, Traffiques and Discoveries of the English Nation, . . . by Richard Hakluyt, Master of Artes and sometime Student of Christ Church in Oxford. Imprinted at London,* 1598. Vol. I., p. 560.

[2] *Sucesos de las Filipinas,* p. 347.

iards had founded in the first three decades of their occupation. These were as follows: —

The City of Nueva Segovia, at the mouth of the
Cagayan, was founded in the governorship of Ronquillo,
when the valley of the Cagayan was first occupied and the
Japanese colonists, who had settled there, were expelled.
It had at the beginning of the seventeenth century two
hundred Spaniards, living in houses of wood. There was
a fort of stone, where some artillery was mounted. Besides the two hundred Spanish inhabitants there were one
hundred regular Spanish soldiers, with their officers and
the alcalde mayor of the province. Nueva Segovia was
also the seat of a bishopric which included all northern
Luzon. The importance of the then promising city has
long ago disappeared, and the pueblo of Lallo, which marks
its site, is an insignificant native town.

The City of Nueva Caceres, in the Camarines, was
founded by Governor La-Sande. It, too, was the seat
of a bishopric, and had one hundred Spanish inhabitants.

The Cities of Cebu and Iloilo. — In the Bisayas were
the Cities of the Holy Name of God (Cebu), and on the
island of Panay, Arévalo (or Iloilo). The first maintained
something of the importance attaching to the first Spanish
settlement. It had its stone fort and was also the seat of
a bishopric. It was visited by trading-vessels from the
Moluccas, and by permit of the king enjoyed for a time
the unusual privilege of sending annually a ship loaded
with merchandise to New Spain. Arévalo had about
eighty Spanish inhabitants, and a monastery of the
Augustinians.

The City of Fernandina, or Vigan, which Salcedo
had founded, was nearly without Spanish inhabitants.

Still, it was the political center of the great Ilocano coast, and it has held this position to the present day.

Manila. — But all of these cities were far surpassed in importance by the capital on the banks of the Pasig. The wisdom of Legaspi's choice had been more than justified. Manila, at the beginning of the seventeenth century, was unquestionably the most important European city of the East. As we have already seen, in 1580 Portugal had been annexed by Spain and with her had come all the Portuguese possessions in India, China, and Malaysia. After 1610, the Dutch were almost annually warring for this colonial empire, and Portugal regained her independence in 1640. But for the first few years of the seventeenth century, Manila was the political mistress of an empire that stretched from Goa to Formosa and embraced all those coveted lands which for a century and a half had been the desire of European states.

The governor of the Philippines was almost an independent king. Nominally, he was subordinate to the viceroy of Mexico, but practically he waged wars, concluded peaces, and received and sent embassies at his own discretion. The kingdom of Cambodia was his ally, and the states of China and Japan were his friends.

The Commercial Importance of Manila. — Manila was also the commercial center of the Far East, and the entrepôt through which the kingdoms of eastern Asia exchanged their wares. Here came great fleets of junks from China laden with stores. Morga fills nearly two pages with an enumeration of their merchandise, which included all manner of silks, brocades, furniture, pearls and gems, fruits, nuts, tame buffalo, geese, horses and mules, all kinds of animals, "even to birds in cages, some of which talk and others sing, and which they make perform a thousand tricks; there are innumerable other gew-gaws and knickknacks, which among Spaniards are in much esteem." [1]

Each year a fleet of thirty to forty vessels sailed with the new moon in March. The voyage across the China Sea, rough with the monsoons, occupied fifteen or twenty days, and the fleet returned at the end of May or the beginning of June. Between October and March there came, each year, Japanese ships from Nagasaki which brought wheat, silks, objects of art, and weapons, and took away from Manila the raw silk of China, gold, deer horns, woods, honey, wax, palm-wine, and wine of Castile.

From Malacca and India came fleets of the Portuguese subjects of Spain, with spices, slaves, Negroes and Kafirs, and the rich productions of Bengal, India, Persia, and Turkey. From Borneo, too, came the smaller craft of the Malays, who from their boats sold the fine palm mats, the best of which still come from Cagayan de Sulu and Borneo, slaves, sago, water-pots and glazed earthenware, black and fine. From Siam and Cambodia also, but less often, there came trading-ships. Manila was thus a great emporium for all the countries of the East, the trade of which seems to have been conducted largely by and through the merchants of Manila.

Trade with Mexico and Spain Restricted. — The commerce between the Philippines, and Mexico and Spain, though it was of vast importance, was limited by action of the crown. It was a commerce which apparently admitted of infinite expansion, but the shortsighted merchants and manufacturers of the Peninsula clamored against its development, and it was subjected to the severest limitations. Four galleons were at first main-

---

[1] *Sucesos de las Filipinas*, p. 352.

tained for this trade, which were dispatched two at a time in successive years from Manila to the port of Acapulco, Mexico. The letter on the Philippine trade, already quoted, states that these galleons were great ships of six hundred and eight hundred tons apiece.[1] They went "very strong with soldiers," and they carried the annual mail, reënforcements, and supplies of Mexican silver for trade with China, which has remained the commercial currency of the East to the present day. Later the number of galleons was reduced to one.

The Rich Cargoes of the Galleons. — The track of the Philippine galleon lay from Luzon northeastward to about the forty-second degree of latitude, where the westerly winds prevail, thence nearly straight across the ocean to Cape Mendocino in northern California, which was discovered and mapped by Biscaino in 1602. Thence the course lay down the western coast of North America nearly three thousand miles to the port of Acapulco.

We can imagine how carefully selected and rich in quality were the merchandises with which these solitary galleons were freighted, the pick of all the rich stores which came to Manila. The profits were enormous, — six and eight hundred per cent. Biscaino wrote that with two hundred ducats invested in Spanish wares and some Flemish commodities, he made fourteen hundred ducats; but, he added, in 1588 he lost a ship, — robbed and burned by Englishmen. On the safe arrival of these ships depended how much of the fortunes of the colony!

Capture of the Galleons. — For generations these galleons were probably the most tempting and romantic prize that ever aroused the cupidity of privateer. The first to profit by this rich booty was Thomas Cavendish,

---

[1] Laws of the Indies, VIII., 45, 46.

who in 1584 came through the Straits of Magellan with a fleet of five vessels. Like Drake before him, he ravaged the coast of South America and then steered straight away across the sea to the Moluccas. Here he acquired information about the rich commerce of the Philippines and of the yearly voyage of the galleon. Back across the Pacific went the fleet of Cavendish for the coast of California.

In his own narrative he tells how he beat up and

Capture of a Galleon (from an old print).

down between Capes San Lucas and Mendocino until the galleon, heavy with her riches, appeared. She fell into his hands almost without a fray. She carried one hundred and twenty-two thousand pesos of gold and a great and rich store of satins, damask, and musk. Cavendish landed the Spanish on the California coast, burned the "Santa Anna," and then returned to the Philippines and made an attack upon the shipyard of Iloilo, but was repulsed. He sent a letter to the governor at Manila, boasting of his capture, and then sailed for the Cape of Good Hope and home.

There is an old story that tells how his seaworn ships came up the Thames, their masts hung with silk and damask sails. From this time on the venture was less safe. In 1588 there came to Spain the overwhelming disaster of her history, — the destruction of the Great Armada. From this date her power was gone, and her name was no longer a terror on the seas. English freebooters controlled the oceans, and in 1610 the Dutch appeared in the East, never to withdraw.

The City of Manila Three Hundred Years Ago. — We can hardly close this chapter without some further reference to the city of Manila as it appeared three hundred years ago. Morga has fortunately left us a detailed description from which the following points in the main are drawn. As we have already seen, Legaspi had laid out the city on the blackened site of the town and fortress of the Mohammedan prince, which had been destroyed in the struggle for occupation. He gave it the same extent and dimensions that it possesses to this day.

Like other colonial capitals in the Far East, it was primarily a citadel and refuge from attack. On the point beween the sea and the river Legaspi had built the famous and permanent fortress of Santiago. In the time of the great Adelantado it was probably only a wooden stockade, but under the governor Santiago de Vera it was built up of stone. Cavendish (1587) describes Manila as "an unwalled town and of no great strength," but under the improvements and completions made by Dasmariñas about 1590 it assumed much of its present appearance. Its guns thoroughly commanded the entrance to the river Pasig and made the approach of hostile boats from the harbor side impossible.

It is noteworthy, then, that all the assaults that have been made upon the city, from that of Limahong, to those of the British in 1763, and of the Americans in 1898, have been directed against the southern wall by an advance from Parañaque. Dasmariñas also inclosed the city with a stone wall, the base from which the present noble rampart has arisen. It had originally a width of from seven and a half to nine feet. Of its height no figure is given. Morga says simply that with its buttresses and turrets it was sufficiently high for the purposes of defense.

The Old Fort. — There was a stone fort on the south side facing Ermita, known as the Fortress of Our Lady of Guidance; and there were two or more bastions, each with six pieces of artillery, — St. Andrew's, now a powder magazine at the southeast corner, and St. Gabriel's, overlooking the Parian district, where the Chinese were settled.

The three principal gates to the city, with the smaller wickets and posterns, which opened on the river and sea, were regularly closed at night by the guard which made the rounds. At each gate and wicket was a permanent post of soldiers and artillerists.

The Plaza de Armas adjacent to the fort had its arsenal, stores, powder-works, and a foundry for the casting of guns and artillery. The foundry, when established by Ronquillo, was in charge of a Pampangan Indian called Pandapira.

The Spanish Buildings of the City. — The buildings of the city, especially the Casas Reales and the churches and monasteries, had been durably erected of stone. Chirino claims that the hewing of stone, the burning of lime, and the training of native and Chinese artisans for this building, were the work of the Jesuit father, Sedeño. He himself fashioned the first clay tiles and built the first stone house, and so urged and encouraged others, himself directing, the building of public works, that the city, which a little before had been solely of timber and cane, had become one of the best constructed and most beautiful in the Indies.[1] He it was also who sought out Chinese painters and decorators and ornamented the churches with images and paintings.

Within the walls, there were some six hundred houses of a private nature, most of them built of stone and tile, and an equal number outside in the suburbs, or "arrabales," all occupied by Spaniards ("todos son vivienda y poblacion de los Españoles").[2]

This gives some twelve hundred Spanish families or establishments, exclusive of the religious, who in Manila numbered at least one hundred and fifty,[3] the garrison, at certain times, about four hundred trained Spanish soldiers who had seen service in Holland and the Low Countries, and the official classes.

The Malecon and the Luneta. — It is interesting at this early date to find mention of the famous recreation drive, the Paseo de Bagumbayan, now commonly known as the Malecon and Luneta. "Manila," says our historian, "has two places of recreation on land; the one, which is clean and wide, extends from the point called Our Lady of Guidance for about a league along the sea, and through the street and village of natives, called Bagumbayan, to

---

[1] *Relacion de las Islas Filipinas,* chap. V., p. 23, and chap. XIII. p. 47.

[2] *Ibid.,* p. 323.

[3] *Ibid.,* p. 321.

a very devout hermitage (Ermita), called the Hermitage
of Our Lady of Guidance, and from there a good distance
to a monastery and mission (doctrina) of the Augustinians, called Mahalat (Malate)." [1]   The other drive lay out
through the present suburb of Concepcion, then called
Laguio, to Paco, where was a monastery of the Franciscans.

The Chinese in Manila. — *Early Chinese Commerce.* —
We have seen that even as long ago as three hundred
years Manila was a metropolis of the Eastern world.   Vessels from many lands dropped anchor at the mouth of the
Pasig, and their merchants set up their booths within her
markets.   Slaves from far-distant India and Africa were
sold under her walls.   Surely it was a cosmopolitan population that the shifting monsoons carried to and from her
gates.

But of all these Eastern races only one has been
a constant and important factor in the life of the Islands.
This is the Chinese.   It does not appear that they settled
in the country or materially affected the life of the Filipinos until the establishment of Manila by the Spaniards.
The Spaniards were early desirous of cultivating friendly
relations with the Empire of China.   Salcedo, on his first
punitive expedition to Mindoro, had found a Chinese junk,
which had gone ashore on the western coast.   He was
careful to rescue these voyagers and return them to their
own land, with a friendly message inviting trading relations.   Commerce and immigration followed immediately
the founding of the city.

The Chinese are without question the most remarkable
colonizers in the world.   They seem able to thrive in
any climate.   They readily marry with every race.   The

---

[1] Morga: *Sucesos*, p. 324,

children that follow such unions are not only numerous but healthy and intelligent. The coasts of China teem with overcrowding populations. Emigration to almost any land means improvement of the Chinese of poor birth. These qualities and conditions, with their keen sense for trade and their indifference to physical hardship and danger, make the Chinese almost a dominant factor wherever political barriers have not been raised against their entrance.

The Chinese had early gained an important place in the commercial and industrial life of Manila. A letter to the king from Bishop Salazar shows that he befriended them and was warm in their praise.[1] This was in 1590, and there were then in Manila and Tondo about seven thousand resident Chinese, and they were indispensable to the prosperity of the city.

Importance of Chinese Labor and Trade. — In the early decades of Spanish rule, the Philippines were poor in resources and the population was sparse, quite insufficient for the purposes of the Spanish colonizers. Thus the early development of the colony was based upon Chinese labor and Chinese trade. As the early writers are fond of emphasizing, from China came not only the finished silks and costly wares, which in large part were destined for the trade to New Spain and Europe, but also cattle, horses and mares, foodstuffs, metals, fruits, and even ink and paper. "And what is more," says Chirino, "from China come those who supply every sort of service, all dexterous, prompt, and cheap, from physicians and barbers to burden-bearers and porters. They are the tailors and shoemakers, metal-workers, silversmiths, sculptors, locksmiths, paint-

---

[1] *Carta Relacion de las Cosas de la China y de los Chinos del Parian de Manila,* 1590; in Retana, *Archivo,* vol. III.

ers, masons, weavers, and finally every kind of servitors in the commonwealth." [1]

Distrust of the Chinese. — In those days, not only were the Chinese artisans and traders, but they were also farmers and fishermen, — occupations in which they are now not often seen. But in spite of their economic necessity, the Chinese were always looked upon with disfavor and their presence with dread. Plots of murder and insurrection were supposedly rife among them. Writers object that their numbers were so great that there was no security in the land; their life was bad and vicious; through intercourse with them the natives advanced but little in Christianity and customs; they were such terrible eaters that they made foods scarce and prices high.

If permitted, they went everywhere through the Islands and committed a thousand abuses and offenses. They explored every spot, river, estero, and harbor, and knew the country better even than the Spaniard himself, so that if any enemy should come they would be able to cause infinite mischief.[2] When we find so just and high-minded a man as the president of the Audiencia, Morga, giving voice to such charges, we may be sure that the feeling was deep and terrible, and practically universal among all Spanish inhabitants.

The First Massacre of the Chinese. — Each race feared and suspected the other, and from this mutual cowardice came in 1603 a cruel outbreak and massacre. Three Chinese mandarins arrived in that year, stating that they had been sent by the emperor to investigate a report that there was a mountain in Cavite of solid precious metal.

---

[1] *Relacion de las Islas Filipinas*, p. 18. See also Salazar, *Carta Relacion.*

[2] *Sucesos de las Islas Filipinas*, p. 364.

This myth was no more absurd than many pursued by the Spaniards themselves in their early conquests, and it doubtless arose from the fact that Chinese wares were largely purchased by Mexican bullion; but the Spaniards were at once filled with suspicion of an invasion, and their distrust turned against the Chinese in the Islands.

How far these latter were actually plotting sedition and how far they were driven into attack by their fears at the conduct of the Spaniards can hardly be decided. But the fact is, that on the evening of Saint Francis day the Chinese of the Parian rose. The dragon banners were raised, war-gongs were beaten, and that night the pueblos of Quiapo and Tondo were burned and many Filipinos murdered.

In the morning a force of 130 Spaniards, under Don Luis Dasmariñas and Don Tomas Bravo, were sent across the river, and in the fight nearly every Spaniard was slain. The Chinese then assaulted the city, but, according to the tradition of the priests, they were driven back in terror by the apparition on the walls of Saint Francis. They threw up forts on the site of the Parian and in Dilao, but the power of their wild fury was gone and the Spaniards were able to dislodge and drive them into the country about San Pablo de Monte. From here they were dispersed with great slaughter. Twenty-three thousand Chinese are reported by Zuñiga to have perished in this sedition. If his report is true, the number of Chinese in the Islands must have increased very rapidly between 1590 and 1603.

Restriction of Chinese Immigration and Travel. — Commerce and immigration began again almost immediately. The number of Chinese, however, allowed to remain was reduced. The Chinese ships that came annually to trade were obliged to take back with them the crews and passengers which they brought. Only a limited number of merchants and artisans were permitted to live in the Islands. They were confined to three districts in the city of Manila, and to the great market, the Alcayceria or Parian.

The word "Parian" seems to have been also used for the Chinese quarter in and adjoining the walled city, but here is meant the district in Binondo about the present Calle San Fernando. A block of stores with small habitations above them had been built as early as the time of Gonsalez. It was in the form of a square, and here were the largest numbers of shops and stores.

They could not travel about the Islands, nor go two leagues from the city without a written license, nor remain over night within the city after the gates were closed, on penalty of their lives. They had their own alcalde and judge, a tribunal and jail ; and on the north side of the river Dominican friars, who had learned the Chinese language, had erected a mission and hospital. There was a separate barrio for the baptized Chinese and their families, to the number of about five hundred.

The Chinese in the Philippines from the earliest time to the present have been known by the name of "Sangleyes." The derivation of this curious word is uncertain; but Navarrete, who must have understood Chinese well, says that the word arose from a misapprehension of the words spoken by the Chinese who first presented themselves at Manila. "Being asked what they came for, they answered, 'Xang Lei,' that is, 'We come to trade.' The Spaniards, who understood not their language, conceiving it to be the name of a country, and putting the two words together, made one of them, by which they still distinguish the Chinese, calling them Sangleyes."

The Japanese Colony. — There was also in these early years quite a colony of Japanese. Their community lay between the Parian and the barrio of Laguio. There were about five hundred, and among them the Franciscans claimed a goodly number of converts.

The Filipino District of Tondo. — We have described at some length the city south of the river and the surrounding suburbs, most of them known by the names they hold to-day. North of the Pasig was the great district of Tondo, the center of that strong, independent Filipino feeling which at an early date was colored with Mohammedanism and to this day is strong in local feeling. This region has thriven and built up until it has long been by far the most important and populous part of the metropolis, but not until very recent times was it regarded as a part of the city of Manila, which name was reserved for the walled citadel alone.

A bridge across the Pasig, on the site of the present Puente de España, connected the two districts at a date later than Morga's time. It was one of the first things noticed by Navarrete, who, without describing it well, says it was very fine. It was built during the governorship of Niño de Tabora, who died in 1632.[1] Montero states that it was of stone, and that this same bridge stood for more than two centuries, resisting the incessant traffic and the strength of floods.[2]

The Decline of Manila during the Next Century. — Such was Manila thirty-five and forty years after its foundation. It was at the zenith of its importance, the capital of the eastern colonies, the mart of Asia, more splendid than Goa, more powerful than Malacca or Macao, more

---

[1] Zuñiga: *Historia de las Filipinas*, p. 252.
[2] *Historia General de Filipinas*, vol. I., p. 187.

populous and far more securely held than Ternate and Tidor. "Truly," exclaimed Chirino, "it is another Tyre, so magnified by Ezekiel." It owed its great place to the genius and daring of the men who founded it, to the freedom of action which it had up to this point enjoyed, and to its superlative situation.

In the years that followed we have to recount for the most part only the process of decline. Spain herself was fast on the wane. A few years later and the English had almost driven her navies from the seas, the Portuguese had regained their independence and lost empire, the Dutch were in the East, harrying Portuguese and Spaniard alike and fast monopolizing the rich trade. The commerce and friendly relations with the Chinese, on which so much depended, were broken by massacre and reprisal; and, most terrible and piteous of all, the awful wrath and lust of the Malay pirate, for decade after decade, was to be visited upon the archipelago.

The colonial policy of the mother-land, selfish, shortsighted, and criminal, was soon to make its paralyzing influence felt upon trade and administration alike. These things were growing and taking place in the next period which we have to consider, — the years from 1600 to 1663. They left the Philippines despoiled and insignificant for a whole succeeding century, a decadent colony and an exploited treasure.

CHAPTER IX.

THE DUTCH AND MORO WARS. 1600-1663.

Loss of the Naval Power of Spain and Portugal. — The seizure of Portugal by Philip II. in 1580 was disastrous in its consequences to both Portugal and Spain. For Portugal it was humiliation and loss of colonial power. Spain was unequal to the task of defending the Portuguese possessions, and her jealousy of their prosperity seems to have caused her deliberately to neglect their interests and permit their decline. In one day Portugal lost possession of that splendid and daring navy which had first found a way to the Indies. Several hundred Portuguese ships, thousands of guns, and large sums of money were appropriated by Spain upon the annexation of Portugal.[1] Most of these ill-fated ships went down in the English Channel with the Great Armada.

When the terrible news of the destruction of this powerful armament, on which rested Spanish hopes for the conquest and humiliation of England, was brought to the Escorial, the magnificent palace where the years of the king were passed, Philip II., that strange man, whose countenance never changed at tidings of either defeat or victory, is reported to have simply said, "I thank God that I have the power to replace the loss." He was fatuously mistaken. The loss could never be made good. The navies of Spain and Portugal were never fully rebuilt. In that year (1588), preëminence on the sea passed to the English and the Dutch.

---

[1] Morris : *The History of Colonization*, vol. I., p. 215 sq.

The Netherlands Become an Independent Country. — Who were these Dutch, or Hollanders? How came they to wrest from Spain and Portugal a colonial empire, which they hold to-day without loss of prosperity or evidence of decline? In the north of Europe, facing the North Sea, is a low, rich land, intersected by rivers and washed far into its interior by the tides, known as Holland, the Low Countries, or the Netherlands. Its people have ever been famed for their industry and hardihood. In manufacture and trade in the latter Middle Age, they stood far in the lead in northern Europe. Their towns and cities were the thriftiest, most prosperous, and most cleanly.

We have already explained the curious facts of succession by which these countries became a possession of the Spanish king, Emperor Charles the Fifth. The Low Countries were always greatly prized by Charles, and in spite of the severities of his rule he held their affection and loyalty until his death. It was in the city of Antwerp that he formally abdicated in favor of his son, Philip II., and, as described by contemporary historians, this solemn and imposing ceremony was witnessed with every mark of loyalty by the assembly.

The Rebellion. — But the oppressions and persecutions of Philip's reign drove the people to rebellion. The Netherlands had embraced the Protestant religion, and when, in addition to plunder, intimidation, the quartering of Spanish soldiery, and the violation of sovereign promises, Philip imposed that terrible and merciless institution, the Spanish Inquisition, the Low Countries faced the tyrant in a passion of rebellion.

War, begun in 1556, dragged on for years. There was pitiless cruelty, and the sacking of cities was accompanied by fearful butchery. In 1575 the seven Dutch counties declared their independence, and formed the republic of the Netherlands. Although the efforts of Spain to reconquer the territory continued until the end of the century, practical independence was gained some years before.

Trade between Portugal and the Netherlands Forbidden. — A large portion of the commerce of the Low Countries had been with Lisbon. The Portuguese did not distribute to Europe the products which their navies brought from the Indies. Foreign merchants purchased in Lisbon and carried these wares to other lands, and to a very large degree this service had been performed by the Dutch. But on the annexation of Portugal, Philip forbade all commerce and trade between the two countries. By this act the Dutch, deprived of their Lisbon trade, had to face the alternative of commercial ruin or the gaining of those Eastern products for themselves. They chose the latter course with all its risks. It was soon made possible by the destruction of the Armada.

The Dutch Expeditions to the Indies. — In 1595 their first expedition, led by one Cornelius Houtman, who had sailed in Portuguese galleons, rounded the Cape of Good Hope and entered the Indian domain. The objective point was Java, where an alliance was formed with the native princes and a cargo of pepper secured. Two things were shown by the safe return of this fleet, — the great wealth and profit of the Indian trade, and the inability of Spain and Portugal to maintain their monopoly.

In 1598 the merchants of Amsterdam defeated a combined Spanish and Portuguese fleet in the East, and trading settlements were secured in Java and Johore. In 1605 they carried their factories to Amboina and Tidor.

Effect of the Success of the Dutch. — The exclusive monopoly over the waters of the Pacific and Indian Oceans, which Portugal and Spain had maintained for a century, was broken. With the concurrence of the Roman See, they had tried to divide the New World and the Orient between them. That effort was now passed. They had claimed the right to exclude from the vast oceans they had discovered the vessels of every other nation but their own.

This doctrine in the History of International Law is known as that of *mare clausum,* or "closed sea." The death-blow to this domination was given by the entrance of the Dutch into the Indies, and it is not a mere coincidence that we find the doctrine of closed sea itself scientifically assailed, a few years later, by the great Dutch jurist, Grotius, the founder of the system of international law in his work, *De Libero Mare.*

The Trading Methods of the Dutch.—The Dutch made no attempts in the Indies to found great colonies for political domination and religious conversion. Commerce was their sole object. Their policy was to form alliances with native rulers, promising to assist them against the rule of the Portuguese or Spaniard in return for exclusive privileges of trade. In this they were more than successful.

In 1602 they obtained permission to establish a factory at Bantam, on the island of Java. This was even then a considerable trading-point. "Chinese, Arabs, Persians, Moors, Turks, Malabars, Peguans, and merchants from all nations were established there," the principal object of trade being pepper.[1]

The character of the treaty made by the Dutch with the king of Bantam is stated by Raffles. "The Dutch stipulated to assist him against foreign invaders, particu-

---

[1] Raffles: *History of Java,* vol. II., p. 116.

larly Spaniards and Portuguese; and the king, on his side, agreed to make over to the Dutch a good and strong fort, a free trade, and security for their persons and property without payment of any duties or taxes, and to allow no other European nation to trade or reside in his territories."

Spanish Expedition against the Dutch in the Moluccas. — The Spaniards, however, did not relinquish the field to these new foes without a struggle, and the conflict fills the history of the eighteenth century. When the Dutch expelled the Portuguese from Amboina and Tidor in February, 1605, many of the Portuguese came to the Philippines and enlisted in the Spanish forces. The governor, Don Pedro Bravo de Acuña, filled with wrath at the loss of these important possessions, with great activity organized an expedition for their conquest.

In the previous year there had arrived from Spain eight hundred troops, two hundred of them being native Mexicans. Thus Acuña was able to organize a powerful fleet that mounted seventy-five pieces of artillery and carried over fourteen hundred Spaniards and sixteen hundred Indians.[1] The fleet sailed in January, 1606. Tidor was taken without resistance and the Dutch factory seized, with a great store of money, goods, and weapons. The Spaniards then assailed Ternate; the fort and plaza were bombarded, and then the town was carried by storm.

Thus, at last was accomplished the adventure which for nearly a century had inspired the ambitions of the Spaniards, which had drawn the fleet of Magellan, which had wrecked the expeditions of Loyasa and Villalobos, for

---

[1] On the history of this notable expedition see Argensola, *Conquista de las Islas Molucas.* Madrid, 1609.

which the Spaniards in the Philippines had prepared expedition after expedition, and for which Governor Dasmariñas had sacrificed his life. At last the Moluccas had been taken by the forces of Spain.

Capture of a Dutch Fleet at Mariveles. — So far from disposing of their enemies, however, this action simply brought the Dutch into the Philippines. In 1609, Juan de Silva became governor of the Islands and in the same year arrived the Dutch admiral, Wittert, with a squadron. After an unsuccessful attack on Iloilo, the Dutch fleet anchored off Mariveles, to capture vessels arriving for the Manila trade.

At this place, on the 25th of April, 1610, the Spanish fleet, which had been hastily fitted at Cavite, attacked the Dutch, killing the admiral and taking all the ships but one, two hundred and fifty prisoners, and a large amount of silver and merchandise. These prisoners seem to have been treated with more mercy than the captives of Van Noort's fleet, who were hung at Cavite. The wounded are said to have been cared for, and the friars from all the religious orders vied with one another to convert these "Protestant pirates" from their heresy.

An Expedition against the Dutch in Java. — Spain made a truce of her European wars with Holland in 1609, but this cessation of hostilities was never recognized in the East. The Dutch and Spanish colonists continued to war upon and pillage each other until late in the century. Encouraged by his victory over Wittert, Silva negotiated with the Portuguese allies in Goa, India, to drive the Dutch from Java. A powerful squadron sailed from Cavite in 1616 for this purpose. It was the largest fleet which up to that date had ever been assembled in the Philippines. The expedition, however, failed to unite with their Portuguese allies, and in April, Silva died at Malacca of malignant fever.

The Dutch Fleets. — *Battles near Corregidor.* — The fleet returned to Cavite to find that the city, while stripped of soldiers and artillery, had been in a fever of anxiety and apprehension over the proximity of Dutch vessels. They were those of Admiral Spilbergen, who had arrived by way of the Straits of Magellan and the Pacific. He has left us a chart of the San Bernadino Straits, which is reproduced here. Spilbergen bombarded Ilolio and then sailed for the Moluccas.

A year later he returned, met a Spanish fleet of seven galleons and two galleras near Manila and suffered a severe defeat.[1] The battle began with cannonading on Friday, April 13, and continued throughout the day. On the following day the vessels came to close quarters, the Spaniards boarded the Dutch vessels, and the battle was fought out with the sword.

The Dutch were overwhelmed. Probably their numbers were few. The *Relacion* states they had fourteen galleons, but other accounts put the number at ten, three vessels of which were destroyed or taken by the Spaniards. One of them, the beautiful ship, "The Sun of Holland," was burned. This combat is known as the battle of Playa Honda. Another engagement took place in the same waters of Corregidor, late in 1624, when a Dutch fleet was driven away without serious loss to either side.

The Dutch Capture Chinese Junks, and Galleons. — But through the intervening years, fleets of the Hollanders

---

[1] An account of this victory, written the following year, *Relacion Verdadera de la Grand Vittoria, que el Armada Espanola de la China tuuo contra los Orlandeses Pirates,* has been reprinted by Retana, *Archivo Bibliófilo Filipino,* vol. II.

were continually arriving, both by the way of the Cape of Good Hope and the Straits of Magellan. Those that came across the Pacific almost invariably cruised up the Strait of San Bernadino, securing the fresh provisions so desirable to them after their long voyage.

The prizes which they made of Chinese vessels, passing Corregidor for Manila, give us an idea of how considerably the Spaniards in the Philippines relied upon China for their food. Junks, or "champans," were continually passing Corregidor, laden with chickens, hogs, rice, sugar, and other comestibles.[1]

The Mexican galleons were frequently destroyed or captured by these lurking fleets of the Dutch, and for a time the route through the Straits of San Bernadino had to be abandoned, the galleons reaching Manila by way of Cape Engaño, or sometimes landing in Cagayan, and more than once going ashore on the Pacific side of the island, at Binangonan de Lampon.

The Dutch in Formosa. — The Dutch also made repeated efforts to wrest from Portugal her settlement and trade in China. As early as 1557 the Portuguese had established a settlement on the island of Macao, one of these numerous islets that fill the estuary of the river of Canton. This is the oldest European settlement in China and has been held continuously by the Portuguese until the present day, when it remains almost the last vestige of the once mighty Portuguese empire of the East. It was much coveted by the Dutch because of its importance in the trade with Canton and Fukien.

---

[1] "Just before the naval engagement of Playa Honda, the Dutch intercepted junks on the way to Manila, bringing, amongst their cargoes of food, as many as twelve thousand capons." — Foreman: *The Philippine Islands*, p. 104.

In 1622 a fleet from Java brought siege to Macao, and, being repulsed, sailed to the Pescadores Islands, where they built a fort and established a post, which threatened both the Portuguese trade with Japan and the Manila trade with Amoy. Two years later, on the solicitation of the Chinese government, the Dutch removed their settlement to Formosa, where they broke up the Spanish mission stations and held the island for the succeeding thirty-five years. Thus, throughout the century, these European powers harassed and raided one another, but no one of them was sufficiently strong to expel the others from the East.

The Portuguese Colonies. — In 1640 the kingdom of Portugal freed itself from the domination of Spain. With the same blow Spain lost the great colonial possessions that came to her with the attachment of the Portuguese. "All the places," says Zuñiga, " which the Portuguese had in the Indies, separated themselves from the crown of Castile and recognized as king, Don Juan of Portugal." "This same year," he adds, "the Dutch took Malacca." [1]

The Moros. — *Increase of Moro Piracy.* — During all these years the raids of the Moros of Maguindanao and Jolo had never ceased. Their piracies were almost continuous. There was no security; churches were looted, priests killed, people borne away for ransom or for slavery. Obviously, this piracy could only be met by destroying it at its source. Defensive fortifications and protective fleets were of no consequence, when compared with the necessity of subduing the Moro in his own lairs. In 1628 and 1630 punitive expeditions were sent against Jolo, Basilan, and Mindanao, which drove the Moros from their forts, burned their towns, and cut down their groves of cocoanut trees.

---

[1] *Historia de Filipinas*, p. 282.

But such expeditions served only to inflame the more the wrathful vengeance of the Moro, and in 1635 the government resolved upon a change of policy and the establishment of a presidio at Zamboanga.

Founding of a Spanish Post at Zamboanga. — This brings us to a new phase in the Moro wars. The governor, Juan Cerezo de Salamanca, was determined upon the conquest and the occupation of Mindanao and Jolo. In taking this step, Salamanca, like Corcuera, who succeeded him, acted under the influence of the Jesuits. Their missions in Bohol and northern Mindanao made them ambitious to reserve for the ministrations of their society all lands that were conquered and occupied, south of the Bisayas.

The Jesuits were the missionaries on Ternate and Siao and wherever in the Moluccas and Celebes the Spanish and Portuguese had established their power. The Jesuits had accompanied the expedition of Rodriguez de Figueroa in 1595, and from that date they never ceased petitioning the government for a military occupation of these islands and for their own return, as the missionaries of these regions. The Jesuits were brilliant and able administrators. For men of their ambition, Mindanao, with its rich soil, attractive productions, and comparatively numerous populations, was a most enticing field for the establishment of such a theocratic commonwealth as the Jesuits had created and administered in America.[1]

On the other hand, the occupation of Zamboanga was strenuously opposed by the other religious orders; but the Jesuits, ever remarkable for their ascendancy in affairs of

---

[1] How attractive the island appeared and how well they knew its peoples is revealed by the accurate descriptions in the first book of Combés' *Historia de Mindanao y Jolo.*

state, were able to effect the establishment of Zamboanga, though they could not prevent its abandonment a quarter of a century later.

Erection of the Forts. — The presidio was founded in 1635, by a force under Don Juan de Chaves. His army consisted of three hundred Spaniards and one thousand Bisaya. The end of the peninsula was swept of Moro inhabitants and their towns destroyed by fire. In June the foundations of the stone fort were laid under the direction of the Jesuit, Father Vera, who is described as being experienced in military engineering and architecture.

To supply the new site with water, a ditch was built from the river Tumaga, a distance of six or seven miles, which brought a copious stream to the very walls of the fort. The advantage or failure of this expensive fortress is very hard to determine. Its planting was a partisan measure, and it was always subject to partisan praise and partisan blame. Sometimes it seemed to have checked the Moros and sometimes seemed only to be stirring them to fresh anger and aggression.

The same year that saw the establishment of Zamboanga, Hortado de Corcuera became governor of the Philippines. He was much under the influence of the Jesuits and confirmed their policy of conquest.

Defeat of the Moro Pirate Tagal. — A few months later a notable fleet of pirates, recruited from Mindanao, Jolo, and Borneo, and headed by a chieftain named Tagal, a brother of the notorious Corcelat, sultan of Maguindanao, went defiantly past the new presidio and northward through the Mindoro Sea. For more than seven months they cruised the Bisayas. The islands of the Camarines especially felt their ravages. In Cuyo they captured the corregidor and three friars. Finally, with

650 captives and rich booty, including the ornaments and services of churches, Tagal turned southward on his return.

The presidio of Zamboanga had prepared to intercept him and a fierce battle took place off the Punta de Flechas, thirty leagues to the northeast of Zamboanga. According to the Spanish writers, this point was one held sacred by Moro superstitions. A deity inhabited these waters, whom the Moros were accustomed to propitiate on the departure and arrival of their expeditions, by throwing into the sea lances and arrows. The victory was a notable one for the Spanish arms. Tagal and more than 300 Moros were killed, and 120 Christian captives were released.

Moro Helmet and Coat of Mail.

Corcuera's Expedition against the Moros at Lamitan. — Corcuera had meanwhile been preparing an expedition which had taken on the character of a holy war. Jesuit and soldier mingled in its company and united in its direction. The Jesuit saint, Francis Xavier, was proclaimed patron of the expedition, and mass was celebrated daily on the ships. Corcuera himself accompanied the expedition, and at Zamboanga, where they arrived February 22, 1637, he united a force of 760 Spaniards and many Bisayans and Pampangas.

From Zamboanga the force started for Lamítan, the stronghold of Correlat, and the center of the power of the

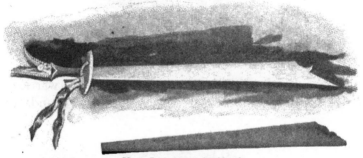

Moro Sword and Scabbard.

Maguindanao. It seems to have been situated on the coast, south of the region of Lake Lanao. The fleet encountered rough weather and contrary winds off Punta de Flechas, which they attributed to the influence of the Moro demon.

To rid the locality of this unholy influence, Padre Marcello, the Jesuit superior, occupied himself for two days. Padre Combés has left us an account of the ceremony.[1] The demon was dispossessed by exorcism. Mass was celebrated. Various articles, representing Moro in-

---

[1] *Historia de Mindanao y Jolo*, lib. IV., chap. 7.

fidelity, including arrows, were destroyed and burnt. Holy relics were thrown into the waters, and the place was finally sanctified by baptism in the name of Saint Sebastian.

On the 14th of March the expedition reached Lamítan,

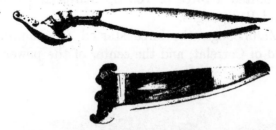

Moro Short Sword and Sheath.

fortified and defended by two thousand Moro warriors. The Spanish force, however, was overwhelming, and the

Moro Spear.

city was taken by storm. Here were captured eight bronze cannon, twenty-seven "versos" (a kind of small howitzer), and over a hundred muskets and arquebuses and a great store of Moro weapons. Over one hundred vessels were destroyed, including a fleet of Malay merchant praos from Java. Sixteen villages were burned, and seventy-two Moros were hung. Correlat, though pursued and wounded, was not captured.[1]

The Conquest of Jolo. — Corcuera returned to Zamboanga and organized an expedition for the conquest of Jolo. Although defended by four thousand Moro warriors and by allies from Basílan and the Celebes, Corcuera took Jolo after some months of siege. The sultan saved

Old Moro Pirate Boat.

himself by flight, but the sultana was taken prisoner. Corcuera reconstructed the fort, established a garrison of two hundred Spaniards and an equal number of Pampangas, left some Jesuit fathers, and, having nominated

---

[1] This important victory was commemorated in a number of writings, some of which have been reprinted by Retana. See *Sucesos Felices, que por Mar y Tierra ha dado N. S. a las armas Españolas*, 1637. Another is published in the Appendix to Barrantes', *Historia de Guerras Piraticas.* The subject is also fully treated by Combés.

Major Almonte chief of all the forces in the south, returned in May, 1638, to Manila, with all the triumph of a conqueror.

Almonte continued the work of subjugation. In 1639 he conquered the Moro dato of Buhayen, in the valley of the Rio Grande, where a small presidio was founded. And in the same year the Jesuits prevailed upon him to invade the territory of the Malanao, now known as the Laguna de Lanao. This expedition was made from the north through Iligan, and for a time brought even this warlike and difficult territory under the authority of the governor and the spiritual administration of the Jesuits.

Loss of the Spanish Settlement on Formosa. — The full military success of Corcuera's governorship was marred by the loss of Macao and the capture of the Spanish settlement on the island of Formosa by the Dutch. In the attempt to hold Macao, Corcuera sent over the encomendero of Pasig, Don Juan Claudio. The populace of Macao, however, rose in tumult, assassinated the governor, Sebastian Lobo, and pronounced in favor of Portugal. Later, by decree of the Portuguese governor of Goa, all the Spanish residents and missionaries were expelled. The Dutch seizure of Formosa, a year later, has already been described.

The Archipelago and the Religious Orders. — During these decades, conflict was almost incessant between the archbishop of Manila and the regular orders. In the Philippines the regulars were the parish curates, and the archbishop desired that all matters of their curacy, touching the administration of the sacraments and other parish duties, should be subject to the direction of the bishops. This question of the "diocesan visit" was fought over for nearly two hundred years.

The Governor and the Archbishop. — Even more serious to the colony were the conflicts that raged between the governor-general and the archbishop. All the points of dissension between Church and State, which vexed the Middle Ages, broke out afresh in the Philippines. The appointment of religious officers; the distribution of revenue; the treatment of the natives; the claim of the church to offer asylum to those fleeing the arm of the law; its claims of jurisdiction, in its ecclesiastical courts, over a large class of civil offenses — these disputes and many others, occasioned almost incessant discord between the heads of civil and ecclesiastical authority.

The "Residencia." — We have seen that the power of the governor was in fact very large. Theoretically, the Audiencia was a limit upon his authority; but in fact the governor was usually the president of this body, and the oidores were frequently his abettors and rarely his opponents. At the end of each governor's rule there took place a characteristic Spanish institution, called the "Residencia." This was a court held by the newly elected governor, for an examination into the conduct of his predecessor. Complaints of every description were received, and often, in the history of the Philippines, one who had ruled the archipelago almost as an independent monarch found himself, at the end of his office, ruined, and in chains.

It was upon the occasion of the Residencia that the ecclesiastical powers, after a governorship stormy with disputes, exercised their power for revenge. Unquestionably many a governor, despite his actual power, facing, as he did, the Residencia at the termination of his rule, made peace with his enemies and yielded to their demands.

Corcuera had continuous troubles with the archbishop and with the religious orders other than the Jesuits. In 1644, when his successor, Fajardo, relieved him, the Franciscans, Augustinians, and Recollects procured his imprisonment and the confiscation of his property. For five years, the conqueror of the Moros lay a prisoner in the fortresses of Santiago and Cavite, when he was pardoned by the Council of the Indies, and appointed governor of the Canaries by the king.

Weakening of the Governor's Power. — This power of private and religious classes to intimidate and overawe the responsible head of the Philippine government was an abuse which continued to the very close of the Spanish rule. This, together with the relatively short term of the governor's office, his natural desire to avoid trouble, his all too frequent purpose of amassing a fortune rather than maintaining the dignity of his position and advancing the interests of the Islands, combined decade after decade to make the spiritual authority more powerful. In the end the religious orders, with their great body of members, their hold upon the Filipinos, their high influence at the court, and finally their great landed wealth, governed the Islands.

The Educational Work of the Religious Orders. — In any criticism of the evils connected with their administration of the Philippines, one must not fail to recognize the many achievements of the missionary friars that were worthy. To the Dominicans and the Jesuits is due the establishment of institutions of learning. The Jesuits in 1601 had planted their College of San José. The Dominicans, here as in Europe, the champions of orthodox learning, had their own institution, the College of Santo Tomas, inaugurated in 1619, and were the rivals of the Jesuits for the privilege of giving higher instruction.

In 1645 the pope granted to the Dominicans the right to
bestow higher degrees, and their college became the "Royal
and Pontifical University of Saint Thomas Aquinas."
This splendid name breathes that very spirit of the Middle
Ages which the Dominican order strove to perpetuate in
the Philippines down to modern days.[1] Dominicans also
founded the College of San Juan de Letran, as a prepara-
tory school to the University.

We should not pass over the educational work of the
religious orders without mention of the early printing-
plants and their publications. The missionary friars were
famous printers, and in the Philippines, as well as in America, some noble volumes were produced by their handi-
craft.

Founding of Hospitals by the Franciscans. — Nor
had the Franciscans in the Philippines neglected the fundamental purpose of their foundation, — that of ministra-
tion to the sick and unprotected. A narrative of their
order, written in 1649, gives a long list of their beneficent
foundations.[2] Besides the hospital of Manila, they had an
infirmary at Cavite for the native mariners and shipbuilders, a hospital at Los Baños, another in the city of
Nueva Caceres. Lay brethren were attached to many of
the convents as nurses.

In 1633 a curious occurrence led to the founding of the
leper hospital of San Lazaro. The emperor of Japan, in
a probably ironical mood, sent to Manila a shipload of
Japanese afflicted with this unfortunate disease. These
people were mercifully received by the Franciscans, and

---

[1] The king did not confer the title of "Royal" until 1735, although
the University was taken under his protection in 1680.

[2] *Entrada de la Seraphica Religion, de Nuestro P. S. Francisco en
las Islas Filipinas*, Retana, vol. I.

cared for in a home, which became the San Lazaro hospital for lepers.

Life and Progress of the Filipinos. — Few sources exist that can show us the life and progress of the Filipino people during these decades. Christianity, as introduced by the missionary friars, was wonderfully successful, and yet there were relapses into heathenism. Old religious leaders and priestesses roused up from time to time, and incited the natives to rebellion against their new spiritual masters. The payment of tribute and the labor required for the building of churches often drove the people into the mountains.

Religious Revolt at Bohol and Leyte. — In 1621 a somewhat serious revolt took place on Bohol. The Jesuits who administered the island were absent in Cebu, attending the fiestas on the canonization of Saint Francis Xavier. The whisper was raised that the old heathen deity, Diwata, was at hand to assist in the expulsion of the Spaniards. The island rose in revolt, except the two towns of Loboc and Baclayan. Four towns were burned, the churches sacked, and the sacred images speared. The revolt spread to Leyte, where it was headed by the old dato, Bancao of Limasaua, who had sworn friendship with Legaspi. This insurrection was put down by the alcalde mayor of Cebu and the Filipino leaders were hung. On Leyte, Bancao was speared in battle, and one of the heathen priests suffered the penalty, prescribed by the Inquisition for heresy — death by burning.

Revolt of the Pampangas. — The heavy drafting of natives to fell trees and build the ships for the Spanish naval expeditions and the Acapulco trade was also a cause for insurrection. In 1660 a thousand Pampangas were kept cutting in the forests of that province alone.

Sullen at their heavy labor and at the harshness of their overseers, these natives rose in revolt. The sedition spread to Pangasinan, Zambales, and Ilocos, and it required the utmost efforts of the Spanish forces on land and water to suppress the rebellion.

Uprising of the Chinese. — In spite of the terrible massacre, that had been visited upon the Chinese at the beginning of the century, they had almost immediately commenced returning not only as merchants, but as colonists. The early restrictions upon their life must have been relaxed, for in 1639 there were more than thirty thousand living in the Islands, many of them cultivating lands at Calamba and at other points on the Laguna de Bay.

In that year a rebellion broke out, in which the Chinese in Manila participated. They seized the church of San Pedro Mecati, on the Pasig, and fortified themselves. From there they were routed by a combined Filipino and Spanish force. The Chinese then broke up into small bands, which scattered through the country, looting and murdering, but being pursued and cut to pieces by the Filipinos. For five months this pillage and massacre went on, until seven thousand Chinese were destroyed. By the loss of these agriculturists and laborers Manila was reduced to great distress.

Activity of the Moro Pirates. — The task of the Spaniards in controlling the Moro datos continued to be immensely difficult. During the years following the successes of Corcuera and Almonte, the Moros were continually plotting. Aid was furnished from Borneo and the Celebes, and they were further incited by the Dutch. In spite of the vigilance of Zamboanga, small piratical excursions continually harassed the Bisayas and the Camarines.

Continued Conflicts with the Dutch. — The Dutch, too, from time to time showed themselves in Manila. In 1646 a squadron attacked Zamboanga, and then came north to Luzon. The Spanish naval strength was quite unprepared; but two galleons, lately arrived from Acapulco, were fitted with heavy guns, Dominican friars took their places among the gunners, and, under the protection of the Virgin of the Rosary, successfully encountered the enemy.

A year later a fleet of twelve vessels entered Manila Bay, and nearly succeeded in taking Cavite. Failing in this, they landed in Bataan province, and for some time held the coast of Manila Bay in the vicinity of Abucay. The narrative of Franciscan missions in 1649, above cited, gives town after town in southern Luzon, where church and convent had been burned by the Moros or the Dutch.

The Abandonment of Zamboanga and the Moluccas. — The threat of the Dutch made the maintenance of the presidio of Zamboanga very burdensome. In 1656 the administration of the Moluccas was united with that of Mindanao, and the governor of the former, Don Francisco de Esteybar, was transferred from Ternate to Zamboanga and made lieutenant-governor and captain-general of all the provinces of the south.

Six years later, the Moluccas, so long coveted by the Spaniards, and so slowly won by them, together with Zamboanga, were wholly abandoned, and to the Spice Islands the Spaniards were never to return. This sudden retirement from their southern possessions was not, however, occasioned by the incessant restlessness of the Moros nor by the plottings of the Dutch. It was due to a threat of danger from the north.

Koxinga the Chinese Adventurer. — In 1644, China was conquered by the Manchus. Pekin capitulated at once and the Ming dynasty was overthrown, but it was only by many years of fighting that the Manchus overcame the Chinese of the central and southern provinces. These were years of turbulance, revolt, and piracy.

More than one Chinese adventurer rose to a romantic position during this disturbed time. One of these adventurers, named It Coan, had been a poor fisherman of Chio. He had lived in Macao, where he had been converted to Christianity, and had been a cargador, or cargo-bearer, in Manila. He afterwards went to Japan, and engaged in trade. From these humble and laborious beginnings, like many another of his persistent countrymen, he gained great wealth, which on the conquest of the Manchus he devoted to piracy.

His son was the notorious Kue-Sing, or Koxinga, who for years resisted the armies of the Manchus, and maintained an independent power over the coasts of Fukien and Chekiang. About 1660 the forces of the Manchus became too formidable for him to longer resist them upon the mainland, and Koxinga determined upon the capture of Formosa and the transference of his kingdom to that island.

For thirty-eight years this island had been dominated by the Dutch, whose fortresses commanded the channel of the Pescadores. The colony was regarded as an important one by the Dutch colonial government at Batavia. The city of Tai-wan, on the west coast, was a considerable center of trade. It was strongly protected by the fortress of Zealand, and had a garrison of twenty-two hundred Dutch soldiers. After months of fighting, Koxinga, with an overpowering force of Chinese, compelled the surrender of the Hollanders and the beautiful island passed into his power.

A Threatened Invasion of the Philippines.—Exalted by his success against European arms, Koxinga resolved upon the conquest of the Philippines. He summoned to his service the Italian Dominican missionary, Ricci, who had been living in the province of Fukien, and in the spring of 1662 dispatched him as an ambassador to the governor of the Philippines to demand the submission of 'the archipelago.

Manila was thrown into a terrible panic by this demand, and indeed no such danger had threatened the Spanish in the Philippines since the invasion of Limahong. The Chinese conqueror had an innumerable army, and his armament, stores, and navy had been greatly augmented by the surrender of the Dutch. The Spaniards, however, were united on resistance. The governor, Don Sabiano Manrique de Lara, returned a defiant answer to Koxinga, and the most radical measures were adopted to place the colony in a state of defense.

All Chinese were ordered immediately to leave the Islands. Fearful of massacre, these wretched people again broke out in rebellion, and assaulted the city. Many were slain, and other bands wandered off into the mountains, where they perished at the hands of the natives. Others, escaping by frail boats, joined the Chinese colonists on Formosa. Churches and convents in the suburbs of Manila, which might afford shelter to the assailant, were razed to the ground. More than all this, the Moluccas were forsaken, never again to be recovered by Spaniards; and the presidios of Zamboanga and Cuyo, which served as a kind of bridle on the Moros of Jolo and Mindanao, were abandoned. All Spanish troops were concentrated in Manila, fortifications were rebuilt, and the population waited anxiously for the attack. But the blow never fell.

Before Ricci arrived at Tai-wan, Koxinga was dead, and the peril of Chinese invasion had passed.

Effects of These Events. — But the Philippines had suffered irretrievable loss. Spanish prestige was gone. Manila was no longer, as she had been at the commencement of the century, the capital of the East. Spanish sovereignty was again confined to Luzon and the Bisayas. The Chinese trade, on which rested the economic prosperity of Manila, had once again been ruined. For a hundred years the history of the Philippines is a dull monotony, quite unrelieved by any heroic activity or the presence of noble character.[1]

---

[1] The Jesuits, on retiring with the Spanish forces from the Moluccas, brought from Ternate a colony of their converts. These people were settled at Marigondon, on the south shore of Manila Bay, where their descendants can still be distinguished from the surrounding Tagálog population.

CHAPTER X.

A CENTURY OF OBSCURITY AND DECLINE.
1663–1762.

Political Decline of the Philippines. — For the hundred years succeeding the abandonment of the Moluccas, the Philippines lost all political significance as a colony. From almost every standpoint they were profitless to Spain. There were continued deficits, which had to be made good from the Mexican treasury. The part of Spain in the conquest of the East was over, and the Philippines became little more than a great missionary establishment, presided over by the religious orders.

Death of Governor Salcedo by the Inquisition. — In 1663, Lara was succeeded by Don Diego de Salcedo. On his arrival, Manila had high hopes of him, which were speedily disappointed. He loaded the Acapulco galleon with his own private merchandise, and then dispatched it earlier than was usual, before the cargoes of the merchants were ready. He engaged in a wearisome strife with the archbishop, and seems to have worried the ecclesiastic, who was aged and feeble, into his grave. At the end of ·a few years he was hated by every one, and a conspiracy against him was formed which embraced the religious, the army, the civil officials, and the merchants. Beyond the reach of the power of ordinary plotters, he fell a victim to the commissioner of the Inquisition.

The Spanish Inquisition, which wrought such cruelty and misery in the Peninsula, was carried also to the Spanish colonies. As we have seen, it was primarily the function of the Dominican order to administer the institution. The powers exercised by an inquisitor can scarcely be understood at the present day. His methods were secret, the charges were not made public, the whole proceedings were closeted, and yet so great were the powers of this court that none could resist its authority, or inquire into its actions. Spain forbade any heretics, Jews, or Moors going to the colonies, and did the utmost to prevent heresy abroad. She also established in America the Inquisition itself. Fortunately, it never attained the importance in the Philippines that it had in Spain. In the Philippines there was no "Tribunal," the institution being represented solely by a commissioner.

Death of the Governor. — In 1667, when the unpopularity of Governor Salcedo was at its height, this commissioner professed to discover in him grounds of heresy from the fact that he had been born in Flanders, and decided to avenge the Church by encompassing his ruin. By secret arrangement, the master of the camp withdrew the guard from the palace, and the commissioner, with several confederates, gained admission. The door of the governor's room was opened by an old woman, who had been terrified into complicity, and the governor was seized sleeping, with his arms lying at the head of his bed.

The commissioner informed the governor that he was a prisoner of the Holy Office. He was taken to the convent of the Augustinians. Here he was kept in chains until he could be sent to Mexico, to appear before the Tribunal there. The government in Mexico annulled the arrest of the commissioner, but Salcedo died at sea on the return of the vessel to the Philippines in 1669.

Colonization of the Ladrone Islands. — In 1668 a Jesuit mission under Padre Diego Luis de Sanvítores was established on the Ladrones, the first of the many mission stations, both Roman Catholic and Protestant, in the South Pacific. The islands at that time were well populated and fertile, and had drawn the enthusiasm of Padre Sanvítores in 1662 when he first sailed to the Philippines.

The hostility of the Manchus in China, the Japanese persecutions, and the abandonment of Mindanao had closed many mission fields, and explains the eagerness with which the Jesuits sought the royal permission to Christianize these islands, which had been so constantly visited by Spanish ships but never before colonized. With Padre Sanvítores and his five Jesuit associates were a number of Christian Filipino catechists.

Settlement of Guam. — The mission landed at Guam, and was favorably received. Society among these islanders was divided into castes. The chiefs were known as chamorri, which has led to the natives of the Ladrones being called "Chamorros." A piece of ground was given the Jesuits for a church at the principal town called Agadna (Agaña), and here also a seminary was built for the instruction of young men. The queen regent of Spain, Maria of Austria, gave an annual sum to this school, and in her honor the Jesuits changed the name of the islands to the Marianas. The Jesuits preached on eleven inhabited islands of the group, and in a year's time had baptized thirteen thousand islanders and given instruction to twenty thousand.

Troubles with the Natives at Guam. — This first year was the most successful in the history of the mission. Almost immediately after, the Jesuits angered the islanders by compulsory conversions. There were quarrels in several places, and priests, trying to baptize children against the wishes of their parents, were killed. In 1670 the Spaniards were attacked, and obliged to fortify themselves at Agaña.

The Jesuits had a guard of a Spanish captain and about thirty Spanish and Filipino soldiers, who, after some slaughter of the natives, compelled them to sue for peace. The conditions imposed by the Jesuits were that the natives should attend mass and festivals, have their children baptized, and send them to be catechised. The hatred of the natives was unabated, however, and in 1672 Sanvítores was killed by them. His biographer claims that at his death he had baptized nearly fifty thousand of these islanders.[1]

Depopulation of the Ladrone Islands. — About 1680 a governor was sent to the islands, and they were organized as a dependency of Spain. The policy of the governors and the Jesuits was conversion by the sword. The natives were persecuted from island to island, and in the history of European settlements there is hardly one that had more miserable consequences to the inhabitants. Disease was introduced and swept off large numbers. Others fell resisting the Spaniards, and an entire island was frequently depopulated by order of the governor, or the desire of the Jesuits to have the natives brought to Guam. Many, with little doubt, fled to other archipelagoes.

If we can trust the Jesuit accounts, there were in the whole group one hundred thousand inhabitants when the Spaniards arrived. A generation saw them almost extinct. Dampier, who touched at Guam in 1686, says then that on the island, where the Spaniards had found thirty thousand people, there were not above one hundred natives. In 1716 and 1721 other voyagers announced the number of inhabitants on Guam at two thousand, but only one other island of the group was populated. When

[1] See the account of the "Settlement of the Ladrones by the Spaniards," in Burney's *Voyages in the Pacific*, vol. III.

Anson in 1742 visited Guam, the number had risen to four thousand, and there were a few hundred inhabitants on Rota; but these seem to have been the whole population. The original native population certainly very nearly touched extinction. The islands were from time to time colonized from the Philippines, and the present population is very largely of Filipino blood.

Conflicts between Governor and Archbishop. — Meanwhile, in the Philippines the conflict of the governor with the archbishop and the friars continued. The conduct of both sides was selfish and outrageous. In 1683 the actions of Archbishop Pardo became so violent and seditious that the Audiencia decreed his banishment to Pangasinan or Cagayan. He was taken by force to Lingayan, where he was well accommodated but kept under surveillance. The Dominicans retaliated by excommunication, and the Audiencia thereupon banished the provincial of the order from the Islands, and sent several other friars to Mariveles.

But the year following, Governor Vargas was relieved by the arrival of his successor, who was favorable to the ecclesiastical side of the controversy. The archbishop returned and assumed a high hand. He suspended and excommunicated on all sides. The oidores were banished from the city, and all died in exile in remote portions of the archipelago. The ex-governor-general, Vargas, being placed under the spiritual ban, sued for pardon and begged that his repentance be recognized.

The archbishop sentenced him to stand daily for the space of four months at the entrances to the churches of the city and of the Parian, and in the thronged quarter of Binondo, attired in the habit of a penitent, with a rope about his neck and carrying a lighted candle in his hand.

He was, however, able to secure a mitigation of this sentence, but was required to live absolutely alone in a hut on an island in the Pasig River. He was sent a prisoner to Mexico in 1689, but died upon the voyage.

The various deans and canons who had concurred in the archbishop's banishment, as well as other religious with whom the prelate had had dissensions, were imprisoned or exiled. The bodies of two oidores were, on their death and after their burial, disinterred and their bones profaned.

Degeneration of the Colony under Church Rule. — Archbishop Pardo died in 1689, but the strife and confusion which had been engendered continued. There were quarrels between the archbishop and the friars, between the prelate and the governor. All classes seem to have shared the bitterness and the hatred of these unhappy dissensions.

The moral tone of the whole colony during the latter part of the seventeenth century was lowered. Corruption flourished everywhere, and the vigor of the administration decayed. Violence went unrebuked, and the way was open for the deplorable tragedy in which this strife of parties culminated. Certainly no governor could have been more supine, and shown greater incapacity and weakness of character, than the one who ruled in the time of Archbishop Pardo and those that succeeded him.

Improvements Made by Governor Bustamante. — *Enrichment of the Treasury.* — In the year 1717, however, came a governor of a different type, Fernando Manuel de Bustamante. He was an old soldier, stern of character and severe in his measures. He found the treasury robbed and exhausted. Nearly the whole population of Manila were in debt to the public funds. Bustamante ordered

these amounts paid, and to compel their collection he
attached the cargo of silver arriving by the galleon from
Acapulco. This cargo was owned by the religious com-
panies, officials, and merchants, all of whom were indebted to the government. In one year of his vigorous
administration he raised the sum of three hundred thousand pesos for the treasury.

With sums of money again at the disposal of the state,
Bustamante attempted to revive the decayed prestige and
commerce of the Islands.

Refounding of Zamboanga.—In 1718 he refounded and
rebuilt the presidio of Zamboanga. Not a year had passed,
since its abandonment years before, that the pirates from
Borneo and Mindanao had failed to ravage the Bisayas.
The Jesuits had petitioned regularly for its reëstablishment, and in 1712 the king had decreed its reoccupation.
The citadel was rebuilt on an elaborate plan under the direction of the engineer, Don Juan Sicarra. Besides the usual
barracks, storehouses, and arsenals, there were, within the
walls, a church, hospital, and cuartel for the Pampangan
soldiers. Sixty-one cannon were mounted upon the defenses. Upon the petition of the Recollects, Bustamante
also established a presidio at Labo, at the southern point
of the island of Paragua, whose coasts were attacked by
the Moros from Sulu and Borneo.

Treaty with Siam. — In the same year he sent an embassy to Siam, with the idea of stimulating the commerce
which had flourished a century before. The reception of
this embassy was most flattering; a treaty of peace, friendship, and commerce was made, and on ground ceded to
the Spaniards was begun the erection of a factory.

Improvements in the City of Manila. — How far this
brave and determined man might have revived the colony

it is impossible to say. The population of Manila, both ecclesiastical and civil, was at this time so sunk in corruption and so degenerate as to make almost impossible any recuperation except under the rule of a man equally determined as Bustamante, but ruling for a long period of time. He had not hesitated to order investigations into the finances of the Islands, which disclosed defalcations amounting to seven hundred thousand pesos. He fearlessly arrested the defaulters, no matter what their station. The whole city was concerned in these peculations, consequently the utmost fear and apprehension existed on all sides; and Bustamante, hated as well as dreaded, was compelled to enforce his reforms single-handed.

His Murder.— He was opposed by the friars and defied by the archbishop, but, notwithstanding ecclesiastical condemnation, he went to the point of ordering the arrest of the prelate. The city rose in sedition, and a mob, headed by friars, proceeded to the palace of the governor, broke in upon him, and, as he faced them alone and without support, killed him in cold blood (October 11, 1719).

The archbishop proclaimed himself governor and president of the Audiencia. The oidores and officials who had been placed under arrest by Bustamante were released, and his work overthrown. The new government had neither the courage nor the inclination to continue Bustamante's policy, and in 1720 the archbishop called a council of war, which decreed the abandonment of the fort at Labo.

When the news of this murder reached Spain, the king ordered an investigation and the punishment of the guilty, and in 1721 Governor Torre Campo arrived to put these mandates into execution. The culprits, however, were so high and so influential that the governor did not dare proceed against them; and although the commands of the king were reiterated in 1724, the assassins of Bustamante were never brought to justice.

Treaty with the Sultan of Jolo. — In spite of the cowardly policy of the successors of Bustamante, the presidio of Zamboanga was not abandoned. So poorly was it administered, however, that it was not effective to prevent Moro piracy, and the attacks upon the Bisaya and Calamianes continued. In 1721 a treaty was formed with the sultan of Jolo providing for trade between Manila and Jolo, the return or ransom of captives, and the restitution to Spain of the island of Basilan.

The Moro Pirates of Tawi Tawi. — To some extent this treaty seems to have prevented assaults from Jolo, but in 1730 the Moros of Tawi Tawi fell upon Paragua and the Calamianes, and in 1731 another expedition from the south spent nearly a whole year cruising and destroying among the Bisayas.

Deplorable State of Spanish Defenses. — The defenses of the Spaniards during these many decades were continually in a deplorable state, their arms were wretched, and, except in moments of great apprehension, no attention was given to fortifications, to the preservation of artillery, nor to the supply of ammunition. Sudden attacks ever found the Spaniards unprepared. Military unreadiness was the normal condition of this archipelago from these early centuries down to the destruction of the Spanish armament by the American fleet.

The Economic Policy of Spain. — *Restrictions of Trade.* — During the closing years of the seventeenth century and the beginning of the eighteenth, commerce seemed to have been actually paralyzed. That brilliant trade which is described by Morga, and which was at its height about

1605, was a few years later defeated by the miserable economic policy of Spain, pandering to the demands of the merchants of Cadiz and Seville.

Spain's economic policy had only in view benefits to the Peninsula. "The Laws of the Indies" abound with edicts for the purpose of limiting and crippling colonial commerce and industry, wherever it was imagined that it might be prejudicial to the protected industries of Spain. The manufacturers of Seville wished to preserve the colonies, both of America and of the Indies, as markets for their monopoly wares; and in this policy, for two centuries, they had the support of the crown. The growing trade between Mexico and the Philippines had early been regarded with suspicion, and legislation was framed to reduce it to the lowest point compatible with the existence of the colony.

None of the colonies of America could conduct commerce with the Philippines except Mexico, and here all communication must pass through the port of Acapulco. This trade was limited to the passage of a single vessel a year. In 1605 two galleons were permitted, but their size was reduced to three hundred tons. They were allowed to carry out 500,000 pesos of silver, but no more than 250,000 pesos' worth of Chinese products could be returned. Neither the Spaniards of Mexico nor any part of America could traffic directly with China, nor could Spanish vessels pass from Manila to the ports of Asia. Only those goods could be bought which Chinese merchants themselves brought to the Philippines.

Selfishness of Merchants in Spain. — Even these restrictions did not satisfy the jealousy of the merchants of Spain. They complained that the royal orders limiting the traffic were not regarded, and they insisted upon so

vexatious a supervision of this commerce, and surrounded
infractions of the law with such terrible penalties, that
the trade was not maintained even to the amount permitted by law. Spanish merchants even went to the
point of petitioning for the abandonment of the Philippines, on the ground that the importations from China
were prejudicial to the industry of the Peninsula.

The colonists upon the Pacific coast of America suffered
from the lack of those commodities demanded by civilized
life, which could only reach them as they came from
Spain through the port of Porto Bello and the Isthmus
of Panama. Without question, an enormous and bene-
ficial commerce could have been conducted by the Philippines with the provinces of western America.[1]

*Trade Between South America and the Philippines
Forbidden.* — But this traffic was absolutely forbidden,
and to prevent Chinese and Philippine goods from entering South America, the trade between Mexico and Peru
was in 1636 wholly suppressed by a decree. This decree,
as it stands upon the pages of the great *Recopilacion,* is
an epitome of the insane economic policy of the Spaniard.
It cites that whereas "it had been permitted that from
Peru to New Spain there should go each year two vessels
for commerce and traffic to the amount of two hundred
thousand ducats [which later had been reduced to one
hundred thousand ducats], and because there had increased in Peru to an excessive amount the commerce in
the fabrics of China, in spite of the many prohibitions
that had been imposed, and in order absolutely to remove

---

[1] Some of the benefits of such a trade are set forth by the Jesuit,
Alonzo de Ovalle, in his *Historical Relation of the Kingdom of Chili,*
printed in Rome, 1649. In Churchill's *Collection of Voyages and
Travels,* vol. III.

the occasion for the future, we order and command the officers of Peru and New Spain that they invariably prohibit and suppress this commerce and traffic between the two kingdoms by all the channels through which it is conducted, maintaining this prohibition firmly and continually for the future." [1]

In 1718 the merchants of Seville and Cadiz still complained that their profits were being injured by even the limited importation of Chinese silks into Mexico. Thereupon absolute prohibition of import of Chinese silks, either woven or in thread, was decreed. Only linens, spices, and supplies of such things as were not produced in Spain could be brought into Mexico. This order was reaffirmed in 1720, with the provision that six months would be allowed the people of Mexico to consume the Chinese silks which they had in their possession, and thereafter all such goods must be destroyed.

Ineffectiveness of These Restrictions. — These measures, while ruining the commerce of the Philippines, were as a matter of fact ineffective to accomplish the result desired. Contraband trade between China and America sprang up in violation of the law. Silks to the value of four million pesos were annually smuggled into America.[2] In 1734 the folly and uselessness of such laws was somewhat recognized by the Council of the Indies, and a cedula was issued restoring the permission to trade in Chinese silks and raising the value of cargoes destined for Acapulco to five hundred thousand pesos, and the quantity of silver for return to one million pesos. The celebrated traffic of the galleon was resumed and continued until the year 1815.

---

[1] *Recopilacion de Leyes de las Indias*, lib. VIII., titulo 45, ley 78.
[2] Montero y Vidal: *Historia de Filipinas*, vol. I., p. 460.

An Attempt to Colonize the Carolines. — Southeastward of the Philippines, in that part of the Pacific which is known as Micronesia, there is an archipelago of small islands called the Carolines. The westernmost portion of the group also bear the name of the Pelews, or Palaos. Inasmuch as these islands were eventually acquired by Spain and remained in her possession down to the year 1898, it may be well to state something at this time of the attempt made by the Jesuits in 1731 to colonize them.

Certain of these little islands were seen several times by expeditions crossing the Pacific as early as the latter part of the sixteenth century, but after the trade between Mexico and the Philippines had been definitely settled upon, a fixed course was followed westward from Acapulco to Guam, from which there was little variation, and during the seventeenth century these islands passed quite out of mind; but in the year 1696 a party of natives, twenty men and ten women, were driven by storms far from their home in the Carolines upon the eastern coast of Samar. It seems that similar parties of castaways from the Pelew and Caroline Islands had been known to reach Mindanao and other parts of the Philippines at an even earlier date. These last came under the observation of the Jesuit priests on Samar, who baptized them, and, learning from them of the archipelago from which they had been carried, were filled with missionary ambition to visit and Christianize these Pacific islanders.

This idea was agitated by the Jesuits, until about 1730 royal permission was granted to the enterprise. A company of Jesuits in the following year sailed for the Ladrones and thence south until the Carolines were discovered. They landed on a small island not far from Yap. Here they succeeded in baptizing numerous natives and in establishing a mission. Fourteen of their number, headed by the priest, Padre Cantava, remained on the island while the expedition returned to secure reënforcements and supplies. Unfortunately, this succor was delayed for more than a year, and when Spanish vessels with missionary reënforcements on board again reached the Carolines in 1733, the mission had been entirely destroyed and the Spaniards, with Padre Cantava, had been killed. These islands have been frequently called the "New Philippines."

Conditions of the Filipinos during the Eighteenth Century. — During the most of the eighteenth century, data are few upon the condition of the Filipino people. There seems to have been little progress. Conditions certainly were against the social or intellectual advance of the native race. Perhaps, however, their material well-being was quite as great during these years, when little was attempted, as during the governorships of the more ambitious and enterprising Spaniards who had characterized the earlier period of Philippine history.

Provincial Governments. — Provincial administration seems to have fallen almost wholly into the hands of the missionaries. The priests made themselves the local rulers throughout the Christianized portion of the archipelago.

Insurrection in Bohol. — Insurrection seems especially to have troubled the island of Bohol during most of the eighteenth century, and in 1750 an insurrection broke out which practically established the independence of a large portion of the island, and which was not suppressed for thirty-five years. The trouble arose in the town of Inabanga, where the Jesuit priest Morales had greatly antagonized and imbittered the natives by his severity. Some apostasized, and went to the hills. One of these men was killed by the orders of the priest and his body refused Christian burial, and left uncared for and exposed.

A brother of this man, named Dogóhoy, infuriated by this indignity, headed a sedition which shortly included three thousand natives. The priest was killed, and his own body left by the road unburied. In spite of the efforts of the alcalde of Cebu, Dogóhoy was able to maintain himself, and practically established a small native state, which remained until the occupation of the island by the Recollects, after the Jesuits had been expelled from the Spanish dominions.

Activity of the Jesuits. — During the eighteenth century the Jesuits alone of the religious orders seemed to have been active in prosecuting their efforts and seeking new fields for conversion. The sloth and inactivity which overcame the other orders place in greater contrast the ambition and the activities, both secular and spiritual, of the Jesuits.

Conversion of the Sultan Alim ud Din. — In 1747 they established a mission even on Joló. They were unable to overcome the intense antagonism of the Moro panditas and datos, but they apparently won the young sultan, Alim ud Din, whose strange story and shifting fortunes have been variously told. One of the Jesuits, Padre Villelmi, was skilled in the Arabic language, and this familiarity with the language and literature of Mohammedanism doubtless explains his ascendency over the mind of the sultan. Alim ud Din was not a strong man. His power over the subordinate datos was small, and in 1748 his brother, Bantilan, usurped his place and was proclaimed sultan of Jolo.

Alim ud Din, with his family and numerous escort, came to Zamboanga, seeking the aid of the Spanish against his brother. From Zamboanga he was sent to Manila. On his arrival, January 3, 1749, he was received with all the pomp and honor due to a prince of high rank. A house for his entertainment and his retinue of seventy persons was prepared in Binondo. A public entrance was arranged, which took place some fifteen days after his reaching the city. Triumphal arches were erected across the streets, which were lined with more than two thousand native militia under arms. The sultan was publicly received in the hall of the Audiencia, where the governor promised to lay his case before the king of Spain. The sultan was showered with presents, which included chains of gold, fine garments, precious gems, and gold canes, while the government sustained the expense of his household.[1]

Following this reception, steps were taken for his conversion. His spiritual advisers cited to him the example of the Emperor Constantine whose conversion enabled him to effect triumphant conquests over his enemies. Under these representations Alim ud Din expressed his desire for baptism. The governor-general, who at this time was a priest, the bishop of Nueva Segovia, was very anxious that the rite should take place; but this was opposed by his spiritual superior, the archbishop of Manila, who, with some others, entertained doubts as to the sincerity of the sultan's profession.

In order to accomplish his baptism, the governor sent him to his own diocese, where at Paniqui, on the 29th of April, 1750, the ceremony took place with great solemnity. On the return of the party to Manila, the sultan was received with great pomp, and in his honor

---

[1] *Relacion de la Entrada del Sultan Rey de Jolo*, in *Archivo del Bibliófilo Filipino*, vol. I.

were held games, theatrical representations, fire-works, and bull-fights. This was the high-water mark of the sultan's popularity.

Failure to Reinstate Alim ud Din. — Meanwhile the usurper, Bantilan, was giving abundant evidence of his hostility. The Spaniards were driven from Jolo, and the fleets of the Moros again ravaged the Bisayas. In July arrived the new governor, the Marquis of Obando, who determined to restore Alim ud Din and suppress the Moro piracy.

An expedition set sail, with the sultan on board, and went as far as Zamboanga, but accomplished nothing. Here the conduct of the sultan served to confirm the doubts of the Spaniards as to the sincerity of his friendship. He was arrested, and returned to Manila, and imprisoned in the fortress of Santiago. With varying treatment he remained in the hands of the Spaniards until 1763, when he was returned to Jolo by the English.

Great Increase in Moro Piracy. — The year 1754 is stated to have been the bloodiest in the history of Moro piracy. No part of the Bisayas escaped ravaging in this year, while the Camarines, Batangas, and Albay suffered equally with the rest. The conduct of the pirates was more than ordinarily cruel. Priests were slain, towns wholly destroyed, and thousands of captives were carried south into Moro slavery. The condition of the Islands at the end of this year was probably the most deplorable in their history.

Reforms under General Arandía. — The demoralization and misery with which Obando's rule closed were relieved somewhat by the capable government of Arandía, who succeeded him. Arandía was one of the few men of talent, energy, and integrity who stood at the head of affairs in these islands during two centuries.

He reformed the greatly disorganized military force, establishing what was known as the "Regiment of the King," made up very largely of Mexican soldiers. He also formed a corps of artillerists composed of Filipinos. These were regular troops, who received from Arandía sufficient pay to enable them to live decently and like an army.

He reformed the arsenal at Cavite, and, in spite of opposition on all sides, did something to infuse efficiency and honesty into the government. At the head of the armament which had been sent against the Moros he placed a Jesuit priest, Father Ducos. A capable officer was also sent to command the presidio at Zamboanga, and while Moro piracy was not stopped, heavy retaliation was visited upon the pirates.

Arandía's most popular act of government was the expulsion of the Chinese from the provinces, and in large part from the city. They seem to have had in their hands then, perhaps even more than now, the commerce or small trade between Manila and provincial towns. To take over this trade, Arandía founded a commercial company of Spaniards and mestizos, which lasted only for a year. The Christianized Chinese were allowed to remain under license, and for those having shops in Manila Arandía founded the Alcayceria of San Fernando. It consisted of a great square of shops built about an open interior. It stood in Binondo, on the present Calle de San Fernando, in what is still a populous Chinese quarter.

Death of Arandía and Decline of the Colony. — Arandía died in May, 1759, and the government was assumed by the bishop of Cebu, who in turn was forced from his position by the arrival of the archbishop of Manila, Don Manuel Rojo. The archbishop revoked the celebrated orders of good government which Arandía had put into force, and the colony promised to relapse once more into its customary dormant condition. This was, however, prevented by an event which brought to an end the long period of obscurity and, inertia under which the colony had been gradually decaying, and introduced, in a way, a new period of its history. This was the capture of the Philippine Islands by the British in 1762.

CHAPTER XI.

THE PHILIPPINES DURING THE PERIOD OF EUROPEAN REVOLUTION. 1762–1837.

The New Philosophy of the Eighteenth Century. — The middle of the eighteenth century in Europe was a time when ideas were greatly liberalized. A philosophy became current which professed to look for its authority not to churches or hereditary custom and privilege, but to the laws of God as they are revealed in the natural world. Men taught that if we could only follow nature we could not do wrong. "Natural law" became the basis for a great amount of political and social discussion and the theoretical foundation of many social rights. The savage, ungoverned man was by many European philosophers and writers supposed to live a freer, more wholesome and more natural life than the man who is bound by the conventions of society and the laws of state.

Most of this reasoning we now know to be scientifically untrue. The savage and the hermit are not, in actual fact, types of human happiness and freedom. Ideal life for man is found only in governed society, where there is order and protection, and where also should be freedom of opportunity. But to the people of the eighteenth century, and especially to the scholars of France, where the government was monarchical and oppressive, and where the people were terribly burdened by the aristocracy, this teaching was welcomed as a new gospel. Nor was it devoid of grand and noble ideas — ideas which, carried out in a conservative way, might have bettered society.

It is from this philosophy and the revolution which

succeeded it that the world received the modern ideas of liberty, equality, fraternity, and democracy. These ideas, having done their work in America and Europe, are here at work in the Philippines to-day. It remains to be seen whether a society can be rebuilt here on these principles, and whether Asia too will be reformed under their influence.

Colonial Conflicts between the Great European Countries. — During the latter half of the eighteenth century there culminated the long struggle for colonial empire between European states which we have been following. We have seen how colonial conquest was commenced by the Portuguese, who were very shortly followed by the Spaniards, and how these two great Latin powers attempted to exclude the other European peoples from the rich Far East and the great New World which they had discovered.

We have seen how this attempt failed, how the Dutch and the English broke in upon this gigantic reserve, drove the Spanish fleets from the seas, and despoiled and took of this great empire almost whatever they would. The Dutch and English then fought between themselves. The English excluded the Dutch from North America, capturing their famous colony of New Amsterdam, now New York, and incorporating it (1674) with their other American colonies, which later became the United States of America. But in the East Indies the Dutch maintained their trade and power, gradually extending from island to island, until they gained — what they still possess — an almost complete monopoly of spice production.

War between England and France. — In India, England in the eighteenth century won great possessions and laid the foundation for what has been an almost complete subjugation of this Eastern empire. Here, however, and even more so than in America, England encountered a royal and brilliant antagonist in the monarch of France.

French exploration in North America had given France claims to the two great river systems of the St. Lawrence and the Mississippi, the latter by far the greatest and richest region of the temperate zone. So, during much of this eighteenth century, England and France were involved in wars that had for their prizes the possession of the continent of North America and the great peninsula of India.

This conflict reached its climax between 1756 and 1763. Both states put forth all their strength. France called to her support those countries whose reigning families were allied to her by blood, and in this way Spain was drawn into the struggle. The monarchs of both France and Spain belonged to the great house of Bourbon. War was declared between England and Spain in 1761. Spain was totally unfitted for the combat. She could inflict no injury upon England and simply lay impotent and helpless to retaliate, while English fleets in the same year took Havana in the west and Manila in the east.

English Victory over French in India and America. — English power in India was represented during these years by the greatest and most striking figure in England's colonial history — Lord Clive. To him is due the defeat of France in India, the capture of her possessions, and the founding of the Indian Empire, which is still regarded as England's greatest possession. The French were expelled from India in the same year that the great citadel of New France in America — Quebec — was taken by the English under General Wolfe.

The Philippines under the English. — *Expedition from India to the Philippines.* — Lord Clive was now free to strike a blow at France's ally, Spain; and in Madras an expedition was prepared to destroy Spanish power in the Philippines. Notice of the preparation of this expedition reached Manila from several sources in the spring and summer of 1762; but with that fatality which pur-

Church at Malate.

sued the Spaniard to the end of his history in the Philippines, no preparations were made by him, until on the 22d of September a squadron of thirteen vessels anchored in Manila Bay.

Through the mist, the stupid and negligent authorities of Manila mistook them for Chinese trading-junks; but it was the fleet of the English Admiral Cornish, with a force of five thousand British and Indian soldiers under the command of General Draper. For her defense Manila had only 550 men of the "Regiment of the King" and eighty Filipino artillerists. Yet the Spaniards determined to make resistance from behind the walls of the city.

Surrender of Manila to the English. — The English disembarked and occupied Malate. From the churches of Malate, Ermita, and Santiago the British bombarded Manila, and the Spaniards replied from the batteries of San Andres and San Diego, the firing not being very effective on either side.

On the 25th, Draper summoned the city to surrender; but a council of war, held by the archbishop, who was also governor, decided to fight on. Thirty-six hundred Filipino militia from Pampanga, Bulacan, and Laguna marched to the defense of the city, and on the 3rd of October two thousand of these Filipinos made a sally from the walls and recklessly assaulted the English lines, but were driven back with slaughter. On the night of the 4th of October a breach in the walls was made by the artillery, and early in the morning of the 5th four hundred English soldiers entered almost without resistance. A company of militia on guard at the Puerto Real was bayoneted and the English then occupied the Plaza, and here received the surrender of the fort of Santiago.

The English agreed not to interfere with religious liberty, and honors of war were granted to the Spanish soldiers. Guards were placed upon the convent of the nuns of Santa Clara and the beaterios, and the city was given over to pillage, which lasted for forty hours, and in which many of the Chinese assisted.

Independent Spanish Capital under Anda at Bulacan. — The English were thus masters of the city, but during their period of occupation they never extended their power far beyond the present limits of Manila. Previous to the final assault and occupation of Manila, the authorities had nominated the oidor, Don Simon de Anda y Salazar, lieutenant-governor and captain-general of the Islands, with instructions to maintain the country in its obedience to the king of Spain. Anda left the capital on the night of October 4, passing in a little banca through the nipa swamps and esteros on the north shore of Manila Bay to the provincial capital of Bulacan.

Here he called together the provincial of the Augustinian monks, the alcalde mayor of the province, and some other Spaniards. They resolved to form an independent government representing Spain, and to continue the resistance. This they were able to do as long as the British remained in the Islands. The English made a few short expeditions into Bulacan and up the Pasig River, but there was no hard fighting and no real effort made to pursue Anda's force. The Chinese welcomed the English and gave them some assistance, and for this Anda slew and hung great numbers of them.

The Philippines Returned to Spain.— By the Treaty of Paris in 1763, peace was made, by which France surrendered practically all her colonial possessions to England; but England returned to Spain her captures in Cuba and the Philippines. In March, 1764, there arrived the Spanish frigate "Santa Rosa," bringing the first "Lieutenant of the King for the Islands," Don Francisco de la Torre, who brought with him news of the Treaty of Paris and the orders to the English to abandon the Islands.

Resistance of the English by the Friars. — In resistance to the English and in the efforts to maintain Spanish authority, a leading part had been taken by the friars. "The sacred orders," says Martinez de Zuñiga,[1]

---

[1] *Historia de Filipinas*, p. 682.

"had much to do with the success of Señor Anda. They maintained the Indians of their respective administrations loyal to the orders; they inspired the natives with horror against the English as enemies of the king and of religion, inciting them to die fighting to resist them; they contributed their estates and their property; and they exposed their own persons to great dangers." The friars were certainly most interested in retaining possession of the Islands and had most to lose by their falling into English hands.

Increase of the Jesuits in Wealth and Power. — In this zealous movement for defense, however, the Jesuits bore no part; and there were charges made against them of treasonable intercourse with the English, which may have had foundation, and which are of significance in the light of what subsequently occurred.

At the close of the eighteenth century, all the governments of Catholic Europe were aroused with jealousy and suspicious hatred against the Jesuits. The society, organized primarily for missionary labor, had gradually taken on much of a secular character. The society was distinguished, as we have seen in its history in the Philippines, by men with great capacity and liking for what we may call practical affairs as distinguished from purely religious or devotional life. The Jesuits were not alone missionaries and orthodox educators, but they were scientists, geographers, financiers, and powerful and almost independent administrators among heathen peoples. They had engaged so extensively and shrewdly in trade that their estates, warehouses, and exchanges bound together the fruitful fields of colonial provinces with the busy marts and money-centers of Europe. Their wealth was believed to be enormous. Properly invested and carefully guarded, it was rapidly increasing.

What, however, made the order exasperating alike to rulers and peoples were the powerful political intrigues in which members of the order engaged. Strong and masterful men themselves, the field of state affairs was irresistibly attractive. Their enemies charged that they were unscrupulous in the means which they employed to accomplish political ends. It is quite certain that the Jesuits were not patriotic in their purposes or plans. They were an international corporation; their members belonged to no one nation; to them the Society was greater and more worthy of devotion than any state, in which they themselves lived and worked.

Dissolution of the Society of Jesus. — Europe had, however, reached the belief, to which it adheres to-day, that a man must be true to the country in which he lives and finds shelter and protection and in which he ranks as a political member, or else incur odium and punishment. Thus it was their indifference to national feeling that brought about the ruin of the Jesuits. It is significant that the rulers, the most devoted to Catholicism, followed one another in decreeing their expulsion from their dominions. In 1759 they were expelled from Portugal, in 1764 from France, and April 2, 1767, the decree of confiscation and banishment from Spain and all Spanish possessions was issued by King Carlos III. Within a year thereafter, the two most powerful princes of Italy, the king of Naples and the Duke of Parma, followed, and then the Grand Master of the Knights of Malta expelled them from that island. The friends of the order were powerless to withstand this united front of Catholic monarchs, and in July, 1773, Pope Clement XIV. suppressed and dissolved the society, which was not restored until 1814.

The Jesuits Expelled from the Philippines.—The order expelling the Jesuits from the Philippines was put into effect in the year 1767. The instructions authorized the governor in case of resistance to use force of arms as against a rebellion.[1] Besides their colleges in Manila, Tondo, Cavite, Leyte, Samar, Bohol, and Negros, the Jesuits administered curacies in the vicinity of Manila, in Cavite province, in Mindoro and Marinduque, while the islands of Bohol, Samar, and Leyte were completely under their spiritual jurisdiction. In Mindanao their missions, a dozen or more in number, were found on both the northern and southern coasts. Outside of the Philippines proper they were the missionaries on the Ladrones, or Marianas. Their property in the Philippines, which was confiscated by the government, amounted to 1,320,000 pesos, although a great deal of their wealth was secreted and escaped seizure through the connivance of the governor, Raon.

Governor Anda's Charges against the Religious Orders. — Don Simon de Anda had been received in Spain with great honor for the defense which he had made in the Islands, and in 1770 returned as governor of the Philippines. His appointment was bitterly resented by the friars. In 1768, Anda had addressed to the king a memorial upon the disorders in the Philippines, in which he openly charged the friars with commercialism, neglect of their spiritual duties, oppression of the natives, opposition to the teaching of the Spanish language, and scandalous interference with civil officials and affairs. Anda's remedy for these abuses was the rigorous enforcement of

---

[1] These orders and other documents dealing with the Jesuit expulsion are printed in Montero y Vidal, *Historia de Filipinas,* vol. II. p. 180 sq.

the laws actually existing for the punishment of such conduct and the return to Spain of friars who refused to respect the law.

He was, however, only partially successful in his policy. During the six years of his rule, he labored unremittingly to restore the Spanish government and to lift it from the decadence and corruption that had so long characterized

Anda Monument.

it. There were strong traits of the modern man in this independent and incorruptible official. If he made many enemies, it is, perhaps, no less to the credit of his character; and if in the few years of his official life he was unable to restore the colony, it must be remembered that he had few assistants upon whom to rely and was without adequate means.

The Moro Pirates. — The Moros were again upon their forays, and in 1771 even attacked Aparri, on the extreme

northern coast of Luzon, and captured a Spanish missionary. Anda reorganized the Armada de Pintados, and
toward the end
of his life created
also the Marina
Sutil, a fleet of light
gunboats for the
defense of the
coasts against the
attacks of pirates.

**Failure of an
English Settle-
ment.** — The hos-
tility of the Moro
rulers was compli-
cated by the inter-
ference of the Eng-
lish, who, after the
evacuation of Ma-
nila, continued to

Calinga Axe.

haunt the Sulu archipelago with the apparent object of
effecting a settlement. By treaty with the Moro datos,

Moro Brass Vessel.

they secured the ces-
sion of the island of
Balanbangan, off the
north coast of Borneo.
This island was forti-
fied and a factory was
established, but in
1775 the Moros at-
tacked the English

with great fury and destroyed the entire garrison, except the governor and five others, who escaped on board

a vessel, leaving a great quantity of arms and wealth to the spoils of the Moros. The English factors, who had taken up business on the island of Jolo, fled in a Chinese· junk; and these events, so unfortunate to the English, ended their attempts to gain a position in the Jolo archipelago until many years later.

Increase in Agriculture. — Anda died in October, 1776, and his successor, Don José Basco de Vargas, was not appointed until July, 1778. With Basco's governorship we see the beginning of those numerous projects for the encouragement of agriculture and industry which characterized the last century of Spanish rule. His "Plan general economico" contemplated the encouragement of cotton-planting, the propagation of mulberry-trees and silk-worms, and the cultivation of spices and sugar. Premiums were offered for success in the introduction of these new products and for the encouragement of manufacturing industries suitable to the country and its people.

Out of these plans grew the admirable Sociedad Economica de Amigos del Pais, which was founded by Basco in 1780. The idea was an excellent one, and the society, although suffering long periods of inactivity, lasted for fully a century, and from time to time was useful in the improvement and development of the country, and stimulated agricultural experiments through its premiums and awards.

Establishment of the Tobacco Industry. — Up to this time the Philippine revenues had been so unproductive that the government was largely supported by a subsidy of $250,000 a year paid by Mexico. Basco was the first to put the revenues of the Islands upon a lucrative basis. To him was due the establishment, in 1782, of the famous tobacco monopoly (estanco de tabacos) which became of great importance many years later, as new and rich tobacco lands like the C a g a y a n were brought under cultivation.

Favorable Commercial Legislation. — The change in economic ideas, which had come over Europe through the liberalizing thought of the eighteenth century, is shown also by a most ra-

Igorrote Drum.

Igorrote Shield.

dical step to direct into new channels the commerce of the Philippines. This was the creation in 1785 of a great trading corporation with special privileges and crown protection, "The Royal Company of the Philippines."

The company was given a complete monopoly of all the commerce between Spain and the Philippines, except the long-established direct traffic between Manila and Acapulco. All the old laws, designed to prevent the importation into the Peninsula of wares of the Orient, were swept away. Philippine products were exempted from all customs duty either on leaving Manila or entering Spain. The vessels of the company were permitted to visit the ports of China, and the ancient and absurd prohibition, which prevented the merchants of Manila from trading with India and China, was removed.

Though still closing the Philippines against foreign trade, this step was a veritable revolution in the commercial legislation of the Philippines. Had the project been ably and heartily supported, it might have produced a development that would have advanced prosperity half a century; but the people of Manila did not welcome the opening of this new line of communication. The ancient commerce with Acapulco was a valuable monopoly to those who had the right to participate in it, and their attitude toward the new company was one either of indifference or hostility.

In 1789 the port of Manila was opened and made free to the vessels of all foreign nations for the space of three years, for the importation and sale exclusively of the wares of Asia; but the products of Europe, with the exception of Spain, were forbidden.

The Royal Company was rechartered in 1805, and enjoyed its monopoly until 1830, when its privileges lapsed and Manila was finally opened to the ships of foreign nations.

Conquest of the Igorrote Provinces of Luzon. — Basco was a zealous governor and organized a number of military expeditions to occupy the Igorrote country in the north. In 1785 the heathen Igorrotes of the missions of Ituy and Paniqui in Nueva Vizcaya revolted and had to be reconquered by a force of musketeers from Cagayan.

Conquest of the Batanes Islands. — Basco also effected the conquest of the Batanes Islands to the north of Luzon, establishing garrisons and definitely annexing them to the colony. The Dominican missionaries long before this time had attempted to convert these islands to Christianity, but the poverty of the people and the fierceness of the typhoons which sweep these little islands prevented the cultivation of anything more than camotes and taro, and had made them unprofitable to hold. Basco was honored, however, for his reoccupation of these islands, and on his return to Spain, at the expiration of his governorship, received the title of "Count of the Conquest of the Batanes."[1]

A Scientific Survey of the Coast of the Islands. — About 1790 the Philippines were visited by two Spanish frigates, the "Descubierta" and the "Atrevida," under the command of Captain Malaspina. These vessels formed an exploring expedition sent out by the Spanish government to make a hydrographic and astronomic survey of the coasts of Spanish America, the Ladrones, and the Philippines. It was one of those creditable enterprises for the widening of scientific knowledge which modern governments have successively and with great honor conducted.

The expedition charted the Strait of San Bernardino, the coasts of several of the Bisayan Islands, and Mindanao. One of the scientists of the party was the young botanist, Don Antonio Pineda, who died in Ilocos in 1792, but whose studies in the flora of the Philippines thoroughly established his reputation. A monument to his memory was erected near the church in Malate, but it has since suffered from neglect and is now falling in ruins.

Establishment of a Permanent Navy in the Philippines. — The intentions of England in this archipelago were still regarded with suspicion by the Spanish government, and

---

[1] But the conquest was almost valueless, and a few years later the inhabitants had to be transported to Cagayan because of the scarcity of food.

in 1795 and 1796 a strong Spanish fleet, sent secretly by way of the coast of South America, was concentrated in the waters of the Philippines under the command of Admiral Alava.   Its object was the defense of the Islands in

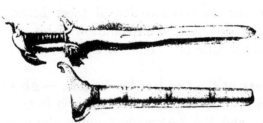

case of a new war with Great Britain.   News of the declaration of war between these two countries reached Manila in March, 1797,

Filipino Creese and Sheath.

but though for many months there was anxiety, England made no attempt at reoccupation.   These events led, however, to the formation of a permanent naval squadron, with head-quarters and naval station at Cavite.[1]

The Climax of Moro Piracy. — The continued presence of the Moros in Min-doro, where they

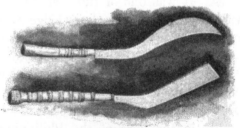

Moro Creeses.

haunted the bays and rivers of both east and west coasts

---

[1] Alava made a series of journeys through the different provinces of the Philippines, and on these trips he was accompanied by Friar Martinez de Zuñiga, whose narrative of these expeditions forms a most interesting and valuable survey of the conditions of the Islands and the people at the beginning of the nineteenth century. *"Estadismo de las Islas Filipinas, ó mis viajes por este pais,* por el Padre Fr. Joaquin Martinez de Zuñiga.   Publica esta obra por primera vez extensamente anotada W. E. Retana."   2 vols.   Madrid, 1893.

for months at a time, stealing out from this island for attack in every direction, was specially noted by Padre Zuñiga, and indicated how feebly the Spaniards repulsed these pirates a hundred years ago.

It was the last severe phase of Malay piracy, when even the strong merchant ships of England and America dreaded the straits of Borneo and passed with caution through the China Sea. Northern Borneo, the Sulu archipelago, and the southern coasts of Mindanao were the centers from which came these fierce sea-wolves, whose cruel exploits have left their many traditions in the American and British merchant navies, just as they periodically appear in the chronicles of the Philippines.

Five hundred captives annually seem to have been the spoils taken by these Moros in the Philippines Islands, and as far south as Batavia and Macassar captive Filipinos were sold in the slave marts of the Malays. The aged and infirm were inhumanly bartered to the savage tribes of Borneo, who offered them

Moro Fish Spear.

up in their ceremonial sacrifices. The measures of the Spanish government, though constant and expensive, were ineffective. Between 1778 and 1793, a million and a half of pesos were expended on the fleets and expeditions to drive back or punish the Moros, but at the end of the century a veritable climax of piracy was attained.

Pirates swarmed continually about the coasts of Mindoro, Burias, and Masbate, and even frequented the esteros of Manila Bay. Some sort of peace seems to have been established with Jolo and a friendly commerce was engaged in toward the end of the century, but the Moros of Mindanao and Borneo were increasing enemies. In 1798 a fleet of twenty-five Moro bancas passed up the Pacific coast of Luzon and fell upon the isolated towns of Paler, Casiguran, and Palanan, destroying the pueblos

and taking 450 captives. The cura of Casiguran was ransomed in Binangonan for the sum of twenty-five hundred pesos. For four years this pirate fleet had its rendezvous on Burias, whence it raided the adjacent coasts and the Catanduanes.

The Great Wars in America and Europe.

Moro Musical Instrument.

— The English reoccupied Balanbangan in 1803, but held the island for only three years, when it was definitely abandoned. For some years, however, the coasts of the Philippines were threatened by English vessels, and there was reflected here in the Far East the tremendous conflicts which were convulsing Europe at this time. The wars which changed Europe at the close of the eighteenth century, following the French Revolution, form one of the most important and interesting periods of European history, but it is also one of the most difficult periods to judge and describe. We will say of it here only so much as will be sufficient to show the effect upon Spain and so upon the Philippines.

The Revolution of the English Colonies in America. — In 1776 the thirteen English colonies on the Atlantic coast of North America declared their independence of Great Britain. In the unfair treatment of the British king and Parliament they had, they believed, just grounds for revolution. For nearly eight years a war continued by which England strove to reduce them again to obedience. But at the end of that time England, having successively lost two armies of invasion by defeat and capture, made peace with the American colonists and recognized their independence. In 1789 the Americans framed their present constitution and established the United States of America.

The French Revolution. — *Condition of the People in France.* — In their struggle for independence the Americans had been aided by France, who hoped through this opportunity to cripple her great colonial rival, England. Between America and France there was close sympathy of political ideas and theories, although in their actual social conditions the two countries were as widely separated as could be. In America the society and government were democratic. All classes were experienced in politics and government. They had behind them the priceless heritage of England's long struggle for free and representative government. There was an abundance of the necessaries of life and nearly complete freedom of opportunity.

France, like nearly every other country of continental Europe, was suffering from the obsolete burden of feudalism. The ownership of the land was divided between the aristocracy and the church. The great bulk of the population were serfs bound to the estates, miserably oppressed, and suffering from lack of food, and despoiled of almost every blessing which can brighten and dignify human life. The life of the court and of the nobility grew more luxurious, extravagant, and selfish as the economic conditions in France became worse. The king was nearly an absolute monarch. His will was law and the earlier representative institutions, which in England had developed into the splendid system of parliamentary government, had in France fallen into decay.

In the other countries of Europe — the German States, Austria, Italy, and Spain — the condition of the people was quite as bad, probably in some places even worse than it was in France. But it was in France that the revolt broke forth, and it was France which led Europe in a movement for a better and more democratic order. Frenchmen had fought in the armies of America; they had experienced the benefits of a freer society, and it is significant that in the same year (1789) that saw the founding of the American state the Revolution in France began. It started in a sincere and conservative attempt to remedy the evils under which France was suffering, but the accumulation of injustice and misery was too great to be settled by slow and hesitating measures. The masses, ignorant, and bitter with their wrongs, broke from the control of statesman and reformer, threw themselves upon the established state and church, both equally detestable to them, and tore them to pieces. Both king and queen died by beheading. The nobility were either murdered or expelled. The revolutionary government, if such it could be called, fell into the hands of wicked and terrible leaders, who maintained themselves by murder and terrorism.

Effects of the Revolution. — These are the outward and terrible expressions of the Revolution which were seized upon by European statesmen and which have been most dwelt upon by historical writers. But, apart from the bloody acts of the years from 1793 to 1795, the Revolution modernized France and brought incalculable gains to the French people. By the seizure of the great estates and their division among the peasantry, the agricultural products of the country were doubled in a single year, and that terrible condition of semi-starvation which had prevailed for centuries was ended.

The other monarchies of Europe regarded the events in France with horror and alarm. Monarchs felt their own thrones threatened, and a coalition of European monarchies was formed to destroy the republic and to restore the French monarchy and old régime. France found herself invaded by armies upon every frontier. It was then that the remarkable effects produced by the Revolution upon the people of France appeared.

With a passionate enthusiasm which was irresistible, the people responded to the call for war; great armies were enlisted, which by an almost uninterrupted series of victories threw back the forces of the allies. Men rose from obscurity to the command of armies, and there was developed that famous group of commanders, the marshals of France. Out of this terrible period of warfare there arose, too, another, who was perhaps, if we except the Macedonian king, Alexander, the greatest man ever permitted to lead armies and to rule men — Bonaparte, later the emperor, Napoleon the First.

The New Republic under Napoleon the First. — From 1795, when Bonaparte was given command of the invasion of Italy, until 1815, when he was finally defeated at Waterloo in Belgium, Europe experienced almost continuous war. The genius of Napoleon reduced to the position of vassal states Italy, Switzerland, Holland, Belgium, Germany, and Austria. In all these countries the ancient thrones were humbled, feudalism was swept away, and the power of a corrupt church and aristocracy was broken. In spite of the humiliation of national pride, these great benefits to Europe of Napoleon's conquests can not be overestimated. Wherever Napoleon's power extended there followed the results of the Revolution—a better system of law, the introduction of the liberal "Code Napoleon," the liberation of the people from the crushing toils of mediævalism, and the founding of a better society. These are the debts which Europe owes to the French Revolution.

The Decline of Spain. — *Lack of Progress.* — In this advance and progress Spain did not share. The empire of Napoleon was never established in the Peninsula. In 1811 the Spaniards, with the assistance of the English under the great general, Wellington, repulsed the armies of the French. This victory, so gratifying to national pride, was perhaps a real loss to Spain, for the reforms which prevailed in other parts of Europe were never carried out in Spain, and she remains even yet unliberated from aristocratic and clerical power.

A liberal constitutional government was, however, set up in Spain in 1812 by the Cortes; but in 1814 King Ferdinand, aided by the Spanish aristocracy and clergy, was able to overthrow this representative government and with tyrannical power to cast reforms aside. Fifty thousand people were imprisoned for their liberal opinions, the Inquisition was restored, the Cortes abolished, and its acts nullified. The effect of these acts upon the Philippines will be noticed presently.

Separation of the Philippines from Mexico. —The events of these years served to separate the Philippines from their long dependency on Mexico. In 1813 the Cortes decreed the suppression of the subsidized Acapulco galleon. The Mexican trade had long been waning and voyages had become less profitable. The last of the galleons left Manila in 1811 and returned from Acapulco in 1815, never again to attempt this classical voyage.

The cessation of these voyages only briefly preceded the complete separation from America. From the first period of settlement, the Philippines had in many respects been a sub-dependency of New Spain. Mexico had until late afforded the only means of communication with the mother-country, the only land of foreign trade. Mexican officials frequently administered the government of the Islands, and Mexican Indians formed the larger part of the small standing army of the Philippines, including the "Regiment of the King." As we have seen, a large subsidy, the situado, was annually drawn from the Mexican treasury to support the deficient revenues of the Philippines.

Rebellion of the South American Countries. — But the grievances of the Spanish American colonists were very great and very real. The revolution which had successively stirred North America and Europe now passed back again to the Spanish countries of the New World, and between 1810 and 1825 they fought themselves free of Spain. The last of the colonies from which the Spaniards were forced to retire was Peru. Mexico achieved her separation in 1820. Spain lost every possession upon the mainland of both Americas, and the only vestiges of her once vast American empire were the rich islands of the Greater Antilles — Cuba and Porto Rico.

Limited Trade with the Philippines. — The Philippines were now forced to communicate by ship directly with Spain. The route for the next fifty years· lay by sailing-vessels around the Cape of Good Hope. It occupied from four to six months, but this route had now become practically a neutral passage, its winds and currents were well understood, and it was annually followed by great numbers of vessels of Europe, England, and the United States.

Trade was still limited to the ships of the Royal Philippine Company, and this shipping monopoly lasted until 1835, when a new era in the commercial and industrial life of the Philippines opened. An English commercial house was established in Manila as early as 1809.

Volcanic Eruptions. — The terrible eruptions of Mount Taal, the last of which occurred in 1754, were followed in the next century by the destructive activity of Mount Mayon. In 1814 an indescribable eruption of ashes and lava occurred, and the rich hemp towns around the base of this mountain were destroyed. Father Francisco Aragoneses, cura of Cagsaua, an eye-witness, states that twelve thousand people perished; in the church of Budiao alone two hundred lay dead.[1]

Rebellions in the Philippines. — *The Liberal Spanish Cortes.* — Two revolts in the Philippines that occurred at this period are of much importance and show the effect in the Philippines of the political changes in Spain. In 1810 the liberal Spanish Cortes had declared that "the kingdoms and provinces of America and Asia are, and ought to have been always, reputed an integral part of the Spanish monarchy, and for that same, their natives

---

[1] Jagor: *Viajes por Filipinas*, p. 81. Translated from the German. Madrid, 1895.

and free inhabitants are equal in rights and privileges to those of the Peninsula."

This important declaration, which if carried out would have completely revolutionized Spain's colonial policy, was published in the Philippines, and with that remarkable and interesting facility by which such news is spread, even among the least educated classes of Filipinos, this proclamation had been widely disseminated and discussed throughout the Islands. It was welcomed by the Filipino with great satisfaction, because he believed it exempted him from the enforced labor of the *polos* and *servicios*. These were the unremunerated tasks required of Filipinos for the construction of public works, bridges, roads, churches, and convents.

Effect of the Repeal of the Declaration of the Cortes. — King Ferdinand VII. in May, 1814, on his return to power, as we have seen, published the famous decree abolishing constitutional government in Spain and annulling all the acts of the Cortes, including those which aimed to liberalize the government of the colonies. These decrees, when published in the Philippines, appeared to the Filipinos to return them to slavery, and in many places their disaffection turned to rebellion. In Ilocos twelve hundred men banded together, sacked convents and churches, and destroyed the books and documents of the municipal archives. Their fury seems to have been particularly directed against the petty tyrants of their own race, the caciques or principales.

The result of Spanish civilization in the Philippines had been to educate, and, to a certain degree, enrich a small class of Filipinos, usually known as principales or the *gente ilustrada*. It is this class which has absorbed the direction of municipal and local affairs, and which almost alone of the Filipino population has shared in those benefits and opportunities which civilized life should bring.

The vast majority of the population have, unfortunately, fallen or remained in a dependent and almost semi-servile position beneath the principales. In Ilocos this subordinate class, or dependientes, is known as *kailian*, and it was these kailian who now fell upon their more wealthy masters, burning their houses and destroying their property, and in some instances killing them. The assignment of compulsory labor had been left to the principales in their positions as gobernadorcillos and cabezas de barangay, and these officials had unquestionably abused their power and had drawn down upon themselves the vengeance of the kailian.[1]

This revolt, it will be noticed, was primarily directed neither against friars nor Spanish authorities, but against the unfortunate social order which the rule of Spain maintained.

A Revolt Lead by Spaniards. — A plot, with far more serious motives, took place in 1823. The official positions in the regiments and provinces had previously been held almost entirely by Spaniards born in America or the Philippines. The government now attempted to fill these positions with Spaniards from Manila. The officials, deprived of their positions, incited the native troops which they had commanded, into a revolt, which began in the walled city in Manila. About eight hundred soldiers followed them, and they gained possession of the Cuartel of the King, of the Royal Palace, and of the Cabildo, but they failed to seize the fortress of Santiago.

---

[1] See *Estado de las Islas Filipinas en 1847*, by D. Sinibaldo de Mas.

It was not properly a revolt of Filipinos, as the people were not involved and did not rise, but it had its influence in inciting later insurrection.

Insurrection on Bohol. — Since the insurrection on Bohol in 1744, when the natives had killed the Jesuit missionaries, a large part of the island had been practically independent under the leader Dogóhoy. After the expulsion of the Jesuits, Recollects were placed in special charge of those towns along the seacoast, which had remained loyal to Spain. An effort was made to secure the submission of the rebels by the proclamation of a pardon, but the power of the revolt grew rather than declined, until in 1827 it was determined to reduce the rebellion by force. An expedition of thirty-two hundred men was formed in Cebu, and in April, 1828, the campaign took place, which resulted in the defeat of the rebels and their settlement in the Christian towns.

The New Provinces of Benguet and Abra. — It is proper to notice also the slow advances of Spanish authority, which began to be made about this time among the heathen tribes of northern Luzon. These fierce and powerful tribes occupy the entire range of the Cordillera Central. Missionary effort in the latter half of the eighteenth century had succeeded in partly Christianizing the tribes along the river Magat in Neuva Vizcaya, but the fierce, head-hunting hillmen remained unsubdued and unchristianized.

Between 1823 and 1829 the mission of Pidigan, under an Augustinian friar, Christianized some thousands of the Tinguianes of the river Abra. In 1829 an expedition of about sixty soldiers, under Don Guillermo Galvey, penetrated into the cool, elevated plateau of Benguet. The diary of the leader recounts the difficult march up the river Cagaling from Aringay and their delight upon emerging from the jungle and cogon upon the grassy, pine-timbered slopes of the plateau.

They saw little cultivated valleys and small culsters of houses and splendid herds of cattle, carabaos, and horses, which to this day have continued to enrich the people of these mountains. 'At times they were surrounded by the yelling bands of Igorrotes, and several times they had to repulse attacks, but they nevertheless succeeded in reaching the beautiful circular depression now known as the valley of La Trinidad.

The Spaniards saw with enthusiasm the carefully separated and walled fields, growing camotes, taro, and sugarcane. The village of about five hundred houses was partly burned by the Spaniards, as the Igorrotes continued hostile. The expedition returned to the coast, having suffered only a few wounds. The commandancia of Benguet was not created until 1846, in which year also Abra was organized as a province.

CHAPTER XII.

PROGRESS AND REVOLUTION.

1837–1897.

Progress during the Last Half-Century of Spanish Rule.— We have now come to the last half-century and to the last phase of Spanish rule. In many respects this period was one of economic and social progress, and contained more of promise than any other in the history of the Islands. During this last half-century the Spanish rulers had numerous plans for the development and better administration of the Philippines, and, in spite of a somewhat wavering policy and the continual sore of official peculation, this was a period of wonderful advancement. Revolution and separation from Spain came at last, as revolutions usually do, not because there was no effort nor movement for reform, but because progress was so discouragingly slow and so irritatingly blocked by established interests that desired no change.

Effect of Opening the Port of Manila to Foreign Trade.— *Increase in Agriculture.* — The opening of the port of Manila to foreign trade, in 1837, was followed by a period of rising industry and prosperity. Up to this time the archipelago had not been a producing and exporting country, but the freeing of trade led to the raising of great harvests for foreign export, which have made world-wide the fame of certain Philippine productions. Chief among these are of course Manila hemp and tobacco. These were followed by sugar and coffee culture, the latter plant enriching the province of Batangas, while the planting of new cocoanut groves yearly made of greater importance the yield of that excellent product, copra. These rich merchandises had entered very little into commerce during the early decades of the century.

Increase in Exports. — In 1810 the entire imports of the Philippines amounted in value to 5,329,000 dollars, but more than half of this consisted of silver sent from Mexico. From Europe and the United States trade amounted to only 175,000 dollars. The exports in the same year amounted to 4,795,000 dollars, but a million and a half of this was Mexican silver exported on to China, and the whole amount of exports to Europe and the United States was only 250,000 dollars.

In 1831 the exportation of hemp amounted to only 346 tons. But the effect upon production of opening Manila to foreign trade is seen in the export six years later of 2,585 tons. By 1858 the exportation of hemp had risen to 412,000 piculs, or 27,500 tons. Of this amount, nearly two thirds, or 298,000 piculs, went to the United States. At this time the North Atlantic seaboard of America was the center of a most active ship-building and ship-carrying trade. The American flag was conspicuous among the vessels that frequented these Eastern ports, and "Manila hemp" was largely sought after by American seamen to supply the shipyards at home. Of sugar, the export in 1858 amounted to 557,000 piculs, of which more than half went to Great Britain.

After 1814 general permission had been given to foreigners to establish trading-houses in Manila, and by 1858 there were fifteen such establishments, of which seven were English and three American.[1]

------

[1] Bowring: *A Visit to the Philippine Islands*, p. 387.

Other Ports Opened to Foreign Commerce. — In 1855 three other ports were opened to foreign commerce — Sual in Pangasinan on the Gulf of Lingayan, Iloilo, and Zamboanga. In 1863, Cebu likewise was made an open port. The exports of Sual consisted only of rice, and in spite of its exceptional harbor this port never flourished, and is to-day no more than an unfrequented village.

Iloilo exported leaf tobacco, sugar, sapan or dyewood (an industry long ago ruined), hemp, and hides. Zamboanga through the Chinese had a small trade with Jolo and the Moro Islands, and exported the produce of these seas — sea-slug (tripang), shark fins, mother-of-pearl, tortoise shell, etc. For some years the customs laws in these ports were trying and vexatious, and prevented full advantage being taken of the privileges of export; but in 1869 this service was, by royal decree, greatly liberalized and improved. Since that date the Philippines have steadily continued to grow in importance in the commercial world.

The Form of Government under the Spanish. — *General Improvements.* — This is perhaps a convenient place to examine for the last time the political system which the Spaniards maintained in the country. In 1850 there were thirty-four provinces and two politico-military commandancias. In these provinces the Spanish administration was still vested solely in the alcalde mayor, who until after 1886 was both governor or executive officer and the judge or court for the trial of provincial cases and crimes.

Many of the old abuses which had characterized the government of the alcaldes had been at least partially remedied. After 1844 they had no longer the much-abused monopoly privilege of trade, nor had they as free a hand in controlling the labor of the inhabitants; but opportunities for illegal enrichment existed in the administration of the treasury and tax system, and these opportunities were not slighted. Up to the very end of Spanish rule the officials, high and low, are accused of stealing public money.

The Pueblo. — The unit of administration was the pueblo, or township, which ordinarily embraced many square miles of country and contained numerous villages, or "barrios." The center of the town was naturally the site where for centuries had stood the great church and the convent of the missionary friars. These locations had always been admirably chosen, and about them grew up the market and trading-shops of Chinese and the fine and durable homes of the more prosperous Filipinos and mestizos.

About 1860 the government began to concern itself with the construction of public buildings and improvements, and the result is seen in many pueblos in the finely laid-out plazas and well-built municipal edifices grouped about the square — the "tribunal," or town house, the jail, and the small but significant schoolhouses. The government of the town was vested in a "gobernadorcillo" and a council, each of the "consejales" usually representing a hamlet or barrio.

But the Spanish friar, who in nearly every pueblo was the parish curate, continued to be the paternal guardian and administrator of the pueblo. In general, no matter was too minute for his dictation. Neither gobernadorcillo nor councillors dared act in opposition to his wishes, and the alcalde of the province was careful to keep on friendly terms and leave town affairs largely to his dictation. The friar was the local inspector of public instruction and ever vigilant to detect and destroy radical ideas. To the humble Filipino, the friar was the visible and only representative of Spanish authority.

The Revolt of 1841. — *Repression of the People by the Friars.* — Unquestionably in the past, the work of the friars had been of very great value; but men as well as institutions may lose their usefulness, as conditions change, and the time was now approaching when the autocratic and paternal régime of the friars no longer satisfied the Filipinos. Their zeal was no longer disinterested, and their work had become materialized by the possession of the vast estates upon which their spiritual charges lived and labored as tenants or dependents. The policy of the religious orders had, in fact, become one of repression, and as the aspirations of the Filipinos increased, the friars, filled with doubt and fear, tried to draw still tighter the bonds of their own authority, and viewed with growing distrust the rising ambition of the people.

Apolinario de la Cruz. — The unfortunate revolution of 1841 shows the wayward and misdirected enthusiasm of the Filipino; and the unwisdom of the friars. Apolinario de la Cruz, a young Filipino, a native of Lukban, Tayabas, came up to Manila filled with the ambition to lead a monastic life, and engaged in theological studies. By his attendance upon lectures and sermons and by imitation of the friar preachers of Manila, Apolinario became, himself, quite an orator, and, as subsequent events showed, was able to arouse great numbers of his own people by his appeals.

It was his ambition to enter one of the regular monastic orders, but this religious privilege was never granted to Filipinos, and he was refused. He then entered a brotherhood known as the Cofradia, or Brotherhood of San Juan de Dios, composed entirely of Filipinos. After some years in this brotherhood, he returned in 1840 to Tayabas and founded the Cofradia de San José, his aim being to form a special cult in honor of Saint Joseph and the Virgin. For this he requested authorization from Manila. It was here that the lack of foresight of the friars appeared.

The Opposition of the Friars.— Instead of sympathizing with these religious aspirations, in which, up to this point, there seems to have been nothing heretical, they viewed the rise of a Filipino religious leader with alarm. Their policy never permitted to the Filipino any position that was not wholly subordinate. They believed that the permanence of Spanish power in these islands lay in suppressing any latent ability for leadership in the Filipino himself. Their influence, consequently, was thrown against Apolinario, and the granting of the authority for his work. They secured not only a condemnation of his plan, but an order for the arrest and imprisonment of all who should attend upon his preaching.

Apolinario Forced to Rebel. — Apolinario thereupon took refuge in independent action. His movement had already become a strong one, and his followers numbered several thousand people of Laguna, Tayabas, and Batangas. The governor of Tayabas province, Don Joaquin Ortega, organized an expedition to destroy the schism. Accompanied by two Franciscan friars, he attacked Apolinario in the month of October, 1840, and was defeated and killed. One account says that Apolinario was assisted by a band of Negritos, whose bowmanship was destructive. There are still a very few of these little blacks in the woods in the vicinity of Lukban.

Apolinario was now in the position of an open rebel, and he fortified himself in the vicinity of Alitao, where he built a fort and chapel.

His religious movement became distinctly independent and heretical. A church was formed, of which he was first elected archbishop and then supreme pontiff. He was also charged with having assumed the title of "King of the Tagálog."

Finally a force under the new alcalde, Vital, and General Huet early in November attacked Apolinario's stronghold and after a fierce struggle defeated the revolutionists. About a thousand Filipinos perished in the final battle. Apolinario was captured and executed. He was then twenty-seven years of age.

Organization of Municipal Governments. — In 1844 an able and liberal governor, General Claveria, arrived, and remained until the end of the year 1849. A better organization of the provincial governments, which we have seen, followed Claveria's entrance into office, and in October, 1847, came the important decree, organizing the municipalities in the form which we have already described, and which remained without substantial modification to the end of Spanish rule, and which has to a considerable extent been followed in the Municipal Code framed by the American government.

Subjection of the Igorrote Tribes. — With Claveria began a decisive policy of conquest among the Igorrote tribes of northern Luzon, and by the end of Spanish rule these mountains were dotted with cuartels and missions for the control of these unruly tribes. The province of Nueva Vizcaya has been particularly subject to the raids of these head-hunting peoples. Year after year the Christian towns of the plains had yielded a distressing sacrifice of life to satisfy the savage ceremonials of the Igorrotes.[1]

In 1847, Claveria nominated as governor of Nueva Vizcaya, Don Mariano Ozcariz, whose severe and telling conquests for the first time checked these Igorrote outrages and made possible the development of the great valleys of northern Luzon.

Spanish Settlements on Mindanao. — *Zamboanga.* — With Claveria's governorship we enter also upon the last phase of Moro piracy. In spite of innumerable expeditions, Spain's occupation of South Mindanao and the Sulu archipelago was limited to the presidio of Zamboanga. She had occupied this strategic point continuously since the reëstablishment of Spanish power in 1763. The great stone fort, which still stands, had proved impregnable to Moro attack, and had long been unmolested.

Distributed for a distance of some miles over the rich lands at this end of the Zamboanga peninsula was a Christian population, which had grown up largely from the descendants of rescued captives of the Moros. Coming originally from all parts of the Bisayas, Calamianes, and Luzon, this mixed population has grown to have a somewhat different character from that of any other part of the Islands. A corrupt Spanish dialect, known as the "Chabucano," has become the common speech, the only instance in the Philippines where the native dialect has been supplanted. This population, loyal and devotedly Catholic, never failed to sustain the defense of this iso-

---

[1] The reports of the Dominican missionaries of Nueva Vizcaya and Isabela show the extent and persistence of these raids. (See the files of the missionary publication, *El Correo Sino-Annamita,* and also the work by Padre Buenaventura Campa, Los Maybyaos y la Raza Ifugao, Madrid, 1895.

lated Spanish outpost, and contributed brave volunteers to every expedition against the Moro islands.

Activity of Other Nations. — But Spain's maintenance of Zamboanga was insufficient to sustain her claims of sovereignty over the Sulu and Tawi-Tawi groups. Both the Dutch and English planned various moves for their occupation and acquisition, and in 1844 a French fleet entered the archipelago and concluded a treaty with the sultan of Sulu for the cession of the island of Basilan for the sum of one million dollars. Writings of the French minister and historian, M. Guizot, show that France hoped, by the acquisition of this island, to obtain a needed naval base in the East and found a great commercial port within the sphere of Chinese trade.[1]

Conquest of the Gulf of Davao. — But this step roused the Spaniards to activity and the occupation of the island. A naval vessel subdued the towns along the north coast, and then proceeding to the mouth of the Rio Grande, secured from the sultan of Maguindanao the cession of the great Gulf of Davao. Spain took no immediate steps to occupy this gulf, but in 1847 a Spaniard, Don José Oyanguran, proposed to the governor, Claveria, to conquer the region at his own expense, if he could be furnished with artillery and munitions and granted a ten years' government of Davao, with the exclusive privilege of trade.

His offer was accepted by the governor and the Audiencia, and Oyanguran organized a company to secure funds for the undertaking. In two years' time he had subdued the coast regions of this gulf, expelled the pirates who harbored there, and founded the settlement of Nueva

---

[1] Montero y Vidal: *Historia de Filipinas*, vol. III., p. 99.

Vergara. He seems to have been making progress toward the conquest and commercial exploitation of this region, when jealous attacks in Manila induced Governor Urbistondo to cancel his privilege and to relieve him by an officer of the government.

In subsequent years the Jesuits had a few mission stations here and made a few converts among the Bagobos; but the region is still an unsubdued and unutilized country, whose inhabitants are mainly pagan tribes, and whose rich agricultural possibilities lie undeveloped and unclaimed.

The Samal Pirates. — *The Sulu.* — The piratical inhabitants of the Sulu archipelago are made of two distinct Malayan peoples — the Sulu (or Sulug), and the Samal, who are known throughout Malaysia as the "Bajau" or "Orang laut" (Men of the Sea). The former appear to be the older inhabitants. They occupy the rich and populous island of Jolo and some islands of the Siassi group, immediately south.

The Samal. — The Samal, or Bajau, are stated to have come originally from Johore. Many of them live almost exclusively in their boats, passing their lives from birth to death upon the sea. They are found throughout most parts of Malaysia, the position of their little fleets changing with the shifting of the monsoons. In the Sulu archipelago and a few points in South Mindanao, many of these Samal have shifted their homes from their boats to the shore. Their villages are built on piles over the sea, and on many of the low coral reefs south of Siassi and east of Tawi-Tawi there are great towns or settlements which have apparently been in existence a long while.

Fifty years ago the Samal were very numerous in the many islands between Jolo and Basilan, and this group is still known as the Islas Samales. Like the Sulu and other Malays, the Samal are Mohammedans, and scarcely less persistent pirates than their fellow-Malays. With the decline of piratical power among the Sulu of Jolo, the focus of piracy shifted to these settlements of the Samal, and in the time of Claveria the worst centers were the islands of Balanguingui and Tonquil, lying just north of the island of Jolo. From here pirate and slaving raids upon the Bisayan Islands continued to be made, and nearly every year towns were sacked and burned and several hundred unfortunate captives carried away. The captives were destined for slavery, and regular marts existed for this traffic at Jolo and on the Bay of Sandakan in Borneo.

Arrival of Steam Warships. — In 1848 the Philippines secured the first steam war vessels. These were the " Magellanes," the " Elcano," and the " Reina de Castilla." They were destined to revolutionize Moro relations.

The Destruction of the Samal Forts. — Hitherto it had been possible for the great Moro war praos, manned by many oarsmen, to drop their masts on the approach of an armed sailing-vessel, and, turning toward the "eye of the wind," where no sailing-ship could pursue, row calmly away from danger. Steam alone was effective in combating these sea-wolves. Claveria took these newly arrived ships, and with a strong force of infantry, which was increased by Zamboangueño volunteers, he entered the Samal group in February, 1848, and landed on the island of Balanguingui.

There were four fortresses situated in the mangrove marshes of the island. These, in spite of a desperate resistance, were carried by the infantry and Zamboangueños and the pirates scattered. The conduct of the campaign appears to have been admirable and the fighting heroic. The Moros were completely overwhelmed; 450 dead were burned or interred; 124 pieces of artillery—for the most part, the small brass cannon called "lantacas" — were captured, and 150 Moro boats were destroyed. The Spaniards cut down the cocoanut groves, and with spoil that included such rich pirate loot as silks, silver vases, ornaments, and weapons of war, and with over two hundred prisoners and three hundred rescued captives, returned to Zamboanga. This was the most signal victory ever won by Europeans in conflict with Malay piracy. The effectiveness of this campaign is shown by the fact that while in the preceding year 450 Filipinos had suffered capture at the hands of Moro pirates, in 1848 and the succeeding year there was scarcely a depredation. But in 1850 a pirate squadron from Tonquil, an island adjacent to Balanguingui, fell upon Samar and Camaguin. Fortunately, Governor Urbistondo, who had succeeded Claveria, vigorously continued the policy of his predecessor, and an expedition was promptly dispatched which destroyed the settlements and strongholds on Tonquil.

Destruction of the Moro Forts at Jolo. — A year later war broke out again with Jolo, and after a varied interchange of negotiations and hostilities, the Spaniards stormed and took the town in February, 1851. The question of permanent occupation of this important site was debated by a council of war, but their forces appearing unequal to the task, the forts of the Moros were destroyed, and the expedition returned. Jolo is described at this time as a very strongly guarded situation. Five forts and a double line of trenches faced the shore. The Moro town is said to have contained about seven thousand souls, and there was a barrio of Chinese traders, who numbered about five hundred.

Treaty with the Sultan of Jolo. — A few months later the governor of Zamboanga concluded a treaty with the sultan of Jolo by which the archipelago was to be considered an incorporated part of the Spanish possessions. The sultan bound himself to make no further treaties with or cessions to foreign powers, to suppress piracy, and to fly the Spanish flag. The Moros were guaranteed the practice of their religion, the succession of the sultan and his descendants in the established order, boats of Jolo were to enjoy the same trading privileges in Spanish ports as other Filipino vessels, and the sultan retained the right to all customs duties on foreign trading-vessels. Finally, "in compensation for the damages of war," the sultan was to be paid an annual subsidy of 1,500 pesos and 600 pesos each to three datos and 360 pesos to a sherif. [1]

The End of Malay Piracy. — In these very years that Malay piracy was receiving such severe blows from the recuperating power and activity of the Spanish government on the north, it was crushed also from the south by the merciless warfare of a great Englishman, the Raja Charles Brooke of Sarawak. The sources of pirate depredation were Maguindanao, the Sulu archipelago, and the north and west coasts of the great island of Borneo. We have seen how these fleets, century after century, swept northward and wasted with fire and murder the fair islands of the Philippines.

But this archipelago was not alone in suffering these ravages. The peaceful trading inhabitants of the great island groups to the south were persistently visited and despoiled. Moreover, as the Chinese trade by the Cape of

---

[1] Montero y Vidal: *Historia de Filipinas,* vol. III., p. 209. The document is given in Appendix 4 of the same volume.

Good Hope route became established in the first half of the nineteenth century, these pirates became a great menace to European shipping. They swarmed the China Sea, and luckless indeed was the ship carried too far eastward on its course. Every American schoolboy is familiar with the stories of fierce hand-to-hand struggles with Malay pirates, which have come down from those years when the American flag was seen everywhere in the ports of the Far East.

About 1839 a young English officer,[1] who had been in the Indian service, Charles Brooke, having armed and equipped a yacht of about 140 tons, set sail for the coast of Borneo, with the avowed intent of destroying Malay piracy and founding an independent state. In all the romantic stories of the East there is no career of greater during than that of this man. In 1841, having engaged in several bloody exploits, Brooke forced from the sultan of Borneo the cession of Sarawak, with the government vested in himself as an independent raja.

Brooke now devoted himself with merciless severity to the destruction of the pirates in the deep bays and swampy rivers, whence they had so long made their excursions. Later he was assisted by the presence of the English man-of-war "Dido," and in 1847 the sultan of Brunei ceded to Great Britain the island of Labuan. In 1849, Brooke visited Zamboanga in the English man-of-war "Mœander,' and concluded a treaty with the sultan of Sulu, which greatly alarmed the Spaniards.

Brooke's private correspondence shows that he was ambitious and hopeful of acquiring for England parts of the Dutch possessions in the south and the Spanish Philip-

---

[1] See *Rajah Brooke,* by Sir Spencer St. John, London, 1899.

pines in the north; but his plans were never followed up by England, although in 1887 North Borneo was ceded to an English company, and all the northern and eastern portions of this great island are now under English protection.[1]

Liberal Ideas among the Filipinos. — The release from Moro piracy, the opening of foreign commerce, and the development of agricultural production were rapidly bringing about a great change in the aspirations of the Filipino people themselves. Nearly up to the middle of the nineteenth century the Filipinos had felt the full effect of isolation from the life and thought of the modern world. But the revolutionary changes in Europe and the struggles for constitutional government in Spain had their influence, even in these far-away Spanish possessions. Spaniards of liberal ideas, some of them in official positions, found their way to the Islands, and an agitation began, originating among Spaniards themselves, against the paternal powers of the friars.

Influence of the Press. — The growth of periodic literature accelerated this liberalizing movement. The press, though suffering a severe censorship, has played a large part in shaping recent thought in these islands and in communicating to the Filipino people those ideas and purposes which ever inspire and elevate men.[2] The first newspaper to make its appearance in the Philippines was in 1822 — "El Philantropo"; but journalism assumed no

---

[1] Keppel: *Expedition to Borneo of H. M. S. Dido for the Suppression of Piracy, with extracts from the Journal of James Brooke, Esq.* 2 vols. London, 1846. Keppel: *A Visit to the Indian Archipelago in H. M. S. Mœandar.* 2 vols. London, 1853.

[2] Spain established a permanent commission of censorship in 1856. It was composed of eight persons, one half nominated by the governor and one half by the archbishop.

real importance until the forties, when there were founded "Semanario Filipino" (1843), and almost immediately after several others — "El Amigo de Pais" (1845), "La Estrella" (1846), and "La Esperanza" (1847), the first daily. These were followed by "Diario de Manila" (1848); in 1858 "El Comercio" appeared, the oldest of the papers still in existence.[1]

Papers conducted by Filipinos and in the Filipino tongues are of more recent origin, but these early Spanish periodicals had a real effect upon the Filipinos themselves, training up a class familiar with the conduct of journalism and preparing a way for the very influential work of the Filipino press in recent years.

Establishment of an Educational System. — *Return of the Jesuits.*— But more important than all other influences was the opening of education to Filipinos. In 1852 a royal decree authorized the Jesuits to return to the Philippines. The conditions under which they came back were that they should devote themselves solely to missions in the unoccupied fields of Mindanao, and to the higher education of the Filipinos.

The Public Schools.— In 1860, O'Donnell, the Spanish minister of war and colonies (Ultramar), founded the system of public primary instruction. A primary school for boys and one for girls was to be established in each pueblo of the Islands. In these schools, instruction was to be given in the Spanish language. A superior commission of education was formed, which consisted of the governor, the archbishop, and seven other members added by the governor himself.

The system was not secular, for it primarily was de-

---

[1] *El Periodismo Filipino*, por W. E. Retana. Madrid, 1895.

voted to the teaching of religious doctrine. The Spanish friar, the pueblo curate, was the local inspector of schools and practically directed their conduct. It was not wholly a free system, because tuition was required of all but the poorest children; nor was it an adequate system, because, even when most complete, it reached only a small proportion of the children of a parish, and these very largely

Cathedral, Manila.

were of the well-to-do families. And yet this system, for what it accomplished, is deserving of great credit.

Besides the church, the convent, and the tribunal, nearly every town in the Philippines, toward the close of Spanish rule, had also, in the public plaza, its public school buildings for boys and for girls. In these towns a number of Filipinos were taught to converse in the Spanish language and at least the rudiments of Spanish education. But this system did not give opportunity for education to the little child of the humble fisherman and the husbandman.

The Manila Normal School. — To prepare Filipino teachers to do this work of primary instruction, a decree of 1863 established the Manila Normal School. In charge of the Jesuits, this school was inaugurated in January, 1865. And about the same date the government decreed the foundation of the Jesuit "Ateneo Municipal" for higher instruction in the classics and sciences that should conduct the student to the degree of bachelor of arts. The influence of these institutions upon the development of the Filipino has been remarkable. In one or the other of them have been trained nearly all of those young men who in recent years have stirred the Filipino people to wide ambitions and demands. At the same time the excellent Jesuit observatory, which has done such important work in meteorology, was established in charge of Padre Faura.

Increase in Spanish Population. — The opening of the Suez Canal in 1869 brought immense changes to the Islands. Previous to this date Spanish residents had been few. Almost the only class deeply interested in the Islands and permanently established here had been the friars. But with communication by steamer in thirty days from Barcelona to Manila, a new interest was felt by Spaniards in the Philippines, though unfortunately this interest was greatest among the politicians. Some of the projects planned and decreed can only be regarded as visionary and beyond the point of serviceability, and others, more unfortunately still, had for their purpose the creation of offices and emoluments for Peninsula politicians; but they all contributed to bring to an end the paternal government under which there was no prospect of further enlightenment or progress for the Filipino.

Increase in the Number of Wealthy, Educated Filipinos. — The Filipino had now become embarked upon a new current of intellectual experience — a course of enlightenment which has been so full of unexpected development, and which has already carried him so far from his ancestor of one hundred years ago, that we can not say what advance another generation or two may bring. Throughout all the towns of the Islands a class was rapidly growing up to which the new industries had brought wealth. Their means enabled them to build spacious and splendid homes of the fine, hard woods of the Philippines, and to surround themselves with such luxuries as the life of the Islands permitted. This class was rapidly gaining education. It acquired a knowledge of the Spanish language, and easily assumed that graceful courtesy which distinguishes the Spaniard.

The only misfortune, as regards this class, was that it was very small. It could embrace but a few families in each populous town. Some of these had Chinese and Spanish blood in their veins, but other notable families were pure Filipinos.

Attitude of the Spanish and the Friars toward Filipino Education. — The great mistake committed by the Spaniard was that he rarely welcomed the further progress of the native population, and the center of this opposition to the general enlightenment of the race was the friars. Thus those who had been the early protectors and educators, little by little, because of their extreme conservatism and their fear of loosening the ties that bound the Filipino to the church and to Spain, changed into opponents of his progress and enemies of his enlightenment;

but the education which the church itself had given to
the Filipino, and which had been fostered by the state
and especially in recent times by the Jesuits, had made
the Filipino passionately ambitious for more enlightenment and freedom.

The Rule of Governor Torre. — *Liberal Reforms.* — In
1868, Queen Isabella II. of Spain was deposed, and a little
later a revolutionary government, the "Republic of Spain,"
was founded. It was the brief triumph of that reforming
and liberal spirit which for so many years had been strug-
gling to free Spain from the burdens of aristocracy and
ecclesiasticism.

The natural consequence was the sending of a liberal
governor to the Philippines and the publication of liberal
principles and reforms. This governor was General de
la Torre. He was a brave and experienced soldier and
a thorough democrat at heart. He dispensed with the
formality and petty pomp with which the governors of
Manila had surrounded themselves; he dismissed the
escort of halberdiers, with their mediæval uniforms and
weapons, which had surrounded the governor-generals
since 1581, and rode out in civilian's clothes and without
ostentation. His efforts were directed to encouraging
the Filipinos and to attaching them to Spain. In the
eyes of the Spanish law, for a brief period, Spaniard and
colonists had become equal, and La Torre tried to enforce
this principle and make no distinction of race or birth.
While Filipinos were encouraged and delighted, it is impossible to describe the disgust of the Spanish population
and the opposition of the friars. La Torre was attacked
and opposed, and the entire course of his governorship
was filled with trouble, in which, naturally, liberal ideas
gained wider and wider currency among the Filipinos.

Effect of the Opposition of the Friars. — The friars, being the most influential opponents of the Filipino, naturally came to be regarded by the Filipinos as their greatest enemies, and the anti-friar spirit daily spread and intensified. A party was formed which demanded that the friars vacate the parishes, and that their places be filled by secular priests, in accordance with the statutes of the Council of Trent. This party was headed by a native priest, Dr. José Burgos.

A Filipino Movement for Reform. — After the fall of the republic in Spain and the restoration of the monarchy, the administration in the Philippines attempted to extirpate the rising tide of liberal thought; but these ideas had taken root and could not be suppressed. The Filipino party, if so we may call it, continued to plan and work for reform. It numbered not only those of Filipino blood, but many of Spanish descent, born in the Philippines. There is no certain evidence that they were at this time plotting for independence, or that their actions were treasonable; but the fear and hatred felt by the Spaniards resulted frequently in the exile and punishment of known advocates of reform.

The Cavite Revolt. — In 1872 there occurred an important outbreak known as the Cavite Revolt. Two hundred native soldiers at the Cavite arsenal rose, killed their officers, and shouted "Death to Spain!" They had fellow-conspirators among the troops in Manila, but owing to mistakes in their plans these failed to rise with them and the revolt was easily suppressed.

It was immediately followed by the arrest of a large number of Filipinos who had been conspicuous in La Torre's time and who were advocates of reform. This number included the three priests, Fathers Burgos, Zamora, and Gomez, besides Don Antonio Regidor, Don Joaquin Pardo de Tavera, Don Pedro Carillo, and others. A council of war condemned to death forty-one of the participants in the Cavite riot, and these were shot on the morning of the 27th of January, 1872, on the Field of Bagumbayan. On the 6th of February a council of war condemned to death eleven more soldiers of the regiment of artillery, but this sentence was commuted by the governor to life imprisonment. On the 15th of February the same council of war sentenced to death upon the garrote, the priests Burgos, Zamora, Gomez, and a countryman, Saldua; and this sentence was executed on the morning of the 17th.

The Spread of Secret Organizations. — *Masonry.* — New ground for fear was now found in the spread of secret organizations, which were denounced as Free Masonry. This is a very ancient institution which, in Protestant countries like England and America, has a very large membership, and in these countries its aims are wholly respectable. It has never in any way been connected with sedition or other unworthy movements. Its services are, in fact, largely of a religious character and it possesses a beautiful and elaborate Christian ritual; but in Latin countries Masonry has been charged with political intrigue and the encouragement of infidelity, and this has resulted in clerical opposition to the order wherever found. The first Masonic lodge in the Philippines was estabilshed about 1861 and was composed entirely of Spaniards. It was succeeded by others with Filipino membership, and in one way or another seems to have inspired many secret organizations.

The "Liga Filipina" and Dr. Rizal. — Large numbers of Filipinos were now working, if not for independence, at least for the expulsion of the friars; and while this feeling should have been met by a statesmanlike and liberal policy of reform, the government constantly resorted to measures of repression, which little by little changed the movement for reformation into revolution.

In 1887 the "Liga Filipina" was formed by a number of the younger Filipino patriots, chief among whom was Dr. José Rizal y Mercado. Rizal, by his gifts, his noble character, and his sad fate, has gained a supreme place in the hearts of Filipinos and in the history of the Islands. He was born in 1861 at Calamba, on Laguna de Bay, and even as a child he was affected with sadness at the memory of the events of 1872 and with the backward and unhappy condition of his countrymen. He was educated by the Jesuits at the Ateneo Municipal in Manila, and his family having means, he was enabled to study in Spain, where he took a degree in medicine, and later to travel and study in France, England, and Germany.

Dr. Rizal.

It was in this latter country that he produced his first novel, *Noli Me Tangere*. He had been a contributor to the Filipino paper published in Spain, "La Solidaridad," and, to further bring the conditions and needs of his country to more public notice, he wrote this novel dealing with Tagálog life as represented at his old home on Laguna de Bay and in the city of Manila. Later he published a sequel, *El Filibusterismo*, in which even more courageously and significantly are set forth his ideas for reform.

His work made him many enemies, and on his return to Manila he found himself in danger and was obliged to leave. He returned again in 1893, and was immediately arrested and sentenced to deportation to Dapitan, Mindanao. Here he remained quietly in the practice of his profession for some years.

The Katipunan.—Meanwhile the ideas which had been agitated by the wealthy and educated Filipinos had worked their way down to the poor and humble classes. They were now shared by the peasant and the fisherman. Especially in those provinces where the religious orders owned estates and took as rental a portion of the tenants' crop, there was growing hatred and hostility to the friars. The "Liga Filipina" had been composed of cultivated and moderate men, who while pressing for reform were not inclined to radical extremes, nor to obtain their ends by violent means.

But there now grew up and gradually spread, until it had its branches and members in all the provinces surrounding Manila, a secret association composed largely of the uneducated classes, whose object was independence of Spain, and whose members, having little to lose, were willing to risk all. This was the society which has since become famous under the name of "Katipunan." This secret association was organized in Cavite about 1892. Its president and founder was Andres Bonifacio. Its objects were frankly to expel the friars, and, if possible, to destroy the Spanish government.

Rebellion of 1896. — A general attack and slaughter of the Spaniards was planned for the 20th of August, 1896. The plot was discovered by the priest of Binondo, Padre Gil, who learned of the movement through the wife of one of the conspirators, and within a few hours the government had seized several hundred persons who were supposed to be implicated. The arrests included many rich and prominent Filipinos, and at the end of some weeks the Spanish prisons contained over five thousand suspects. Over one thousand of these were almost immediately exiled to far-distant Spanish prisons — Fernando Po, on the west coast of Africa, and the fortress of Ceuta, on the Mediterranean.

Meanwhile the Katipunan was organizing its forces for struggle. On the 26th of August, one thousand insurgents attacked Caloocan, and four days later a pitched battle was fought at San Juan del Monte. In this last fight the insurgents suffered great loss, their leader, Valenzuela, was captured and, with three companions, shot on the Campo de Bagumbayan. The rising continued, however, and the provinces of Pampanga, Bulacan, and Nueva Ecija were soon in full rebellion. The center of revolt, however, proved to be Cavite. This province was almost immediately cleared of Spaniards, except the long neck of land containing the town of Cavite and protected by the fleet. Here the insurgents received some organization under a young man, who had been prominent in the Katipunan — Emilio Aguinaldo.

The governor-general, Blanco, a humane man, who afterwards for a short time commanded in Cuba, was recalled, and General Polavieja replaced him. The Spanish army at the beginning of the revolt had consisted of but fifteen hundred troops, but so serious was the revolt regarded

that Spain, although straining every energy at the moment to end the rebellion in Cuba, strengthened the
forces in the Philippines, until Polavieja had an army of
twenty-eight thousand Spaniards assisted by several loyal
Filipino regiments.
With this army a
fierce campaign in
C a v i t e province
was conducted,
which after fifty-
two days' hard
fighting ended in
the defeat of the
insurgents and the
scattering of their
forces.

Emilio Aguinaldo.

*Death of Dr.
Rizal.* — For the
moment it looked
as though the re-
bellion might pass.
Then the Spanish
government of Po-
lavieja disgraced
itself by an act as
wanton and cruel
as it was inhuman
and impolitic.

Four years Dr. Rizal had spent in exile at Dapitan. He
had lived quietly and under surveillance, and it was impossible that he could have had any share in this rebellion
of 1898. Wearied, however, with his inactivity, he so-
licited permission to go as an army doctor to the dreadful

Spanish hospitals in Cuba. This request was granted in July, and Rizal had the misfortune to arrive in Manila at the very moment of discovery of the rebellion in August. Governor Blanco hastened to send him to Spain with a most kindly letter to the minister of war, in which he vouched for his independence of the events which were taking place in Manila.

His enemies, however, could not see him escape. Their persecution followed him to the Peninsula, and, upon his arrival in Spain, Rizal was at once arrested and sent back to Manila a prisoner. His friend Blanco had gone. Polavieja, the friend and tool of the reactionary party, was busy punishing by imprisonment, banishment or death all Filipinos who could be shown to have the slightest part or association in the movement for reform. And by this clique Dr. Rizal was sentenced to execution. He was shot early on the morning of December 30, 1896.[1] At his death the insurrection flamed out afresh. It now spread to Pangasinan, Zambales, and Ilocos.

End of the Revolt by Promises of Reform. — Polavieja returned to Spain, and was succeeded by Gen. Primo de Rivera, who arrived in the spring of 1897. The Spanish troops had suffered several recent reverses and the country swarmed with insurgents. The policy of Primo de Rivera was to gain by diplomacy where the energy of his predecessor had failed. In July, 1897, an amnesty proclamation was issued, and in August the governor-general opened negotiations with Aguinaldo, whose headquarters were now in the mountains of Angat in Bulacan. Primo de Rivera urged the home govern-

---

[1] An account of Rizal's trial and execution, together with many papers on the revolution, is printed by Retana. See *Archivo, Tomo IV. Documentos politicos de Actualidad.*

ment to make some reforms, which would greatly lessen the political importance of the friars. He was vehemently opposed by the latter, but it was probably upon the promise of reform that Aguinaldo and his fellow-insurgents agreed, for the payment of 1,700,000 pesos, to surrender their arms, dismiss the insurgent forces, and themselves retire from the Islands. This agreement was made, and on December 27, 1897, Aguinaldo left the port of Sual for Hongkong.

The Spanish Misrule Ended. — Conditions in the provinces still continued very unsatisfactory, and in its very last hours the Spanish government lost the remnant of its prestige with the people by a massacre in Calle Camba, Binondo, of a company of Bisayan sailors. Ten days after this occurrence a revolt blazed out on the island of Cebu. Had events taken their course, what would have been the final conclusion of the struggle between Spaniards and Filipinos it is impossible to say. On the 25th day of April the United States declared war upon Spain, and the first day of May an American fleet reached Manila harbor, and in the naval fight off Cavite, Spanish dominion, which had lasted with only one brief interruption for 332 years, was broken.

CHAPTER XIII.

AMERICA AND THE PHILIPPINES.

Beginning of a New Era. — With the passing of the Spanish sovereignty to the Americans, a new era began in the Philippines. Already the old Spanish rule seems so far removed that we can begin to think of it without feeling and study it without prejudice.

Development of the United States of America. — The American nation is the type of the New World. Beginning in a group of colonies, planted half a century later than the settlement of the Philippines, it has had a development unparalleled in the history of states. Although peopled by emigrants from Europe, who rigidly preserved both their purity of race and pride of ancestry, the American colonists, at the end of a century, were far separated in spirit and institutions from the Old World.

Struggle with the wilderness and with the savage produced among them a society more democratic and more independent than Europe had ever known; while their profound religious convictions saved the colonists from barbarism and intellectual decline. It can truthfully be held, that in 1775, at the outbreak of the American Revolution, the colonists had abler men and greater political ability than the mother-country of England. It was these men who, at the close of the Revolution, framed the American Constitution, the greatest achievement in the history of public law. This nation, endowed at its commencement with so precious an inheritance of political genius, felt its civil superiority to the illiberal or ineffective governments of Europe, and this feeling has

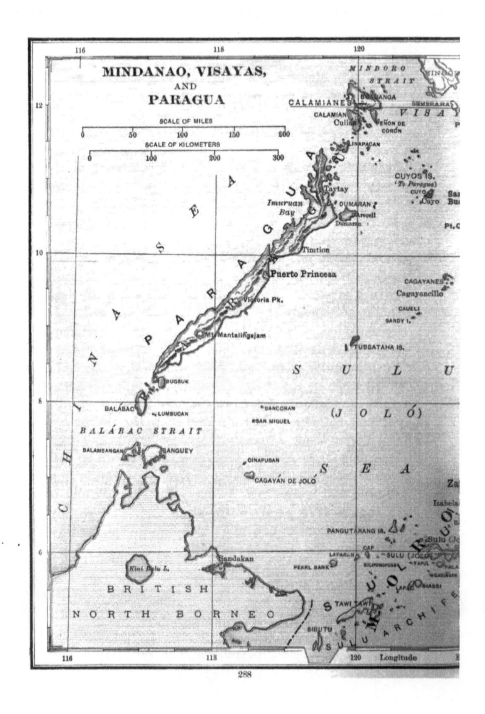

MINDANAO, VISAYAS,
AND
PARAGUA

SCALE OF MILES

0   50   100   150   200

SCALE OF KILOMETERS

0   100   200   300

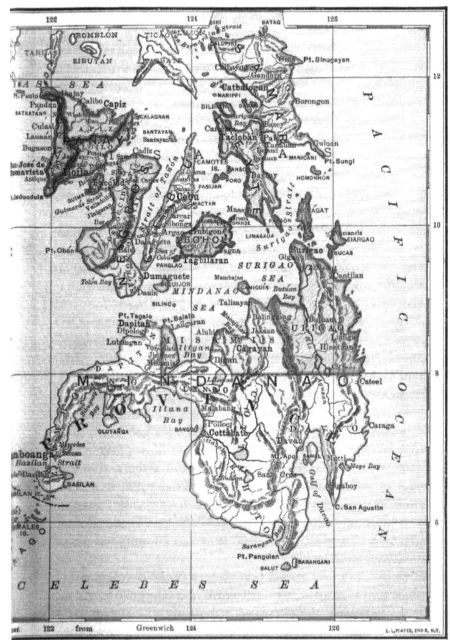

produced in Americans a supreme and traditional confidence in their own forms of government and democratic standards of life. Certainly their history contains much to justify the choice of their institutions.

A hundred and twenty-five years ago, these colonies were a small nation of 2,500,000 people, occupying no more than the Atlantic coast of the continent. Great mountain chains divided them from the interior, which was overrun by the fiercest and most warlike type of man that the races have produced — the American Indian. With an energy which has shown no diminishing from generation to generation, the American broke through these mountain chains, subdued the wilderness, conquered the Indian tribes, and in the space of three generations was master of the continent of North America.

Even while engaged in the War for Independence, the American frontiersman crossed the Appalachians and secured Kentucky and the Northwest Territory, and with them the richest and most productive regions of the Temperate Zone, — the Mississippi Valley. In 1803, the great empire of Louisiana, falling from the hand of France, was added to the American nation. In 1818, Florida was ceded by Spain, and in 1857, as a result of war with Mexico, came the Greater West and the Pacific seaboard. This vast dominion, nearly three thousand miles in width from east to west, has been peopled by natural increase and by immigration from Europe, until, at the end of the nineteenth century, the American nation numbered seventy-four million souls.

This development has taken place without fundamental change in the constitution or form of government, without loss of individual liberty, and constantly increasing national prosperity. Moreover, the States have survived the

Civil War, the most bloody and persistently fought war of all modern centuries — a war in which a million soldiers fell, and to sustain which three and a half billion dollars in gold were expended out of the national treasury. This war accomplished the abolition of negro slavery, the greatest economic revolution ever effected by a single blow.

Such in brief is the history of the American nation, so gifted with political intelligence, so driven by sleepless energy, so proud of its achievements, and inwardly so contemptuous of the more polished but less liberal life of the Old World. Europe has never understood this nation, and not until a few years ago did Europeans dream of its progress and its power.

Relation of the United States to South American Republics. —Toward the republics of Spanish America the United States has always stood in a peculiar relation. These countries achieved their independence of Spain under the inspiration of the success of the United States. Their governments were framed in imitation of the American, and in spite of the turbulence and disorder of their political life, the United States has always felt and manifested a strong sympathy for these states as fellow-republics. She has moreover pledged herself to the maintenance of their integrity against the attacks of European powers. This position of the United States in threatening with resistance the attempt of any European power to seize American territory is known as the Monroe Doctrine, because it was first declared by President Monroe in 1823.

Sympathy of American People for the Oppressed Cubans. — The fact that the American nation attained its own independence by revolution has made the American people give ready sympathy to the cause of the revolutionist.

The people of Cuba, who made repeated ineffective struggles against Spanish sovereignty, always had the good wishes of the American people. By international usage, however, one nation may not recognize or assist revolutionists against a friendly power until their independence is practically effected.

Thus, when rebellion broke out afresh in Cuba in 1894, the United States government actively suppressed the lending of assistance to the Cubans, as was its duty, although the American people themselves heartily wished Cuba free. The war in Cuba dragged along for years and became more and more merciless. The passions of Cubans and Spaniards were so inflamed that quarter was seldom given, and prisoners were not spared. Spain poured her troops into the island until there were 120,000 on Cuban soil, but the rebellion continued.

The Spanish have always been merciless in dealing with revolutionists. Americans, on the other hand, have always conceded the moral right of a people to resist oppressive government, and in the entire history of the United States there has scarcely been a single punishment for political crime. Although probably the fiercest war in history was the American Civil War from 1861 to 1865, there was not a single execution for treason. Thus the stories of the constant executions of political prisoners, on an island in sight of its own shores, greatly exasperated America, as did the policy of Governor-general Weyler, which was excessive in its severity.

War with Spain. — *Destruction of the "Maine."* — As the contest proceeded without sign of termination, the patience of the American people grew less. Then, February 15, 1898, occurred one of the most deplorable events of recent times. The American battleship "Maine," lying in the harbor of Havana, was, in the night, blown to destruction by mine or torpedo, killing 266 American officers and sailors. It is impossible to believe that so dastardly an act was done with the knowledge of the higher Spanish officials; but the American people rightly demanded that a government such as Spain maintained in Cuba, unable to prevent such an outrage upon the vessel of a friendly power, and that could neither suppress its rebellion nor wage war humanely, should cease.

Declaration of War. — On April 19th the American Congress demanded that Spain withdraw from the island and recognize the independence of Cuba. This was practically a declaration of war. Spain indignantly refused, and resolved upon resistance. Unfortunately, the ignorant European press claimed for Spain military and naval superiority.

The war was brief, and was an overwhelming disaster to Spain. Every vessel of her proud navy that came under the fire of American guns was destroyed.

For a few months battle raged along the coasts of Cuba, and then Spain sued for peace.

Dewey's Victory in Manila Bay. — But meanwhile the war, begun without the slightest reference to the Philippine Islands, had brought about surprising consequences here.

At the opening of the war, both Spain and the United States had squadrons in Asiatic waters. The Spanish fleet lay at Cavite, the American ships gathered at Hongkong. Immediately on the declaration of war, the American naval commander, Dewey, was ordered to destroy the Spanish fleet, which was feared on the Pacific coast of America. Dewey entered the Bay of Manila in darkness on the morning of May 1st, and made direct for the

Spanish vessels at Cavite. His fleet was the more powerful and immeasurably the more efficient. In a few hours
the Spanish navy was utterly destroyed and Manila lay
at the mercy of his guns.

A New Insurrection under Aguinaldo. — At this signal catastrophe to Spain, the smoldering insurrection in
the Islands broke out afresh. The Spanish troops not in
Manila were driven in upon their posts, and placed in a
position of siege. The friars, so hated by the revolutionists, were captured in large numbers and were in some
cases killed. With the permission and assistance of the
American authorities, Aguinaldo returned from Singapore,
and landed at Cavite. Here he immediately headed anew
the Philippine insurrection.

Capture of Manila. — Troops were dispatched from
San Francisco for the capture of Manila. By the end of
July, 8,500 men lay in the transports off Cavite. They
were landed at the little estuary of Parañaque, and advanced northwards upon Fort San Antonio and the defenses of Malate. The Spaniards behind the city's defenses,
although outnumbering the Americans, were sick and
dispirited. One attempt was made to drive back the
invading army, but on the following day the Americans
swept through the defenses and line of blockhouses, and
Manila capitulated (August 13, 1898).

The Filipinos had scarcely participated in the attack
on the city, and they were excluded from occupying it
after its surrender. This act was justified, because the
Filipino forces had been very recently raised, the soldiers were undisciplined, and had they entered the city,
with passions as they were inflamed, it was feared by the
Americans that their officers might not be able to keep
them from looting and crime.

Misunderstanding between Americans and Filipinos. —
Up to this point, the relations between the American and
Filipino armies had been friendly. But here began that
misunderstanding and distrust which for so many months
were to alienate these two peoples and imbitter their
intercourse.

Provisional Government of the Filipinos. — In the
interval between the destruction of the Spanish fleet and
the capture of Manila, the Filipinos in Cavite had organized a provisional government and proclaimed the independence of the archipelago.

American Ideas in Regard to the Philippines. — The
idea of returning these islands to the Spanish power was
exceedingly repugnant to American sentiment. Spain's
attitude toward revolutionists was well understood in
America, and the Filipinos had acted as America's friends
and allies. On the other hand, the American government
was unwilling to turn over to the newly organized Filipino
republic the government of the archipelago. It was felt
in America, and with reason, that this Filipino government was not truly representative of all the people in the
Philippines, that the Filipino leaders were untried men,
and that the people themselves had not had political
training and experience. The United States, having overthrown the Spanish government here, was under obligation to see that the government established in its place
would represent all and do injustice to none. The Filipinos were very slightly known to Americans, but their
educated class was believed to be small and their political
ability unproven. Thus, no assurances were given to the
Filipino leaders that their government would be recognized,
or that their wishes would be consulted in the future of
the Islands. In fact, these matters could be settled only

by action of the American Congress, which was late in assembling and slow to act.

The Terms of Peace. — Spain and America were now negotiating terms of peace. These negotiations were conducted at Paris, and dragged on during many critical weeks. The Filipinos were naturally very much concerned over the outcome.

General Luna.

Finally, the American government demanded of Spain that she cede the Islands to the United States and accept the sum of $20,000,000 gold, for public works and improvements which she had made.

Suspicions of the Filipino Leaders. — These terms became known in December, 1898. They served to awaken the worst suspicions of the Filipino leaders. Many believed that they were about to exchange the oppressive domination of Spain for the selfish and equally oppressive domination of America. There is reason to believe that some leaders counseled patience, and during the succeeding months made a constant effort to maintain the peace, but the radical party among the Filipinos was led by a man of real gifts and fiery disposition, Antonio Luna. He had received an education in Europe, had had some instruction in military affairs, and when in September the Filipino government was transferred to Malolos, Luna became the general in chief of the military forces. He was also editor of the most radical Filipino newspaper, "La Independencia."

Apolinario Mabini.

New Filipino Government. — On January 4, 1899, President McKinley issued a special message to General Otis, commanding the armies of the United States in the Philippines, declaring that American sovereignty must be recognized without conditions. It was thought in the United States that a firm declaration of this kind would be accepted by the Filipinos and that they would not dare to make resistance. The intentions of the American president and nation, as subsequent events have proven, were to deal with the Filipinos with great liberality; but the president's professions were not trusted by the Filipinos, and the result of Mr. McKinley's message was to move them at once to frame an independent government and to decide on war.

This new government was framed at Malolos, Bulacan, by a congress with representatives from most of the provinces of central Luzon. The "Malolos Constitution" was proclaimed January 23, 1899, and Don Emilio Aguinaldo was elected president. The cabinet, or ministry, included Don Apolinario Mabini, secretary of state ; Don Teodoro Sandico, secretary of interior ; General Baldomero Aguinaldo, secretary of war; General Mariano Trias, secretary of treasury ; Don Engracio Gonzaga, secretary of public instruction and agriculture.

War with the Americans. — *Battle of Manila.* — The Filipino forces were impatient for fighting, and attack on the American lines surrounding Manila began on the night of February 4th. It is certain that battle had been decided upon and in preparation for some time, and that fighting would have been begun in any case, before the arrival of reënforcements from America; but the attack was precipitated a little early by the killing at San Juan Bridge of a Filipino officer who refused to halt when challenged by an American sentry. On that memorable and dreadful night, the battle raged with great fury along the entire circle of defenses surrounding the city, from Tondo on the north to Fort San Antonio de Abad, south of the suburb of Malate. Along three main avenues from the north, east, and south the Filipinos attempted to storm and enter the capital, but although they charged with reckless bravery, and for hours sustained a bloody combat, they had fatally underestimated the fighting qualities of the American soldier.

The volunteer regiments of the American army came almost entirely from the western United States, where young men are naturally trained to the use of arms, and are imbued by inheritance with the powerful and aggressive qualities of the American frontier. When morning broke, the Filipino line of attack had, at every point, been shattered and thrown back, and the Americans had advanced their positions on the north to Caloocan, on the east to the Water Works and the Mariquina Valley, and on the south to Pasay.

Declaration of War. — Unfortunately, during the night attack and before the disaster to Filipino arms was apparent, Aguinaldo had launched against the United States a declaration of war. This declaration prevented the Americans from trusting the Filipino overtures which followed this battle, and peace was not made.

The Malolos Campaign. — On March 25th began the American advance upon the Filipino capital of Malolos. This Malolos campaign, as it is usually called, occupied six days, and ended in the driving of the Filipino army and government from their capital. Hard fighting took place in the first days of this advance, and two extremely worthy American officers were killed, Colonels Egbert and Stotsenberg.

The Filipino army was pursued in its retreat as far as Calumpit, where on the southern bank of the Rio Grande de Pampanga the American line rested during the height of the rainy season. During this interval the volunteer regiments, whose terms of service had long expired, were returned to the States, and their places taken by regiments of the regular army.

The American Army. — The American army at that time, besides the artillery, consisted of twenty-five regiments of infantry and ten of cavalry. Congress now authorized the organization of twenty-four new regiments of infantry, to be known as the 26th to the 49th Regiments of U. S. Volunteers, and one volunteer regiment of cavalry, the 11th, for a service of two years. These regiments were largely officered by men from civil life, familiar with a great variety of callings and professions, — men for the most part of fine character, whose services in the months that followed were very great not only in the field, but in gaining the friendship of the Filipino people and in representing the character and intentions of the American government.

Anti-War Agitators in America. — Through the summer of 1899 the war was not pressed by the American general, nor were the negotiations with the Filipino leaders conducted with success. The Filipinos were by no means dismayed. In spite of their reverses, they believed the conquest of the Islands impossible to foreign troops. Furthermore, the war had met with tremendous opposition in America. Many Americans believed that the war was against the fundamental rights of the Filipino people. They attacked the administration with unspeakable bitterness. They openly expressed sympathy for the Filipino revolutionary cause, and for the space of two years their encouragement was an important factor in sustaining the rebellion.

Spread of the Insurrection. — In these same summer months the revolutionary leaders spread their cause among the surrounding provinces and islands. The spirit of resistance was prominent at first only among the Tagálog, but gradually nearly all the Christianized population was united in resistance to the American occupation.

Occupation of Negros. — The Americans had meanwhile occupied Iloilo and the Bisayas, and shortly afterwards the presidios in Mindanao surrendered by the Spaniards. In Negros, also, exceptional circumstances had transpired. The people in this island invited American sovereignty; and Gen. James Smith, sent to the island in March as governor, assisted the people in forming a liberal government, through which insurrection and disorder in that island were largely avoided.

Death of General Luna. — With the cessation of heavy rains, the fighting was begun again in northern Luzon. The Filipino army had its headquarters in Tarlac, and its lines occupied the towns of the provinces of Pangasinan and Nueva Ecija, stretching in a long line of posts from the Zambales Mountains almost to the upper waters of the Rio Pampanga. It was still well armed, provisioned, and resolute; but the brilliant, though wayward, organizer of this army was dead. The Nationalist junta, which had directed the Philippine government and army, had not been able to reconcile its differences. It is reported that Luna aspired to a dictatorship. He was killed by soldiers of Aguinaldo at Cabanatuan.

The Campaign in Northern Luzon. — The American generals now determined upon a strategic campaign. General MacArthur was to command an advance up the railroad from Calumpit upon Tarlac; General Lawton, with a flying column of swift infantry and cavalry, was to make a flanking movement eastward through Nueva Ecija and hem the Filipino forces in upon the east. Meanwhile, General Wheaton was to convey a force by transport to the Gulf of Lingayen, to throw a cordon across the Ilocano coast that should cut off the retreat of the Filipino army northward. As a strategic movement, this

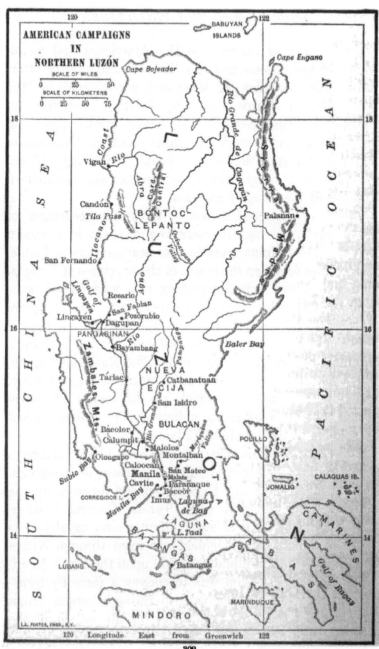

AMERICAN CAMPAIGNS
IN
NORTHERN LUZÓN

SCALE OF MILES
0   25   50

SCALE OF KILOMETERS
0   25   50   75

BABUYAN
ISLANDS

Cape Engaño

Cape Bojeador

S O U T H   C H I N A   S E A

Vigan

Candón

Tila Pass

San Fernando

Rosario
San Fabian
Pozorubio
Lingayen
Dagupan

PANGASINAN

Bayambang

Tárlac

BONTOC
LEPANTO

L U Z O N

Palanan

NUEVA
ECIJA

Catbanatuan

San Isidro

BULACAN

Bacolor
Calumpit
Olongapo
Caloocan
Manila
Cavite
Bacoor
Imus

Malolos
Montalban
San Mateo
Malate
Parañaque

Laguna
de Bay

LAGUNA
L. Taal

BATANGAS
Batangas

LÚBANG

MINDORO

Baler Bay

POLILLO

JOMALIG

CALAGUAS IS.

CAMARINES

Gulf of Ragay

MARINDUQUE

P A C I F I C   O C E A N

CORREGIDOR I.

Manila Bay

Subic Bay

Zambales Mts.

Gulf of Lingayen

Rio Grande de Cagayán

120   Longitude   East   from   Greenwich   122

302

campaign was only partially successful. MacArthur swept northward, crushing the Filipino line on his front, his advance being led by the active regiment of General J. Franklin Bell. Lawton's column scoured the country eastward, marching with great rapidity and tremendous exertions. Swollen rivers were crossed with great loss of life, and the column, cutting loose from its supplies, was frequently in need of food. It was in this column that the Filipino first saw with amazement the great American cavalry horse, so large beside the small pony of the Philippines. Lawton's descent was so swift that the Philippine government and staff narrowly escaped capture.

On the night of November 11th, the Filipino generals held their last council of war at Bayambang on the Rio Agno, and resolved upon dispersal. Meanwhile, Wheaton had landed at San Fabian, upon the southern Ilocano coast, but his force was insufficient to establish an effective cordon, and on the night of November 15th Aguinaldo, with a small party of ministers and officers, closely pursued by the cavalry of Lawton under the command of General Young, slipped past, through the mountains of Pozorubio and Rosario, and escaped up the Ilocano coast.

Then began one of the most exciting pursuits in recent wars. The chase never slackened, except in those repeated instances when for the moment the trail of the Filipino general was lost. From Candon, Aguinaldo turned eastward through the comandancias of Lepanto and Bontoc, into the wild Igorrote country of the Cordillera Central. The trail into Lepanto leads over the lofty mountains through the precipitous Tila Pass. On the summit, in what was regarded as an impregnable position, Gregorio del Pilar, little more than a boy, but a brigadier-general, with a small force of soldiers, the remnant of his command, attempted to cover the retreat of his president. But a battalion of the 33d Infantry, under Major March, carried the pass, with the total destruction of Pilar's command, he himself falling amid the slain.

General Pilar.

Capture of Aguinaldo.— Major March then pursued Aguinaldo into Bontoc and thence southward into the wild and mountainous territory of Quiangan. On Christmas night, 1899, the American soldiers camped on the crest of the Cordillera, within a few miles of the Igorrote village where the Filipino force was sleeping. Both parties were broken down and in dire distress through the fierceness of the flight and pursuit, but for several weeks longer Aguinaldo's party was able to remain in these mountains and elude its pursuers. A month later, his trail was finally lost in the valley of the Cagayan. He and his small party had passed over the exceedingly difficult trail through the

Sierra Madre Mountains, to the little Tagálog town of Palanan near the Pacific coast. Here, almost entirely cut off from active participation in the insurrection, Aguinaldo remained until June of 1901, when he was captured by the party of General Funston.

For some weeks following the disintegration of the Filipino army, the country appeared to be pacified and the insurrection over. The new regiments arriving from the United States, an expedition was formed under General Schwan, which in December and January marched southward through Cavite and Laguna provinces and occupied Batangas, Tayabas, and the Camarines. Other regiments were sent to the Bisayas and to northern Luzon, until every portion of the archipelago, except the islands of Mindoro and Palawan, contained large forces of American troops.

Reorganization of the Filipino Army. — The Filipinos had, by no means, however, abandoned the contest, and this period of quiet was simply a calm while the insurgent forces were perfecting their organization and preparing for a renewal of the conflict under a different form. It being found impossible for a Filipino army to keep the field, there was effected a secret organization for the purpose of maintaining irregular warfare through every portion of the archipelago. The Islands were partitioned into a great number of districts or " zones." At the head of each was a zone commander, usually with the rank of general. The operations of these men were, to a certain extent, guided by the counsel or directions of the secret revolutionary juntas in Manila or Hongkong, but, in fact, they were practically absolute and independent, and they exercised extraordinary powers. They recruited their own forces and commissioned subordinate com-

manders. They levied "contributions" upon towns, own-
ers of haciendas, and individuals of every class, and there
was a secret civil or municipal organization for collecting
these revenues. The zone commanders, moreover, exercised the terrible power of execution by administrative
order.

Assassination of Filipinos. — Many of the Filipino
leaders were necessarily not well instructed in those
rules for the conduct of warfare which civilized peoples
have agreed upon as being humane and honorable. Many
of them tried, especially in the latter months of the war,
when understanding was more widely diffused, to make
their conduct conform to international usage; but the
revolutionary junta had committed the great crime of
ordering the punishment by assassination of all Filipinos
who failed to support the insurgent cause. No possible
justification, in the light of modern morality, can be found
for such a step as this. The very worst passions were
let loose in carrying out this policy. Scores of unfortunate men were assassinated, many of them as the results
of private enmity. Endless blackmail was extorted and
communities were terrorized from one end of the archipelago to the other.

Irregular Warfare of the Filipinos. — Through the
surrender of Spanish forces, the capture of the arsenals
of Cavite and Olongapo, and by purchase through Hongkong, the revolutionary government possessed between
thirty thousand and forty thousand rifles. These arms
were distributed to the different military zones, and the
secret organization which existed in each municipality
received its proportion. These guns were secreted by the
different members of the command, except when occasion
arose for effecting a surprise or making an attack. There

were no general engagements, but in some towns there was almost nightly shooting. Pickets and small detachments were cut off, and roads became so unsafe throughout most of the archipelago that there was no travel by Americans except under heavy escort. For a long time, also, the orders of the commanding general were so lenient that it was impossible to punish properly this conduct when it was discovered.

Death of General Lawton. — The American army, in its attempt to garrison every important town in the Islands, was cut up into as many as 550 small detachments of post garrisons. Thus, while there were eventually sixty thousand American soldiers in the Islands, it was rare for as many as five hundred to take the field, and most of the engagements of the year 1900 were by small detachments of fifty to one hundred men.

It was in one of these small expeditions that the American army suffered the greatest single loss of the war. A few miles east of Manila is the beautiful Mariquina Valley, from which is derived the city's supply of water, and the headwaters of this pretty stream lie in the wild and picturesque fastness of San Mateo and Montalban. Although scarce a dozen miles from the capital and the headquarters of a Filipino brigade, San Mateo was not permanently occupied by the Americans until after the 18th of December, 1899, when a force under General Lawton was led around through the hills to surprise the town.

Early in the morning the American force came pouring down over the hills that lie across the river from the village. They were met by a brisk fire from the insurgent command scattered along the banks of the river and in a sugar hacienda close to the stream. Here Lawton, conspicuous in white uniform and helmet, accompanying, as was his custom, the front line of skirmishers, was struck by a bullet and instantly killed.

Filipino Leaders Sent to Guam. — In November, 1900, after the reëlection in the United States of President McKinley, a much more vigorous policy of war was inaugurated. In this month General MacArthur, commanding the division, issued a notable general order, defining and explaining the laws of war which were being violated, and threatening punishment by imprisonment of those guilty of such conduct. Some thousands of Filipinos under this order were arrested and imprisoned. Thirty-nine leaders, among them the high-minded but irreconcilable Mabini, were in December, 1900, sent to a military prison on the island of Guam.

Campaigning was much more vigorously prosecuted in all military districts. By this time all the American officers had become familiar with the insurgent leaders, and these were now obliged to leave the towns and establish cuartels in remote barrios and in the mountains.

These measures, pursued through the winter of 1900–01, broke the power of the revolution.

The Philippine Civil Commission. — Another very influential factor in producing peace resulted from the presence and labors of the Civil Philippine Commission. These gentlemen, Judge William H. Taft, Judge Luke E. Wright, Judge Henry C. Ide, Professor Dean C. Worcester, and Professor Bernard Moses, were appointed by the president in the spring of 1900 to legislate for the Islands and to prepare the way for the establishment of civil government. President McKinley's letter of instructions to this commission will probably be ranked as one of the ablest and most notable public papers in American history.

The commission reached the Islands in June and began

their legislative work on September 1st. This body of men, remarkable for their high character, was able at last to bring about an understanding with the Filipino leaders and to assure them of the unselfish and honorable purposes of the American government. Thus, by the early winter of 1900–01 many Filipino gentlemen became convinced that the best interests of the Islands lay in accepting American sovereignty, and that they could honorably advocate the surrender of the insurgent forces. These men represented the highest attainments and most influential positions in the Islands. In December they formed an association known as the Federal Party, for the purpose of inducing the surrender of military leaders, obedience to the American government, and the acceptance of peace.

Governor Taft.

End of the Insurrection. — Under these influences, the insurrection, in the spring of 1901, went rapidly to pieces. Leader after leader surrendered his forces and arms, and took the oath of allegiance and quietly returned home. By the end of June there were but two zone commanders who had not surrendered, — General Malvar in Batangas, and General Lukban in Samar.

The First Civil Governor. — Peaceful conditions and security almost immediately followed these surrenders and determined the president to establish at once civil government. On July 4, 1901, this important step was taken, Judge Taft, the president of the Philippine Commission, taking office on that date as the first American civil governor of the Philippines. On September 1st, the Philippine Commission was increased by the appointment of three Filipino members, — the Hon. T. H. Pardo de Tavera, M. D., the Hon. Benito Legarda, and.the Hon. José Luzuriaga of Negros.

The Philippine Commission has achieved a remarkable amount of legislation of a very high order. From September, 1900, to the end of December, 1902, the commission passed no less than 571 acts of legislation. Some of these were of very great importance and involved long preparation and labor. Few administrative bodies have ever worked harder and with greater results than the Philippine Commission during the first two years of its activity. The frame of government in all its branches had to be organized and set in motion, the civil and criminal law liberalized, revenue provided, and public instruction remodeled on a very extensive scale.

The New Government. — The government is a very liberal one, and one which gives an increasing opportunity for participation to the Filipinos. It includes what is called local self-government. There are in the Islands about 1,132 municipalities. In these the residents practically manage their own affairs. There are thirty-eight organized provinces in the archipelago, in which the administration rests with the Provincial Board composed of the governor, treasurer, and supervisor or engineer. The governor is elected for the term of one year by the councilors of all the towns united in assembly. The treasurer and supervisor are appointed by the governor of the

Philippine archipelago under the rules of the Civil Service Board. The civil service is a subject which has commanded the special consideration of the Commission. It gives equal opportunity to the Filipino and to the American to enter the public service and to gain public promotion; and the Filipino is by law even given the preference where possessed of the requisite ability.

The Palace, Manila. Headquarters of the Government.

The Insular Government.—For the purposes of administration, the insular, or central government of the Islands is divided into four branches, called departments, each directed by a secretary who is also a member of the Philippine Commission. These departments are, interior, Secretary Worcester; finance and justice, Secretary Ide; commerce and police, Secretary Wright; and public instruction, Secretary Moses, until January 1, 1903, and since

that date Secretary Smith.   Under each of these departments are a large number of bureaus, by which the many
important activities of the government are performed.

We have only to examine a list of these bureaus to see
how many-sided is the work which the government is
performing.   It is a veritable commonwealth, complete in
all the branches which demand the attention of modern
governments.   Thus, under the Department of the Interior, there is the Bureau of Public Health, with its extremely important duties of combating epidemic diseases
and improving public sanitation, with its public hospitals,
sanitariums, and charities;   the Bureau of Government
Laboratories for making bacteriological and chemical investigations;   a Bureau of Forestry;   a Bureau of Mining;
the Philippine Weather Bureau;   a Bureau of Agriculture;
a Bureau of Non-Christian Tribes for conducting the government work in ethnology and for framing legislation for
pagan and Mohammedan tribes;   and a Bureau of Public
Lands.

Under the department of Commerce and Police are
the Bureau of Posts;   Signal Service;   the Philippines
Constabulary, really an insular army, with its force of
some sixty-five hundred officers and men;   Prisons;   the
Coast Guard and Transportation Service, with a fleet of
about twenty beautiful little steamers, nearly all of them
newly built for this service and named for islands of the
archipelago;   the Coast and Geodetic Survey, doing the
much-needed work of charting the dangerous coasts and
treacherous waters of the archipelago;   and the Bureau of
Engineering, which has under its charge great public
works, many of which are already under way.

Under the Department of Finance and Justice are the
Insular Treasurer;   the Insular Auditor;   the Bureau of

Customs and Immigration; the Bureau of Internal Revenue; the Insular Cold Storage and Ice Plant; and the great Bureau of Justice.

Under the Department of Public Instruction there is the Bureau of Education in charge of the system of public schools; a Bureau of Printing and Engraving, with a new and fully equipped plant; a Bureau of Architecture; a Bureau of Archives; a Bureau of Statistics; and the Philippine Museum.

Revenues and Expenditures. — The maintenance of these numerous activities calls for an expenditure of large sums of money, but the insular government and the Filipino people are fortunate in having had their finances managed with exceptional ability. The revenues of the Islands for the past fiscal year have amounted to about $10,638,-000, gold. Public expenditures, including the purchase of equipment such as the coast-guard fleet and the forwarding of great public works such as the improving of the harbor of Manila, amounted during fiscal year of 1903 to about $9,150,000, gold. The government has at all times preserved a good balance in its treasury; but the past year has seen some diminution in the amount of revenues, owing to the great depreciation of silver money, the falling off of imports, the wide prevalence of cholera, and the poverty of many parts of the country as a result of war and the loss of livestock through pest. To assist the government of the Philippines, the Congress of the United States in February, 1903, with great and characteristic generosity appropriated the sum of $3,000,000, gold, as a free gift to the people and government of the Philippines.

The Judicial System. — Especially fortunate, also, have been the labors of the commission in establishing a judicial system and revising the Spanish law. The legal ability of the commission is unusually high. As at present constituted, the judicial system consists of a Supreme Court composed of seven justices, three of whom at the present time are Filipinos, which, besides trying cases over which it has original jurisdiction, hears cases brought on appeal from the Courts of First Instance, fifteen in number, which sit in different parts of the Islands. Each town, moreover, has its justices of the peace for the trial of small cases and for holding preliminary examinations in cases of crimes. By the new Code of Civil Procedure, the administration of justice has been so simplified that there are probably no courts in the world where justice can be more quickly secured than here.

System of Public Schools. — Probably no feature of the American government in the Islands has attracted more attention than the system of public schools. Popular education, while by no means wholly neglected under the Spanish government, was inadequate, and was continually opposed by the clerical and conservative Spanish forces, who feared that the liberalizing of the Filipino people would be the loosening of the control of both Spanish state and church. On the contrary, the success of the American government, as of any government in which the people participate, depends upon the intelligence and education of the people. Thus, the American government is as anxious to destroy ignorance and poverty as the Spanish government and the Spanish church were desirous of preserving these deeply unfortunate conditions.

Americans believe that if knowledge is generally spread among the Filipino people, if there can be a real understanding of the genius and purpose of our American institutions, there will come increasing content and satisfaction to dwell under American law. Thus, education was early encouraged by the American army, and it received the first attention of the commission. The widespread system of public schools which now exists in these islands was organized by the first General Superintendent of Public Instruction, Dr. Fred W. Atkinson, and by Professor Bernard Moses of the Philippine Commission.

Instruction in the English Language. — The basis of this public instruction is the English language. This was early decided upon in view of the great number of Filipino dialects, the absence of a common native language or literature, and the very moderate acquaintance with Spanish by any except the educated class.

It is fortunate for the Filipino people that English has been introduced here and that its knowledge is rapidly spreading. Knowledge of language is power, and the more widely spoken the tongue, the greater the possession of the individual who acquires it. Of all the languages of the world, English is to-day the most widely spoken and is most rapidly spreading. Moreover, English is preeminently the language of the Far East. From Yokohama to Australia, and from Manila to the Isthmus of Suez, English is the common medium of communication. It is the language alike of business and of diplomacy. The Filipino people, so eager to participate in all the busy life of eastern Asia, so ambitious to make their influence felt and their counsels regarded, will be debarred from all this unless they master this mighty English tongue.

The Filipino Assembly. — Thus, after four and a half years of American occupation, the sovereignty of the United States has been established in the archipelago, and a form of government, unique in the history of colonial administration, inaugurated. One other step in the contemplation of Congress, which will still further make the government a government of the Filipino people, remains to be taken. This is the formation of a Filipino assembly of delegates or representatives, chosen by popular vote from all the Christianized provinces of the archipelago. The recent census of the Philippines will form the basis for the apportionment of this representation. This assembly will share the legislative power on all matters pertaining to the Christian people of the Philippines and those parts of the Islands inhabited by them. When this step shall have been taken, the government of the Philippine Islands will be like the typical and peculiarly American form of government known as territorial.

Territorial Form of Government in the United States. — The American Union is composed of a number of states or commonwealths which, while differing vastly in wealth and population, are on absolutely equal footing in the Union. The inhabitants of these states form politically the American sovereignty. They elect the president and Congress, and through their state legislatures may change or amend the form of the American state itself.

Besides these states, there have always been large possessions of the nation called territories. These territories are extensive countries, too sparsely inhabited or too undeveloped politically to be admitted, in the judgment of the American Congress, to statehood in the Union. Their inhabitants do not have the right to vote for the president; neither have they representation in the American Congress. These territories are governed by Congress, through territorial governments, and over them Congress has full sovereign powers. That is, as the Supreme Court of the United States has decided and explained, while Congress when legislating for the states in the Union has only those powers of legislation which have been specifically granted by the Constitution, in legislating for the territories it has all the powers which the Constitution has not specifically denied. The only limitations on Congress are those which, under the American system of public law, guarantee the liberty of the individual, — his freedom of religious belief and worship; his right to just, open, and speedy trial; his right to the possession of his property; and other precious privileges, the result of centuries of development in the English-speaking race, which make up civil liberty. These priceless securities, which no power of the government can take away, abridge, or infringe, are as much the possession of the inhabitants of a territory as of a state.[1]

The government of these territories has varied greatly in form and may be changed at any time by Congress, but it usually consists of a governor and supreme court, appointed by the president of the United States, and a legislature elected by the people. Since 1783 there has always been territory so held and governed by the United States, and if we may judge from the remarkable history of these regions, this form of government of dependent possessions is the most successful and most advantageous to the territory itself that has ever been devised.

At the present time, the territories of the United States are Oklahoma, the Indian Territory, New Mexico, Ari-

---

[1] See the decisions of the Supreme Court in the cases of *American Insurance Co.* v. *Canter* (1 Peters, 511), decided in 1828; *National Bank* v. *County of Yankton* (101 U. S. Reports, 129), decided in 1879; *The Mormon Church* v. *United States* (136 U. S. Reports, 1), decided May, 1890. On the domain of personal liberty possessed by the inhabitants of a territory, in addition to above cases, see also the cases of *Reynolds* v. *United States* (98 U. S. Reports, 154), 1878; and *Murphy* v. *Ramsey* (114 U. S. Reports, 15), 1884.

zona, Alaska, the Hawaiian Islands, Porto Rico, the Philippines, and Guam.

The territorial form of government has frequently been regarded by American statesmen as a temporary condition to be followed at a comparatively early date by statehood. But after more than a century of development, territorial government, as shaped by Congress and as defined by the Supreme Court, shows itself so flexible and advantageous that there is no reason why it should not be regarded as a permanent and final form. Whether it will long prevail in the Philippines, depends very largely upon the political development and ultimate desires of the Filipino people themselves. For the present, it is the only suitable form of government and the only form which it is statesmanlike to contemplate.

Filipino Independence. — The events of the last few years seem to indicate that the American nation will not intrust the Philippines with independence until they have immeasurably gained in political experience and social self-control. The question is too great to be discussed here, but this much may be said: The rapid march of international politics in this coming century will not be favorable to the independence of the small and imperfectly developed state. Independence, while it may fascinate the popular leader, may not be most advantageous for this people. Independence, under present tendencies of international trade, means economic isolation. Independence, in the present age, compels preparedness for war; preparedness for war necessitates the maintenance of strong armies, the building of great navies, and the great economic burdens required to sustain these armaments. Especially would this be true of an archipelago so exposed to attack, so surrounded by ambitious powers, and so near the center of coming struggle, as are the Philippines. Japan, with a population of forty-two million, wonderful for their industry and economy, and passionately devoted to their emperor, is independent, but at great cost. The burden of her splendid army and her modern navy weighs heavily upon her people, consumes a large proportion of their earnings, and sometimes seems to be threatening to strain the resources of the nation almost to the point of breaking.

Advantages of American Control. — Surely, a people is economically far more privileged if, like the Philippines under the American government, or Australia under the British, they are compelled to sustain no portion of the burden of exterior defense. The navies of the United States to-day protect the integrity of the Philippine archipelago. The power of a nation so strong and so terrible, when once aroused, that no country on the globe would think for a minute of wantonly molesting its territory, shields the Filipino from all outside interference and permits him to expend all his energy in the development of those abilities to which his temperament and endowment inspire him.

American government means freedom of opportunity. There is no honorable pursuit, calling, or walk of life under heaven in which the Filipino may not now engage and in which he will not find his endeavors encouraged and his success met with generous appreciation. In politics, his progress may be slow, because progress here is not the development of the individual nor of the few, but of the whole. But in the no less noble pursuits of science, literature, and art, we may in this very generation see Filipinos achieving more than notable success and distinction, not only for themselves but for their land.

Patriotic Duty. — Patriotic duty, as regards the Philippines, means for the American a wholesome belief in the uprightness of the national purposes; a loyal appreciation of the men who have here worked wisely and without selfishness, and have borne the brunt of the toil; a loyalty to the government of the Philippines and of the United States, so long as these governments live honestly, rule justly, and increase liberty; and a frank and hearty recognition of every advance made by the Filipino people themselves. And for the Filipinos, patriotic duty means a full acceptance of government as it has now been established, as better than what has preceded, and perhaps superior to what he himself would have chosen and could have devised; a loyalty to his own people and to their interests and to the public interests, that shall overcome the personal selfishness that has set its cruel mark on every native institution in this land; and a resolution to obey the laws, preserve the peace, and use faithfully every opportunity for the development of his own character and the betterment of the race.

APPENDIX.

SPANISH GOVERNORS OF THE PHILIPPINES.

(1571–1898.)

1571–1572	Don Miguel Lopez de Legaspi.
1572–1575	(Tesorero) Guido de Labezares.
1575–1580	Don Francisco La-Sande.
1580–1583	Don Gonzalo Ronquillo.
1583–1584	Don Diego Ronquillo.
1584–1590	Dr. Don Santiago de Vera.
1590–1593	Don Gomez Perez de Dasmariñas.
1593–1595	Luis Perez Dasmariñas.
1595–1596	Don Antonio de Morga.
1596–1602	Don Francisco Tello de Guzman.
1602–1606	Don Pedro Bravo de Acuña.
1606–1608	Royal Audiencia.
1608–1609	Don Rodrigo Vivero.
1609–1616	Don Juan de Silva.
1616–1618	Don Andres Alcazar.
1618–1624	Don Alonso Faxardo y Tenza.
1624–1625	Royal Audiencia.
1625–1626	Don Fernando de Silva.
1626–1632	Don Juan Niño de Tabora.
1632–1633	Royal Audiencia.
1633–1635	Don Juan Zerezo de Salamanca.
1635–1644	Don Sebastian Hurtado de Corcuera.
1644–1653	Don Diego Faxardo y Chacon.
1653–1663	Sabiano Manrique de Lara.
1663–1668	Don Diego Salcedo.
1668–1669	Señor Peña Bonifaz.
1669–1677	Don Manuel de Leon.
1677–1678	Royal Audiencia.
1678–1684	Don Juan de Vargas.
1684–1689	Don Gabriel de Curuzalequi.
1689–1690	Don Alonso de Avila Fuertes.

1690–1701	Don Fausto Cruzat y Gongora.
1701–1709	Don Domingo Zabalburu.
1709–1715	Conde de Lizarraga.
1715–1717	Royal Audiencia.
1717–1719	Don Fernando Manuel de Bustamante.
1719–1721	Archbishop Cuesta.
1721–1729	Don Toribio José de Cosio y Campo (Marqués de Torre Campo).
1729–1739	Don Fernando Valdes y Tamon.
1739–1745	Don Gaspar de la Torre.
1745–1750	Bishop Father Juan de Arrechedra.
1750–1754	Don Francisco José de Obando y Solis.
1754–1759	Don Pedro Manuel de Arandia y Santisteban.
1759–1761	Don Miguel Lino de Ezpeleta (Bishop of Zebu).
1761–1764	Archbishop Don Manuel Antonio Rojo del Rio y Vieyra.
1764–1764	Dr. Don Simon de Anda y Salazar.
1164–1765	Don Francisco de la Torre.
1765–1770	Don José Raon.
1770–1778	Dr. Don Simon de Anda y Salazar.
1778–1787	Don José Basco y Vargas.
1787–1788	Don Pedro Sarrio.
1788–1793	Don Felix Berenguer de Marquina.
1793–1806	Don Rafael Maria de Aguilar y Ponce de Leon.
1806–1810	Don Mariano Fernandez de Folgueras.
1810–1813	Don Manuel Gonzalez Aguilar.
1813–1816	Don José de Gardoqui Jaraveitia.
1816–1822	Don Mariano Fernandez de Folgueras.
1822–1825	Don Juan Antonio Martinez.
1825–1830	Don Mariano Ricafort Palacio y Abarca.
1830–1835	Don Pascual Enrile y Alcedo.
1835–1836	Don Gabriel de Torres.
1836–1838	Don Andres Garcia Camba.
1838–1841	Don Luis Lardizabal y Montojo.
1841–1843	Don Marcelino de Oraa Lecumberri.
1843–1844	Don Francisco de Paula Alcalá de la Torre.
1844–1850	Don Narciso Clavería y Zaldua.
1850–1850	Don Antonio Maria Blanco.
1850–1853	D. Antonio de Urbiztondo, Marqués de la Solana y Teniente General.

1853–1854   El Mariscal de Campo de Ramon Montero, General Segundo Cabo (acting).

1854–1854   El Teniente General Marqués de Novaliches.

1854–1854   El Mariscal de Campo de Ramon Montero (acting).

1854–1856   El Teniente General de Manuel Crespo.

1856–1857   El Mariscal de Campo de Ramon Montero (acting).

1857–1860   El Teniente General de Fernando de Norzagaray.

1860–1860   El Mariscal de Campo de Ramon Solano y Llánderal (acting).

1860–1861   El Brigadier de Artilleria de Juan Herrera Dávila (acting).

1861–1862   El Teniente General de José Lemery.

1862–1865   El Teniente General de Rafael Echagüe.

1865–1865   El Mariscal de Campo de Joaquin Solano (acting).

1865–1866   El Teniente General de Juan de Lara é Irigoyen.

1866–1866   El Mariscal de Campo de Juan Laureano Sanz (acting).

1866–1866   El Comandante General de Marina de Antonio Ossorio (acting).

1866–1866   El Mariscal de Campo de Joaquin Solano (acting).

1866–1866   El Teniente General de José de la Gándara.

1866–1869   El Mariscal de Campo de Manuel Maldonado (acting).

1869–1871   El Teniente General de Carlos de la Torre.

1871–1873   El Teniente General de Rafael Izquierdo.

1873–1873   El Comandante General de Marina de Manuel Mac-Crohon (acting).

1873–1874   El Teniente General de Juan Alaminos y Vivar.

1874–1874   El Mariscal de Campo de Manuel Blanco Valderrama (acting).

1874–1877   El Contra Almirante de la Armada de José Malcampo y Monje.

1877–1880   El Teniente General de Domingo Moriones y Murillo.

1880–1880   El Comandante General de Marina de Rafael Rodriguez Arias (acting).

1880–1883   El Teniente General de Fernando Primo de Rivera, Marqués de Estella.

1883–1883   El Mariscal de Campo de Emilio de Molins, General Segundo Cabo (acting).

1883–1885   El Capitan General del Ejercito de Joaquin Jovellar y Soler.

1885–1885　El Mariscal de Campo de Emilio de Molins (acting).

1885–1888　El Teniente General de Emilio Terrero.

1888–1888　El Mariscal de Campo de Antonio Molto (acting).

1888–1888　El Cotra Almirante de la Armada de Federico Lobatón (acting).

1888–1891　El Teniente General de Valeriano Weyler.

1891–1893　El Teniente General de Eulogio Despojol, Conde de Caspe.

1893–1893　El General de Division de Federico Ochando, General Segundo Cabo (acting).

1893–1896　El Teniente General de Ramon Blanco y Erenas, Marqués de Peña-Plata.

1896–1897　El Teniente General de Camilo G. de Polavieja, Marqués de Polavieja.

1897–1897　de José de Lachambre y Dominguez, Teniente General (acting).

1897–1898　de Fernando Primo de Rivera, Capitan General, Marqués de Estella.

1898–1898　de Basilio Augustin Teniente General del Ejercito.

1898–1898　El General Segundo Cabo de Fermin Jaudenes y Alvarez.

INDEX.

325

Milne's Arithmetics

By WILLIAM J. MILNE, Ph.D., LL.D.

President of the New York State Normal College, Albany, N. Y.

TWO-BOOK SERIES		THREE-BOOK SERIES	
Elements of Arithmetic	$0.30	Primary Arithmetic .	$0.25
		Intermediate Arithmetic	.30
Standard Arithmetic .	.65	Standard Arithmetic .	.65

IT is not enough for pupils to understand arithmetical processes; they must be able to use them accurately and rapidly. It is evident, therefore, that the best text-books in arithmetic are those which give the pupil a thorough and practical knowledge of the study, and, following this, readiness in applying this knowledge to the common affairs of everyday life.

Milne's Arithmetics meet all these conditions and requirements in a natural, logical, and practical manner.

In Either a Two-Book or a Three-Book Series. To meet the varying needs of teachers these arithmetics are now issued in two editions—a two-book series and a three-book series. Other books of a similar nature have been published from time to time, but none have ever attained the extraordinary popularity of Milne's Arithmetics. Their success has been entirely without precedent. The method employed is inductive for the most part, yet it is neither tedious nor redundant. The large number and practical character of the problems included, and the application of business methods of computation in their solution, form noteworthy and valuable features of the books. Other important characteristics are their admirable arrangement, their use of sound pedagogical principles, the absence of all useless matter, their comprehensive character, and their exact statements. No other arithmetics are more modern in every respect.

AMERICAN BOOK COMPANY

NEW YORK   CINCINNATI   CHICAGO

Webster's School Dictionaries

REVISED EDITIONS

WEBSTER'S SCHOOL DICTIONARIES in their revised form constitute a progressive series, carefully graded and especially adapted for Primary Schools, Common Schools, High Schools, Academies, and private students. These Dictionaries have all been thoroughly revised, entirely reset, and made to conform in all essential respects to that great standard authority in English— Webster's International Dictionary.

WEBSTER'S PRIMARY SCHOOL DICTIONARY . . $0.48

Containing over 20,000 words and meanings, with over 400 illustrations.

WEBSTER'S COMMON SCHOOL DICTIONARY . . $0.72

Containing over 25,000 words and meanings, with over 500 illustrations.

WEBSTER'S HIGH SCHOOL DICTIONARY . . . $0.98

Containing about 37,000 words and definitions, and an appendix giving a pronouncing vocabulary of Biblical, Classical, Mythological, Historical, and Geographical proper names, with over 800 illustrations.

WEBSTER'S ACADEMIC DICTIONARY

Cloth, $1.50; Indexed, $1.80
Half Calf, 2.75; Indexed, 3.00

Abridged directly from the International Dictionary, and giving the orthography, pronunciations, definitions, and synonyms of the large vocabulary of words in common use, with an appendix containing various useful tables, with over 800 illustrations.

SPECIAL EDITIONS

Webster's Countinghouse Dictionary . Sheep, Indexed, $2.40

Webster's Condensed Dictionary . Cloth, $1.44; Indexed, 1.75

The Same . . . Half Calf, 2.75; Indexed, 3.00

Webster's Handy Dictionary 15

Webster's Pocket Dictionary. Cloth 57

The Same. Roan Flexible 69

The Same. Roan Tucks 78

The Same. Morocco, Indexed 90

Webster's Practical Dictionary 80

Copies of any of Webster's Dictionaries will be sent, prepaid, to any address on receipt of the price by the Publishers:

AMERICAN BOOK COMPANY

NEW YORK   CINCINNATI   CHICAGO

(104)